Photoshop Elements 2024

Image Manipulation Mastery Course on Photoshop Elements 2024 for Beginners, Seniors and Professionals

Robinson Cortez

Copyright © 2024 *Robinson Cortez*

All Rights Reserved

This book or parts thereof may not be reproduced in any form, stored in any retrieval system, or transmitted in any form by any means—electronic, mechanical, photocopy, recording, or otherwise—without prior written permission of the publisher, except as provided by United States of America copyright law and fair use.

Disclaimer and Terms of Use

The author and publisher of this book and the accompanying materials have used their best efforts in preparing this book. The author and publisher make no representation or warranties with respect to the accuracy, applicability, fitness, or completeness of the contents of this book. The information contained in this book is strictly for informational purposes. Therefore, if you wish to apply ideas contained in this book, you are taking full responsibility for your actions.

Printed in the United States of America

TABLE OF CONTENTS

- TABLE OF CONTENTS III
- INTRODUCTION 1
- CHAPTER ONE 2
- GETTING STARTED 2
  - OVERVIEW 2
  - NEW ADDITIONS 2
    - *Match tone and color to create new feeling* 2
    - *Create and share fast-moving Photo Reels* 2
    - *Enjoy a completely new editing experience with a new appearance* 3
    - *Choose an image sky or background with one click for easier editing* 3
    - *Discover one-click photo Quick Actions in one place* 3
    - *Remove JPEG artifacts for a more natural appearance* 4
  - GROW YOUR SKILLS ALONG THE WAY WITH GUIDED EDITS 4
  - ACCESS FREE ADOBE STOCK PICTURES TO BROADEN YOUR CREATIVE OPTIONS 4
    - *With the new Artistic Effect settings, you can turn images into works of art* 5
  - THINGS YOU NEED TO KNOW 5
  - PRINCIPLES OF PHOTO AND GRAPHICS EDITING 5
    - *Pixels* 5
  - PIXEL CHARACTERISTICS 5
    - *Color Information* 5
    - *Transparency and Brightness* 5
  - PIXELS' FUNCTION IN IMAGE EDITING 6
    - *Image Resolution* 6
    - *Editing and Manipulation* 6
  - PIXEL DIFFICULTIES 6
    - *Pixilation* 6
    - *File Size* 6
    - *Loss of Detail* 6
  - HOW TO USE PIXELS IN PHOTOSHOP 7
    - *Pixel Selection* 7
    - *Pixel Editing* 7
    - *Pixel Manipulation and Layers* 7
    - *Pixel Filters* 7
    - *Retouching with Pixels* 7
  - PIXEL OUTPUT AND EXPORT 7
    - *Image File Formats* 7
  - PRINT RESOLUTION VS. WEB RESOLUTION 8
    - *Resolution* 8
  - CHOOSING THE CORRECT RESOLUTION FOR YOUR IMAGE 9

- PRINTING RESOLUTION 9
  - *Professional Publications* 9
  - *Non-Professional* 9
  - *Screen Resolution* 9
  - *Web* 9
  - *Projector / Powerpoint* 10
- RASTER VS. VECTOR GRAPHICS 10
  - *What is a raster file?* 10
  - *Key attributes* 10
  - *Limitations* 11
  - *What is a vector file?* 11
  - *Key attributes* 11
  - *Limitations* 12
- WHAT IS THE DIFFERENCE BETWEEN RASTER AND VECTOR FILES? 12
  - *Resolution* 12
  - *Uses* 13
  - *File sizes* 13
  - *Compatibility and conversion* 13
  - *Types of Files and Extensions* 14
  - *Vector File Types* 14
- RASTER VS. VECTOR FILES: FREQUENTLY ASKED QUESTIONS 15
  - *How do you know if an image is a vector?* 15
  - *Is a Portable Document Format (PDF) classified as a raster or vector format?* 15
  - *Is it possible to convert a JPEG image into a vector file?* 15
  - *Is Adobe Photoshop vector-based software?* 15
- IMAGE SIZE VS. CANVAS SIZE 16
  - *What Is Photoshop Canvas Size?* 16
  - *Is the size of an artboard and a canvas the same?* 16
  - *What is an Image Size?* 17
- WHAT IS THE DISTINCTION BETWEEN CANVAS AND IMAGE SIZE? 17
- CHANGING IMAGE SIZE AND RESOLUTION 18
- CHANGING THE CANVAS SIZE 20
  - *Selections* 20
  - *Layers* 21
- KEY CONCEPTS 21
  - *Background Layer* 21
  - *Adding Layers* 21
  - *Layer Visibility* 21
  - *Layer Opacity* 21
  - *Layer Styles* 21
  - *Layer Mask* 22
  - *Blending Modes* 22
  - *Grouping Layers* 22

Usage	22
Photo Editing	*22*
Graphic Design	*22*
Digital Art	*22*
Alpha	*22*
What is an Alpha Channel?	23
How to create and edit an alpha channel	*23*
Creating an Alpha Channel	*24*
RGB Color	25
Color Channels	*25*
Color Picker	*25*
Color Modes	*25*
Adjustment Layers	*25*
Blending Modes	*26*
Color Correction	*26*
Exporting to the Web	*26*
The Tools Options Bin	26
What is a native PSD file?	27
Recognizing the PSD File Format	*27*
Different Types of Layers	*28*
PSD Files in the Photographic Process	29
PSD File Conversion to Other Formats	30
PSD File Alternatives	*30*
PSD File Benefits and Drawbacks	31
Pros	*31*
Cons	*31*
How to Open PSD Files	31
How to Create and Edit a PSD File	32
PSD File FAQs	32
How can I open a PSD file if I don't have Photoshop?	*32*
Is a PSD identical to a PNG?	*32*
Is it possible to edit PSD files without Photoshop?	*32*
System Requirements	33
Windows	*33*
macOS	*33*
How to download and install Adobe Photoshop Elements 2024	33
Install Photoshop Elements	34
Frequently Asked Questions	38
CHAPTER TWO	**39**
GET TO KNOW PHOTOSHOP ELEMENTS 2024	**39**
Overview	39
The Elements Hub	39

- *Adobe Photoshop Elements' Elements Hub* 39
- THE EDITOR WORKSPACE 40
  - *Home Screen* 40
  - *Begin with the Home screen* 41
- EXPLORE AND CUSTOMIZE AUTO CREATIONS 41
  - *The Welcome Screen* 41
  - *Quick Mode* 42
  - *Guided Mode* 42
  - *Advanced Mode* 43
- CUSTOMIZE WORKSPACE 43
  - *Use Context Menus* 43
  - *Use keyboard commands and modifier keys* 43
- EXIT PHOTOSHOP ELEMENTS 44
- LIGHT OR DARK INTERFACE? 44
- GUIDES AND RULERS 45
  - *Types of Guides* 45
  - *Adding Guides* 45
- TYPES OF RULERS 46
  - *Measuring Units* 46
  - *Using Rulers for Accuracy* 46
- CHANGE THE RULERS' ZERO ORIGIN AND SETTINGS 46
- CHANGE THE GUIDES AND GRID SETTINGS 47
- THE TOOLBOX 47
  - *Toolbox in the Quick mode* 47
  - *Toolbox in the Advanced Mode* 48
- TOOLS IN THE ADVANCED MODE TOOLBOX'S VIEW GROUP 49
  - *Zoom (Z) tool* 49
  - *Hand Tool (H)* 49
- TOOLS IN THE ADVANCED MODE TOOLBOX'S SELECT GROUP 49
  - *Move tool (V)* 49
  - *Rectangular Marquee (M) tool* 50
  - *Elliptical Marquee (M) tool* 50
  - *Lasso (L) tool* 50
  - *Magnetic Lasso (L) tool* 50
  - *Polygonal Lasso Tool (L)* 50
  - *Quick Selection Tool (A)* 50
  - *Selection Brush tool (A)* 50
  - *Magic Wand tool (A)* 50
  - *Refine Selection Brush tool (A)* 50
  - *Auto Selection tool (A)* 50
- TOOLS IN THE ADVANCED MODE TOOLBOX'S ENHANCE GROUP 51
  - *Eye tool (Y)* 51
  - *(Spot Healing Brush tool (J)* 51

- *Healing Brush tool (J)* *51*
- *Smart Brush tool (F)* *51*
- *Detail Smart Brush tool (F)* *51*
- *Clone Stamp tool (S)* *51*
- *Pattern Stamp tool (S)* *51*
- *Blur tool (R)* *51*
- *Sharpen tool (R)* *51*
- *Smudge tool (R)* *51*
- *Sponge tool (O)* *52*
- *Dodge tool (O)* *52*
- *Burn tool (O)* *52*

TOOLS IN THE ADVANCED MODE TOOLBOX'S DRAW GROUP 52
- *(Brush tool (B)* *52*
- *Impressionist Brush tool (B)* *52*
- *Color Replacement tool (B)* *52*

ERASER TOOL (E) 52
- *Background Eraser tool (E)* *52*
- *Magic Eraser tool (E)* *52*

PAINT BUCKET TOOL (K) 52
- *Pattern tool (K)* *53*

GRADIENT TOOL (G) 53
COLOR PICKER TOOL (I) 53
CUSTOM SHAPE TOOL (U) 53
TYPE TOOL (T) 53
PENCIL TOOL (N) 54
TOOLS IN THE ADVANCED MODE TOOLBOX'S MODIFY GROUP 54
- *Cropping tool (C)* *54*
- *Cookie Cutter tool (C)* *54*
- *Perspective Crop tool (C)* *54*

RECOMPOSE TOOL (W) 54
CONTENT-AWARE MOVE TOOL (Q) 54
STRAIGHTEN TOOL (P) 54
- *Use a tool* *54*
- *Choose a tool* *54*

SELECT OPTIONS FROM THE TOOL OPTIONS BAR 55
CHANGE THE TOOL PREFERENCES 55
- *Change your general preferences* *55*
- *Set the appearance of a pointer* *56*

DRAG TO RESIZE OR MODIFY THE SHARPNESS OF PAINTING CURSORS (WINDOWS ONLY) 56
RESTORE THE TOOL'S DEFAULT SETTINGS 56
THE PANEL BIN 57
PANEL MENUS 58
- *Pop-up sliders within panels* *58*

  Work with Panels 58
   Panels in the Advanced Mode 58
 BASIC WORKSPACE 58
  Custom Workspace 59
 USE THE TASKBAR 60
 THE PHOTO BIN 61
 WHAT DO THESE PANELS DO? 62
 OTHER PANELS 63
 SAVE FILES TO THE CLOUD 64
  The Save/Save As dialog box and how to use it 64
 HOW TO SAVE FILES FOR THE WEB 66
 SUPPORTED FILE FORMATS FOR SAVING 66
  BMP 67
  GIF (Graphics Interchange Format) on CompuServe 67
  JPEG (Joint Photographic Experts Group) 67
  Adobe Photoshop (PSD) 67
  PSE (Photo Creations Format) 67
  Photoshop PDF (Portable Document Format) 67
  Pixar 68
  PNG (Portable Network Graphics) 68
  TIFF (Tagged-Image File Format) 68
  File Compression 68
  RLE (Run Length Encoding) 68
  LZW (Lemple-Zif-Welch) 68
  JPEG 69
  CCITT 69
  ZIP 69
 FREQUENTLY ASKED QUESTIONS 69

PART II 70

QUICK AND GUIDED PHOTO EDITING 70

CHAPTER THREE 71

QUICK FIXES AND EFFECTS 71
 OVERVIEW 71
 THE QUICK FIX TOOLBOX 71
 ADJUSTMENTS, EFFECTS, TEXTURES, AND FRAMES 72
  Effects 72
  Artistic Effects 73
  Classic Effects 74
  Textures 75
  Frames 76
 APPLY AN EFFECT, TEXTURE, OR FRAME 77

  Frequently Asked Questions 77

CHAPTER FOUR 78
GUIDED EDITS 78

 Overview 78
 Guided mode and Guided Edits 78
 How to Use the Guided Edit Mode in Photoshop Elements 79
 Search Guided Edits 80
 Basics 81
  Add Text guided edit *81*
 Advanced Type Tools 83
  Use the Text on the Selection tool *83*
 Use the Text on Shape Tool 83
 Use the Text on Path tool 84
 The Move & Scale Object Guided Edit 85
 Object Removal Guided Edit 85
 Resize Guided Edit 86
 Vignette Effect Guided Edit 88
 Color Guided Edits 89
  Enhance Colors guided edit *89*
  Editing using the Lomo Camera Effect *89*
 Remove a Color Cast guided edit 90
 Remove a color cast using Levels 91
  Adjust color curves *91*
 Black & White Edits 92
 B&W Color Pop guided edit 93
 B&W Selection guided edit 95
  High Key guided edit *97*
 Low Key guided edit 98
 Fun Edits 99
  The Meme Maker Guided Edit *99*
 Multi-Photo Text Guided Editing 101
 The Double Exposure Guided Edit 103
 The Painterly Guided Edit effect 103
 The "Out of Bounds" Guided Edit effect 105
 Save as: Save/Save As 106
 Continue editing in Quick / Advanced Mode 106
  Share on Flickr or Twitter *107*
 Create a Picture Stack 107
 Create a Puzzle Effect 108
 Special Edits 109
  Depth of Field Guided Editing *109*
  Simple Method *109*

ix

- *Custom Method* 110
- THE TEXT AND BORDER OVERLAY GUIDED EDIT 110
- .THE PERFECT PORTRAIT GUIDED EDIT 112
- PHOTOMERGE GUIDED EDITS 113
  - *Use Photomerge Group Shot* 113
  - *Show Strokes* 113
  - *Show Regions* 113
  - *Advanced Options* 113
  - *Alignment Tool* 114
  - *Pixel Blending* 114
- USE PHOTOMERGE SCENE CLEANER 114
  - *Show Strokes* 115
  - *Show Regions* 115
  - *Alignment Tool* 115
  - *Pixel Blending* 115
- PHOTOMERGE FACES 116
  - *Show Strokes* 116
  - *Show Regions* 116
- PHOTOMERGE EXPOSURE 117
- AUTOMATIC PHOTOMERGE EXPOSURE 118
  - *Simple Blending* 119
  - *Smart Blending* 119
  - *Highlight* 119
  - *Shadows* 119
  - *Saturation* 119
- MANUAL PHOTOMERGE EXPOSURE 119
  - *Show Strokes* 120
  - *Show Regions* 120
- COMBINE PHOTOS WITH PHOTOMERGE PANORAMA 121
- AUTO PANORAMA 121
  - *Perspective* 121
  - *Cylindrical* 122
  - *Spherical* 122
  - *Collage* 122
  - *Reposition* 122
  - *Blend Images* 122
  - *Vignette Removal* 122
- CORRECTION OF GEOMETRIC DISTORTION 122
  - *Content-Aware Fill Transparent Areas* 123
- THE ACTIONS PANEL 123
- MANAGE ACTION FILES 124
  - *Add actions* 124
  - *Remove actions* 124

Reset actions	*124*
FREQUENTLY ASKED QUESTIONS	**124**

PART III 125

THE ADVANCED PHOTO EDITING WORKSPACE 125

CHAPTER FIVE 126

GET TO KNOW THE PHOTOSHOP ELEMENTS TOOLBOX 126

OVERVIEW	126
THE TOOL OPTIONS	126
The Color Picker	*126*
THE EYEDROPPER/SAMPLER TOOL	127
HOW TO USE THE EYEDROPPER TOOL	127
The Eyedropper tool's options	*129*
THE COLOR SWATCH PANEL	131
SELECT A COLOR WHILE USING THE COLOR SWATCHES WINDOW	131
ADD A COLOR TO THE COLOR SWATCHES PANEL	132
SAVE AND USE CUSTOM SWATCH LIBRARIES	132
Reset a swatch library to its default color swatches	*133*
Delete a color from the Color Swatches panel	*133*
ADDITIONAL FOREGROUND/BACKGROUND COLOR OPTIONS	134
The Zoom Tool	*134*
DISPLAY AN IMAGE AT 100%	135
FIT AN IMAGE TO THE SCREEN	135
RESIZE THE WINDOW WHILE ZOOMING	135
USING THE NAVIGATOR PANEL	136
OPEN MULTIPLE WINDOWS OF THE SAME IMAGE	136
View and arrange multiple windows	*136*
CLOSE THE WINDOWS	137
THE MOVE TOOL	137
MOVE TOOL OPTIONS	138
Auto Select Layer	*138*
Show Bounding Box	*138*
Display Highlights on Rollover	*138*
Arrange menu	*138*
Align menu	*139*
Distribute menu	*139*
Copying selections or layers	*139*
Copy selections with the Move tool	*139*
Copy a selection using commands	*140*
Paste one selection into another	*140*
MOVE TOOL OPTIONS	141
Auto Select Layer	*141*

- *Display Bounding Box* 141
- *Display Highlights on Rollover* 141
- *Arrange menus* 141
- *Menu alignment* 141
- *Distribute the menu* 141
- *Copying selections or layers* 142
- *Copy selections with the Move tool* 142
- *Copy a selection using commands* 142
- *Paste one selection into another* 143
- *Add to and subtract from a selection* 143

REFINING THE EDGES OF A SELECTION 144
THE MARQUEE SELECTION TOOLS 146
- *Selection Brush* 146

QUICK SELECTION TOOLS 151
THE REFINE SELECTION BRUSH AND PUSH TOOL 152
- *Using the Refine Selection Brush Tool* 152

HOW TO USE THE ADD TO OR SUBTRACT FROM SELECTION MODE 152
- *How to Use the Push Selection Mode* 153
- *Smooth Selection Mode: How to Use It* 153

EYE TOOLS: THE RED EYE REMOVAL TOOL 154
OPEN CLOSED EYES 155
THE SPOT HEALING BRUSH TOOL 156
- *Remove spots and small imperfections* 156

PROXIMITY MATCH 156
- *Create Texture* 156

REMOVE UNWANTED OBJECTS WITH CONTENT-AWARE HEALING 157
- *Removing an unwanted object* 157

WHAT IS ANTI-ALIASING? 157
CONTENT-AWARE FILL 158
THE HEALING BRUSH TOOLS 159
- *Healing Brush Tool* 160

THE SMART BRUSH TOOLS 161
THE CLONE STAMP TOOL 161
THE PATTERN STAMP TOOL 163
BLUR, SMUDGE, AND SHARPEN 164
- *The Blur Tool* 164
- *Use the Blur Tool* 164
- *Blur Tool Tips* 165
- *The Smudge Tool* 165

SMUDGE YOUR IMAGE 167
EXPERIMENT WITH DIFFERENT TECHNIQUES 167
- *The Sharpen Tool* 167
- *Sharpening the Tool* 168

- THE SPONGE, DODGE, AND BURN TOOLS 169
  - The Sponge Tool 169
  - Using the Sponge Tool 170
- TIPS 170
  - Apply a Light Touch 170
  - Experiment with Strength 170
  - Zoom in for more detail 171
- THE DODGE TOOL 171
- UNDERSTANDING THE DODGE TOOL 171
  - Location 171
  - Function 171
  - Tonal Range 171
  - Exposure Settings 171
  - How to Use the Dodge Tool 171
- TIPS 172
  - Experiment on a Duplicate Layer 172
  - Merge with Selections 172
  - Experiment with Blend Modes 172
  - The Burn Tool 172
  - Use the Burn Tool 172
  - Tips 173
- THE BRUSH TOOLS 173
  - The Impressionist Brush 173
  - How to Use Adobe Photoshop Elements' Impressionist Brush 174
- THE COLOR REPLACEMENT BRUSH 174
- BRUSH SETTINGS AND OPTIONS 175
- ERASER TOOLS 175
  - The Eraser 175
  - Mode Options 176
- THE BACKGROUND ERASER TOOL 177
- ADVANCED BRUSH TOOL SETTINGS 178
  - Tablet Settings 178
- TABLET CONFIGURATION OPTIONS 178
  - Tablet Input 178
  - Pressure Sensitivity 178
  - Tilt Sensitivity 178
  - Customizable Buttons 179
  - Eraser Settings 179
- USING TABLET SETTINGS 179
  - Brush Control 179
  - Precision Editing 179
  - Tilt for Realism 179
  - Workflow Customization 179

The Magic Eraser Tool	*179*
THE PAINT BUCKET (FILL) TOOL	180
THE GRADIENT TOOL	182
THE SHAPE TOOLS	183
The Rectangle Tool, Ellipse Tool, and sss Tool	*183*
Rectangle Tool	*183*
How to Use It	*183*
ELLIPSE TOOL	183
How to use it	*183*
ROUNDED RECTANGLES TOOL	184
How to Use It	*184*
TIPS	184
Fill and Stroke Variations	*184*
Editing Shapes	*184*
The Polygon Tool	*185*
How to Use the Polygon Tool	*185*
TIPS	186
Hold the Shift Key	*186*
Adjust After Creation	*186*
Combine Shapes	*186*
THE LINE TOOL	186
Draw a line	*186*
SET THE WIDTH OF YOUR LINE	187
Shape mode	*187*
PATH OR PIXELS MODE:	188
SHAPE MODE OPTIONS	188
Line Mode	*188*
Fill Color	*188*
Stroke Color	*188*
Stroke Width	*188*
Weight	*188*
Additional Options	*189*
PIXEL MODE OPTIONS	189
Line Mode	*189*
Mode	*189*
Opacity	*189*
Weight	*189*
ADDITIONAL OPTIONS	189
DRAW AN ARROW	190
MAKING A CURVED LINE IN PHOTOSHOP ELEMENTS	191
TYPING TOOLS	194
The Pencil Tool	*194*
How to Find the Pencil Tool	*194*

- Using the Pencil Tool 195
  - Freehand Drawing 195
  - Brush Size Adjustment 195
  - Adjusting Opacity 195
  - Changing Blending Modes 195
  - Erasing with a Pencil 195
  - Undo and Redo 195
  - Save your Work 196
- The Crop Tool 196
  - No Restriction 196
  - Use the Photo Ratio 196
- Crop to a selection boundary 197
- Automatic cropping recommendations 198
- Use grids to improve cropping results 199
  - Grid Overlay 199
  - The Cookie Cutter Tool 199
- The Perspective Crop Tool 200
- The Recompose Tool 202
- The Content-Aware Move Tool 202
  - How to Use Photoshop Elements' Content-Aware Move 202
- The Straighten Tool 203
  - Straighten a picture manually in Advanced Mode 204
- Grow or Shrink Canvas to Fit 204
  - Crop to Remove Background 204
  - Crop to Original Size 204
- Automatically Fill Empty Edges 205
  - Straighten a picture manually in Quick mode 205
- Keep the Canvas Size 205
  - Maintain the Image Size 205
  - Automatically Fill Empty Edges 206
  - Straighten a picture automatically 206
- Frequently Asked Questions 206

CHAPTER SIX 207

SELECT AND ISOLATE AREAS IN YOUR PHOTOS 207

- Overview 207
- Working with Selections 207
- Why Do You Need to Use "Select" and "Isolate" in Adobe Photoshop Elements: 207
  - Selecting Editing 207
  - Complex Image Manipulation 207
- Masking and Layering 208
  - Detailed Corrections 208
- How to Use Adobe Photoshop Elements' "Select" and "Isolate" Functions: 208

- Feathering ... 209
  - Smooth the edges of a selection by anti-aliasing ... 209
- Define a feathered edge for a selection tool ... 209
- Define a feathered edge for an existing selection ... 210
  - The Select menu ... 210
- One-Click Select Subject, Background, or Sky ... 211
  - Refine the automatic selection ... 213
  - Refine the edge of your selection ... 213
  - Refine Edge Adjustments ... 215
- Use a selection to protect an area ... 216
- Cut and paste a selection into another photo ... 217
- Tips ... 218
  - Use layers ... 218
  - Redo and Undo ... 218
  - Try something new ... 218
- Fill or stroke a selection ... 218
  - Filling a Selection ... 218
  - Stroking a Selection ... 218
- Additional Suggestions ... 219
  - Redo and Undo ... 219
  - Adjusting Selections ... 219
  - Layers ... 219
- Frequently Asked Questions ... 219

CHAPTER SEVEN ... 220

RESIZE YOUR IMAGES ... 220

- Overview ... 220
- Image Size vs. Canvas Size ... 220
  - Image Size ... 220
  - Accessing Image Size ... 220
  - Resampling ... 220
  - Measurement Units ... 220
  - Constraining Proportions ... 221
  - Resolution ... 221
- Canvas Size ... 221
  - Accessing Canvas Size ... 221
  - Anchor Points ... 221
- Absolute vs. Relative ... 221
  - Adding a Border ... 221
  - Image Resizing ... 222
  - Recommendations ... 222
  - Canvas Resizing ... 223
- Frequently Asked Questions ... 223

CHAPTER EIGHT ... 224
FIX AND ENHANCE YOUR PHOTOS ... 224

Overview ... 224
Auto Smart Tone ... 224
Apply Auto Smart Tone to a photograph ... 225
- Auto Smart Tone Learning ... 225
- Reset Auto Smart Tone Learning ... 225
- Adjust Color ... 225
- Adjust Color ... 226
- Color Variations ... 226
- Choose a Tone Range ... 226
- Adjust Color Balance ... 226
- Adjust Saturation ... 226
- Hue/Saturation Adjustment Layer ... 227

Preview Changes ... 227
- Adjust Hue/Saturation ... 228

Remove Color and Replace Color ... 229
- Color Removal ... 229

Using the "Color Range" Tool ... 230
- Replacing Color ... 230

Adjust Color Curves ... 230
Adjust Color for Skin Tone ... 231
- Adjusting Skin Tone in Photoshop Elements ... 231

Defringe Layer ... 232
Brightness/Contrast ... 232
Shadows/Highlights ... 233
Levels ... 234
Making tonal adjustments using Levels in Photoshop Elements ... 235
Histogram ... 235
Quick Fixes and Guided Fixes ... 237
- Convert to Black and White ... 237

Colorize Photo ... 238
Change colors in specific areas of a photo ... 239
Haze Removal ... 240
- How to Apply Haze Removal in Photoshop Elements ... 240

Adjust Sharpness ... 242
- Remove imperfections ... 242
- Duplicate your layer ... 242
- Create a high-pass layer ... 242
- Remove the color ... 242
- Blend it in ... 243
- Mask it off ... 244

Unsharp Mask	244
Smooth Skin	245
Adjust Facial Features	246
Shake Reduction	247
How to Use the Shake Reduction Tool	*247*
Frequently Asked Questions	248

CHAPTER NINE 249
WORK WITH PHOTOSHOP ELEMENTS LAYERS 249

Overview	249
How layers work	249
Fill layers	249
Adjustment layers	*250*
Type layers and shape layers	*250*
About the Layers panel	*250*
Adding layers	*250*
Create and name a new blank layer	*251*
Create a new layer from part of another layer	*251*
Convert the Background layer into a regular layer	252
Make a layer the Background layer	*253*
Create a new layer group	*253*
Assign a color to a layer or a group	*253*
Select a layer to edit	*253*
Select the Layer	*254*
Use the Move Tool	*254*
Use the Tab Key	*254*
Right-click on the document and select	*254*
The Layer Panel	254
The Name Tab	255
The Layer Row	256
The Layer Name	256
The Preview Thumbnail	257
The Active Layer	*257*
The Layer Visibility Icon	258
Changing a Layer's Blend Mode	259
Locking Layers	260
The Layer Search Bar	*261*
Changing the Thumbnail Image Size	263
Simplify or Flatten a Layer	265
How to Simplify a Photoshop Layer	*265*
Using Photoshop's Layers (F7) Panel to Simplify a Layer	*265*
Simplifying a Layer in Photoshop Using the "Layer" Option in the Top Menu	*266*
Copy layers from one image file to another	266

Layering Images in Photoshop Elements 266
Merging and flattening layers 267
Add transparency with Layer Masks 268
Layer masks 269
    Editing a layer mask *269*
Creating a new layer mask 270
Using layer masks with adjustment layers 271
    Removing a layer mask *271*
Create non-square graphics 271
Tips 272
    Use layers *272*
    Transform Tool *272*
    Guides *272*
    Save As Copy *272*
File formats that support alpha 273
Transform and warp a layer 274
    Transforming a Layer *274*
    Warping a Layer *274*
Frequently Asked Questions 275

CHAPTER TEN 276

CREATE AND EDIT TEXT 276

Overview 276
The Type Tools 276
Edit type in a type layer 277
Select characters 278
Choose a font family and style 279
    Choose a font size *279*
    Change text color *280*
    Apply style to text *280*
    Warp type *281*
    Unwarp type *282*
Change the orientation of a type layer 282
    Placing text on a layer *282*
Formatting a text layer 283
    Use your arrow keys *284*
    Editing a text layer *284*
The Type Tool Options Bin 285
    Font Family *285*
    Font Style *286*
    Font Size *286*
    Color Menu *286*
    Leading Menu *286*

- *Tracking* 286
- *Faux Bold* 286
- *Faux Italic* 286
- *Underline* 286
- *Strikethrough* 286
- *Align Text* 286
- *Toggle Text Orientation* 287
- *Warp Text* 287
- *Anti-aliased* 287
- *Shape and resize your text* 287
- OTHER TRANSFORM OPTIONS 288
- TYPE ON A SELECTION, SHAPE, OR PATH 288
  - *Use the Text on the Shape tool* 288
- USE THE TEXT ON THE SELECTION TOOL 289
- MAKE USE OF THE TEXT ON CUSTOM PATH TOOL. 289
- FREQUENTLY ASKED QUESTIONS 290

CHAPTER ELEVEN 291

ADD PHOTO EFFECTS AND FILTERS 291

- OVERVIEW 291
- THE FILTER/ADJUSTMENTS MENU 291
  - *Filter menu* 291
  - *Filter Gallery* 291
  - *Filters Panel* 291
- TIPS FOR USING FILTERS 292
- TIPS FOR CREATING FILTERED VISUAL EFFECTS 292
  - *Apply a filter* 293
- FILTER CATEGORIES 294
  - *Correct Camera Distortion* 294
  - *Adjustment Filters* 294
  - *Artistic Filters* 295
  - *Blur Filters* 295
  - *Brush Stroke Filters* 295
  - *Distort Filters* 295
  - *Noise Filters* 295
  - *Pixelate Filters* 295
  - *Render Filters* 295
  - *Sketch Filters* 295
  - *Stylize Filters* 295
  - *Texture Filters* 295
- OTHER FILTERS 296
  - *Digimarc Filter* 296
  - *The Gallery of Filters* 296

Texture and glass surface options	296
Texture	296
Scaling	296
Relief (If available)	296
Light (if available)	296
Invert	297
Enhance performance by using filters and effects	297
The Effects, Filters, and Styles panels	297
The Effects panel	297
Using the Graphics panel	297
Add stylized shapes or graphics to an image	298
Add an artistic background to an image	298
Add a frame or theme to an image	299
About photo effects	299
Frame	299
Image Effects	299
Textures	299
Artistic effects	300
Classic Effects	301
Color Match effects	301
Apply Color Match effect in Quick mode	301
Apply Color Match effect in advanced mode	303
Add stylized text to an image	304
Add graphics or effects to Favorites	304
Frequently Asked Questions	304

CHAPTER TWELVE 305

PHOTOSHOP ELEMENTS TRICKS 305

Overview	305
Swap out a face	305
Swap out a background	306
Remove warts and blemishes	307
Remove big things from your photos	308
Add things to your photos	309
Frequently Asked Questions	311

CHAPTER THIRTEEN 312

ADVANCED PHOTO EDITING TOOLS 312

Overview	312
Scan your photos	312
Screen captures	313
Windows	313
Mac	313

- Divide Scanned Photos 314
- Download photos from your digital camera 315
- Camera RAW Installation 316
  - Download and install the Adobe Camera Raw plug-in 316
- An Overview of Photoshop Elements' Camera Raw Dialog Box 316
  - Buttons at the top of Photoshop Elements' Camera Raw Dialog Box 316
  - Tools at the Right Side of the Camera Raw Dialog Box in Photoshop Elements 317
  - Buttons in the lower-left corner of Photoshop Elements' Camera Raw Dialog Box 317
  - Buttons underneath/below the Preview Image in Photoshop Elements' Camera Raw Dialog Box ... 318
  - Buttons at the bottom of Photoshop Elements' Camera Raw Dialog Box 318
- Edit in Camera RAW 319
  - Open and process camera raw files 319
- Adjust sharpness in camera raw files 320
  - Reducing noise in camera raw images 321
  - Save changes to camera raw images 321
- Open a camera raw image in the Edit workspace 322
- Camera raw settings 322
  - Zoom tool 322
  - Hand tool 322
  - White Balance tool 322
  - Crop tool 322
  - Straighten tool 323
  - Red Eye Removal 323
- Open the Preferences dialog box 323
  - Rotate Buttons 323
  - Set custom camera settings 323
- Process Multiple Files 323
- Photoshop Elements Preferences and Presets 324
  - New File Presets 324
  - Use preset tool options 325
- Change the display of items in a pop-up panel menu 326
  - Text Only 326
  - Large Thumbnail or Small Thumbnail 326
  - Small or Large List 326
  - Stroke Thumbnail 326
- Use the Preset Manager 326
- Load a library 327
  - Restore the default library or replace the currently displayed library 327
  - Reset 327
  - Save a library subset 327
  - Change the name of a preset 327
- Frequently Asked Questions 328

CHAPTER FOURTEEN **329**

LEARN ABOUT YOUR PHOTOSHOP ELEMENTS FILE ... 329
Overview ... 329
The Info Bar ... 329
Why does a "100% zoom" video fill only part of my computer screen? ... 330
Mismatch in Resolution ... 330
Pixel Aspect Ratio ... 330
Project Settings ... 330
Display Settings ... 331
Zoom Controls ... 331
Software Restrictions ... 331
Hardware Acceleration ... 331
Update Software ... 331
File Format Compatibility ... 331
Examine the Output Settings ... 331
The Status Bar ... 332
Document Information ... 332
Zoom Level ... 332
Tool Information ... 332
Scratch Sizes ... 332
Color Resolution and Mode ... 333
Notification and Status Area ... 333
The Info Panel ... 333
Activating the Info Panel ... 333
Understanding the Info Panel ... 333
Coordinates ... 333
Color Information ... 334
Document Information ... 334
Using the Info Panel ... 334
Cursor Position ... 334
Color Sampling ... 334
Measuring Distance ... 334
Setting Preferences ... 334
Closing the Information Panel ... 334
File Info ... 335
Frequently Asked Questions ... 335

CHAPTER FIFTEEN ... 336

MANAGE YOUR FILES WITH THE ORGANIZER ... 336
Overview ... 336
Adaptive Grid vs. Details View ... 336
Adaptive Grid ... 336
Grid Functionality ... 336

>   *Zoom Level Sensitivity* *336*
>   *Friendly User Interface* *336*
>   *Customization* *336*
>   DETAILS VIEW 337
>   *Zooming in for Precision* *337*
>   *Pixel-Level Editing* *337*
>   *Previewing Changes* *337*
>   *Navigating within the Detail* *337*
>   *Contextual Controls* *337*
>   AUTO CURATE 337
>   *Using Auto Curate* *338*
>   THE MEDIA BROWSER AREA 339
>   THE BACK OR ALL MEDIA BUTTONS 339
>   *Back Button* *339*
>   *All Media Button* *339*
>   MANUALLY ADD TO AND UPDATE YOUR ORGANIZER CATALOG 339
>   *Manually add photos* *339*
>   UPDATE THE ORGANIZER CATALOG 340
>   SWITCH BETWEEN ALBUM AND FOLDER VIEWS 340
>   *Changing the Album and Folder Views* *340*
>   SYNC YOUR MEDIA TO THE CLOUD 341
>   *Using Cloud Storage Services* *341*
>   *Using Adobe Creative Cloud (if Elements is available)* *341*
>   ADD YOUR METADATA 342
>   *Add Metadata* *342*
>   COMMON METADATA TYPES 342
>   *IPTC Metadata* *342*
>   *EXIF Metadata* *342*
>   *XMP Metadata* *343*
>   SEARCH YOUR CATALOG USING FILTERS 343
>   MANAGE YOUR FILES WITH KEYWORD TAGS 343
>   *Adding Keyword Tags* *343*
>   *Searching and Managing Keywords* *344*
>   *Manage your photos by Place* *344*
>   MANAGE YOUR MEDIA FILES BY DATE OR EVENT 345
>   *Organizing by Date* *345*
>   *Organizing by Event* *345*
>   INSTANT FIX A PHOTO 346
>   BACK UP YOUR ORGANIZER CATALOG 346
>   FREQUENTLY ASKED QUESTIONS 347

CHAPTER SIXTEEN **348**

CREATE FUN PIECES **348**

OVERVIEW 348
CREATE AN ORGANIZER SLIDESHOW 348
    Create slideshows 348
MANUALLY SELECT PHOTOS AND VIDEOS 349
CREATE A PHOTO COLLAGE 349
    Create photo collages 349
CREATE A PHOTO REEL 351
CREATE A QUOTE GRAPHIC 353
CREATE PHOTO PRINTS 354
    Select the Print Layout 355
    Set Print Options 355
    Preview and Adjust 355
    Print 355
CREATE A PHOTO BOOK 355
CREATE A GREETING CARD 357
CREATE A PHOTO CALENDAR 358
CREATE PRINTS AND GIFTS 360
FREQUENTLY ASKED QUESTIONS 361

CHAPTER SEVENTEEN 362

SHARE YOUR PHOTOS AND VIDEOS 362

OVERVIEW 362
SAVE CHANGES 362
    Save changes with a different file format, name, or location 362
    File Name 362
    File Format 362
    Add the Elements Organizer 363
SAVE IN VERSION SET WITH ORIGINAL 363
    Layers 363
    As a Copy 363
    ICC Profile 363
    Thumbnail 363
    Use Lower Case Extension 363
SHARE YOUR PHOTOS VIA EMAIL 364
    Using Photoshop Elements Organizer 364
    Using Adobe Photoshop Elements Editor 364
SHARE YOUR PHOTOS ON FLICKR 365
    Using Flickr 365
    Share your video on Vimeo 366
    Setting up a Vimeo upload 366
SHARE AS A PDF SLIDESHOW 367
    Exporting as Images 367
CREATING A PDF FROM IMAGES 367

  Use External Software...*367*
  Online Converters..*368*
 STORING MEDIA IN THE CLOUD... 368
 FREQUENTLY ASKED QUESTIONS 368
 CONCLUSION 369

INDEX **370**

INTRODUCTION

Adobe has announced the 2024 version of Photoshop Elements, a basic image editing application. The revised version, powered by AI, now has an enhanced UI and a slew of additional capabilities that make picture editing a breeze. Similarly, the business has released Premium Elements 2024, a straightforward video editing application. Photoshop Element 2024 is available for both Windows and Mac. A companion app is also available for smartphones operating on the Android and iOS platforms. Unlike full-fledged Photoshop, the Elements edition does not need a subscription and costs $99.99 for a one-time license. Keep in mind that if you already have a Photoshop Elements 2023 license, Adobe will give you a discount on the current license purchase. Photoshop Elements 2024 has a redesigned user interface with a dedicated dark mode and easy-to-use features. The new match color tool, which enables users to fine-tune the color of a photo using built-in presets or a custom one with a single click, is one of the edition's primary attractions. Photoshop Elements 2024 by Adobe was designed with a small program size in mind, using very little space on a computer and launching rapidly for best usage. Photoshop Elements 2024, with new and upgraded capabilities, is the most powerful and sophisticated version of the popular consumer photo editing program to date. With Adobe Sensei AI, automation, and a new editing experience, you can easily go from small picture tweaks to entire makeovers.

CHAPTER ONE
GETTING STARTED

Overview

Chapter One discusses the new additions in Photoshop Elements 2024, the system requirements to download and install the new software, and the actual process of downloading and installing Photoshop Elements 2024.

New additions

This current edition offers new AI-powered functionality as well as a new editing experience with a new design, making it simpler than ever to go from small adjustments to entire makeover.

Match tone and color to create new feeling

Simply select from a wide range of built-in presets or use your picture, then click once to fine-tune brightness, hue, or saturation.

Create and share fast-moving Photo Reels

Reels of your best photos, each with its text, effects, and graphics, will be played again. You can now save new Photo Reels as MP4s or GIFs for simple sharing on all of your favorite social channels.

Enjoy a completely new editing experience with a new appearance

Discover eye-catching contemporary fonts, icons, buttons, and colors. You can also choose between bright and dark modes.

Choose an image sky or background with one click for easier editing

New automated selections powered by Adobe AI make it easy to improve or replace just one part of a picture.

Discover one-click photo Quick Actions in one place

Popular one-click changes are now available, making picture editing faster and more seamless. Blur or erase a background in an instant, smooth skin, dehaze or colorize a shot and more.

Remove JPEG artifacts for a more natural appearance

Powered by Adobe AI, this new option in the Quick Actions panel allows you to improve compressed JPEGs with a single click.

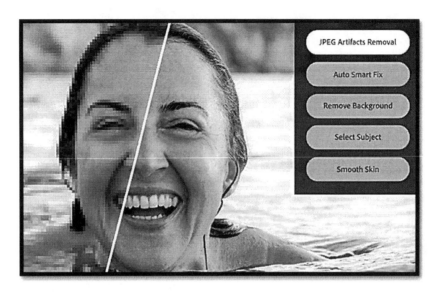

Grow your skills along the way with Guided Edits

With 62 step-by-step Guided Edits in Photoshop Elements 2024, you can make modest edits, creative creations, or eye-catching effects.

What's new is as follows:

- **Create stylish photo text for shareable posts** - Text options have been streamlined into an easy-to-follow guided edit, allowing you to customize your posts in seconds.
- **Using Guided Edits, you can make your subjects stand out by using new backgrounds** in the Replace Background Guided Edit, new sky in the Perfect Landscape Guided Edit, and new patterns in the Pattern Brush Guided Edit.

Access free Adobe Stock pictures to broaden your creative options

With access to hundreds of great stock photos from inside Photoshop Elements, you can try a new background, assemble a collage, or create an inspirational Quote Graphic.

With the new Artistic Effect settings, you can turn images into works of art

Using Adobe AI, simply click to apply effects inspired by legendary works of art or popular art styles.

Things you need to Know

Principles of photo and graphics editing

Pixels

A pixel is the smallest constituent of a digital picture, typically a dot that holds color and brightness information. Each pixel is a small brushstroke that, when merged with millions of others, produces the whole image.

Pixel Characteristics

Color Information

- **RGB Values**: Pixels in Photoshop Elements are commonly specified using the RGB color model (Red, Green, and Blue). These three colors have values in each pixel, which determines its overall color.
- **Color Depth**: The color depth is determined by the number of bits supplied to each pixel. Higher color depth provides for a wider spectrum of colors, but it also means bigger file sizes.

Transparency and Brightness

- **Brightness**: Pixels also contain brightness or intensity information, which affects how light or dark a pixel looks in an image.
- **Transparency**: Some pixels may be partly or completely translucent, enabling the background or layers underneath them to be seen. This is very handy for making overlays and composites.

Pixels' Function in Image Editing

Image Resolution

- **Resolution**: An image's resolution is defined by the number of pixels per inch (PPI) or pixels per centimeter (PPCM). More pixels equal a sharper and more detailed picture with higher resolution.
- **Image Dimensions:** The dimensions of an image are proportional to the number of pixels. Increasing dimensions without increasing pixels may result in pixelation and a loss of quality.

Editing and Manipulation

- **Brushes and Tools:** Photoshop Elements has several tools for manipulating individual pixels. Brushes, for example, can be used to paint or remove pixels, modifying the image's look.
- **Filters and Effects**: In Photoshop Elements, applying filters and effects entails altering pixel values to produce desired artistic or corrective consequences.

Pixel Difficulties

Pixilation

- **Image Enlargement**: Increasing the scale of an image without keeping a sufficient number of pixels may cause pixelation, in which individual pixels become visible, resulting in a loss of clarity.

File Size

- **Large Files**: Images with a high pixel count and color depth might have enormous file sizes, which can affect storage and loading speeds.

Loss of Detail

- **Downsizing**: Image downsizing may result in a loss of detail when pixels are deleted or averaged, thus impacting overall quality.

How to Use Pixels in Photoshop

Pixel Selection

- Photoshop has several tools for choosing pixels, including the Marquee, Lasso, and Magic Wand tools. You can use these tools to isolate certain sections of a picture for modification.

Pixel Editing

- Once you've picked pixels, you can make a variety of changes. This covers color, brightness, contrast, and other changes. The Brush and Eraser tools are often used for pixel-level editing.

Pixel Manipulation and Layers

- Photoshop has a layered technique, enabling you to stack distinct picture components on top of each other. Each layer comprises pixels, which you may edit separately to have fine control over your design.

Pixel Filters

- Photoshop has a plethora of filters that can be applied to pixels. These filters can be used to create effects such as blurring, sharpening, distorting, or stylizing pixels in a variety of ways.

Retouching with Pixels

- The Clone Stamp and Healing Brush tools are popular retouching tools. These programs replicate pixels from one section of a picture to another, assisting in the removal of flaws or undesired features.

Pixel Output and Export

Image File Formats

- Photoshop users can save their work in a variety of picture formats, each of which handles pixels differently. JPEG, PNG, and TIFF are common formats. Each format has its own compression and quality settings, which have an impact on pixel fidelity.

Print Resolution vs. Web Resolution

- Different resolutions may be required depending on the intended purpose (print or online). Print projects often need a higher quality (300 PPI), although online photos may sometimes be lower (72 PPI).

Resolution

The resolution of an image is determined by the number of pixels it contains. The resolution is determined by the pixel count along a one-inch horizontal line in your image. Having stated that, if you possess a total of 72 pixels spanning one horizontal inch, the resolution of said image would amount to 72 ppi, which stands for pixels per inch. Optimal printing results are achieved with higher resolutions. The recommended resolution for printing an image is 300 pixels per inch (ppi). When using an image solely for online purposes or display on a screen, it is advisable to opt for a lower resolution rather than printing it. This is to ensure that the resolution of the image aligns with screen resolutions, also known as display resolutions. The recommended resolution for an onscreen image is 72 pixels per inch (ppi). When adjusting the resolution of an image, one is essentially determining the desired pixel density per inch within the image. An image with a resolution of 600 ppi will consist of 600 pixels per inch. A resolution of 600 pixels per inch (ppi) is considered high, resulting in images that exhibit exceptional clarity and intricate details. Now, let us proceed to compare the aforementioned image with a resolution of 72 pixels per inch (ppi), which exhibits a significantly lower pixel density. As it can be inferred, the visual quality of the image will not be comparable to that of the 600 ppi version. It is advisable to aim for capturing images at the highest possible resolution and quality when scanning or capturing. It is advisable to possess a greater quantity of information rather than an insufficient amount. Image editing applications, such as Photoshop, possess a greater facility in eliminating undesired image data, thereby reducing the image size, as opposed to generating new pixel information to enlarge an image.

Choosing the Correct Resolution for your Image

Printing Resolution

Professional Publications

Certain professional-grade printers have a specific requirement for images to possess a resolution of up to 600 pixels per inch (ppi) to achieve optimal print quality. It is advisable to consult with your printer or publisher regarding the necessary image resolution before submitting any images.

Non-Professional

Printers that are not considered professional-grade, such as inkjet, laser, and other commonly used printers, are most suitable for printing images with a minimum resolution of 200 to 300 pixels per inch (ppi) or higher. A resolution of 200 pixels per inch (PPI) is suitable for images that are intended to have an aesthetically pleasing appearance without any specific technical requirements. It is highly recommended that photographic prints have a resolution of at least 300 pixels per inch (ppi). The recommended resolution for images intended for large-format poster printing typically ranges from 150 to 300 pixels per inch (ppi), with the exact value depending on the intended viewing distance of the image.

Screen Resolution

The characteristics of screen images diverge from those intended for printing due to the need to consider pixel dimensions specific to monitors, TVs, projectors, or displays, as opposed to PPI. The usage of PPI (pixels per inch) is recommended for printed images, while the pixel dimensions of an image are the primary factors that determine its size and quality when displayed on the web or various devices.

Web

It has long been conventionally held that images should be saved with a resolution of 72 PPI. However, it is important to clarify that the prevailing misconception pertains to the notion that image quality for web images is primarily determined by resolution or PPI value. In reality, the key determinant lies in the pixel dimensions of the image. The variability in monitor specifications, including resolution, poses a challenge when designing websites that aim to achieve optimal image display across all types of displays.

Over time, advancements in technology have led to notable enhancements in the quality of our display systems. The most widely favored displays currently in the market are Apple's latest retina displays, which are featured on their most recent line of Macbooks, iPhones, and iPads.

Projector / Powerpoint

Similar to web images, it is important for images intended for projectors to align with the pixel dimensions of the respective projector. Similar to computer monitors, projectors also possess their unique display dimensions. In the context of projectors with a 4:3 aspect ratio, it is common for the display to have a resolution of 1024 x 768 pixels. Therefore, an image with the same dimensions and a resolution of 72 pixels per inch (PPI) would be considered an optimal size for projection.

Raster vs. vector graphics

Raster images and vector graphics serve distinct purposes in design, necessitating a comprehensive comprehension of their appropriate applications and contexts.

What is a raster file?

A raster file refers to a type of digital image file that is composed of a grid of pixels, each containing specific color information. Raster files are composed of pixels, which are small colored squares. These pixels, when combined in large numbers, can create intricate and detailed images, such as photographs. The resolution of an image directly correlates with its quality, meaning that a higher pixel counts results in superior visual fidelity, while a lower pixel count yields a lower-quality output. The pixel count within an image is contingent upon the specific file format employed, such as JPEG, GIF, or PNG.

Key attributes

1. Raster images possess a resolution that is fixed, and any attempts to resize them may result in a degradation of detail or the occurrence of pixelation.
2. Raster graphics are well-suited for the creation of intricate and lifelike images, thereby rendering them highly suitable for the representation of photographs.

There are several advantages to consider

1. **Realism**: Raster graphics demonstrate exceptional proficiency in accurately depicting intricate details and textures commonly observed in photos.
2. **Photo editing software** such as Photoshop Elements is highly proficient in enhancing raster images, providing a wide array of tools including brushes, filters, and layer effects.

Limitations

1. **Scalability**: The issue of scalability arises when enlarging raster images, as this process often leads to degradation in quality, with pixels becoming more apparent.
2. **File Size**: Raster images may exhibit larger file sizes, particularly when rendered at higher resolutions.

What is a vector file?

A vector file is a type of digital graphic that is composed of mathematical equations and geometric shapes, rather than pixels. It is commonly used in graphic design and illustration, as it allows for scalability and flexibility without loss of image quality. Furthermore, vector files use mathematical equations, lines, and curves that are anchored to specific points on a grid to generate a visual representation. Vector files do not contain pixels. A vector file uses mathematical equations to accurately represent the shape, outline, and color fill of an image. Due to the inherent flexibility of the mathematical formula, it is possible to adjust the size of a vector image without compromising its quality.

Key attributes

1. Vector graphics possess the advantageous quality of being resolution-independent, enabling them to be resized without any loss in quality. This attribute renders them exceptionally suitable for applications such as logos and illustrations.
2. The vector graphic comprises editable objects, affording meticulous control over shapes and paths.

There are several advantages to consider, including

1. **Scalability** is a notable advantage of vector graphics, particularly for logos and designs that require frequent resizing.
2. The **editable elements** within a vector graphic possess the capability to be effortlessly manipulated, reshaped, or recolored.

Limitations

1. In terms of intricate and lifelike visuals, vector graphics may not be as well-suited as other formats, particularly when it comes to highly **detailed and realistic images**, such as photos.
2. **Learning Curve**: The usage of vector graphics frequently necessitates the acquisition of a distinct skill set and comprehension in contrast to raster graphics.

What is the difference between raster and vector files?

Raster and vector files are widely recognized as the predominant formats utilized for the representation of visual content. The two options present distinct approaches to representing images, thus necessitating careful consideration when determining the most suitable choice. There are several key distinctions between raster and vector graphics.

Resolution

One of the primary distinctions between raster and vector files lies in their respective resolutions. The resolution of a raster file is commonly denoted in DPI (dots per inch) or PPI (pixels per inch). When the scale of a raster image is increased, either through zooming in or expanding its dimensions, the discrete pixels that comprise the image become perceptible to the viewer. Raster files offer a broader spectrum of colors, enable more extensive color manipulation, and exhibit more intricate light and shading details compared to vector files.

However, it is important to note that raster files experience degradation in image quality when resized. A straightforward method for discerning whether an image is raster or vector in nature is to enlarge its dimensions. If the image experiences blurring or pixelation, the file format in question is probably a raster file. When working with vector image files, resolution is not a concern. Vectors can be resized, rescaled, and reshaped without any degradation in image quality, allowing for infinite adjustments. Vector files are widely used for images that require versatility in size, such as logos that must be adaptable for both business cards and billboards.

Uses

Typically, digital photographs are commonly stored as raster files. Numerous digital cameras possess the capability to autonomously capture and store photographs in the form of raster files. Additionally, it is worth noting that the majority of images encountered on the internet are also presented in raster format. Raster files are frequently utilized in the realm of image, photo, and graphic editing. Vector files are more suitable for digital illustrations, intricate graphics, and logos. The reason for this is that the resolution of vectors remains consistent when resized, rendering them highly compatible with a diverse range of printed formats. Certain projects may incorporate a combination of raster and vector images. In the context of brochure design, it is common practice to use vector graphics for the company logo, while using raster files for incorporating photography.

File sizes

In general, raster files tend to have larger file sizes compared to vector files. These devices can incorporate millions of pixels, resulting in exceptionally high levels of detail. The substantial dimensions of these entities may have an adverse effect on the available storage capacity of the device, as well as impede the expeditious loading of web pages. Raster files can be compressed to enhance storage efficiency and optimize web performance, thereby facilitating faster and more convenient sharing. Vector files are significantly more efficient in terms of file size compared to raster files, as they solely consist of mathematical formulas that define the design.

Compatibility and conversion

Raster files can be conveniently accessed, edited, and shared across various applications and web browsers. Vector files are not easily accessible, as they often necessitate the use of specialized software for both opening and editing purposes. While there may be certain difficulties involved, it is indeed feasible to perform the conversion of vector files to raster or vice versa, as required.

Types of Files and Extensions

The software typically identifies the file type, distinguishing between raster and vector formats. There exist various types and extensions of both raster and vector files, each possessing distinct characteristics and functionalities.

Vector File Types

Vector graphics, commonly referred to as scalable vector graphics (SVG), are a type of digital image format. The graphics in question comprise fixed dots that are interconnected by lines and curves, reminiscent of the connect-the-dot exercises commonly encountered during childhood. The graphics in question are referred to as resolution-independent, as they are not reliant on pixels. This characteristic allows for infinite scalability. The lines exhibit a remarkable level of precision, maintaining their integrity and level of detail regardless of their scale. The graphics in question are device-independent, indicating that their quality remains consistent regardless of the printer's dot density or the screen's pixel count. Due to their composition of lines and anchor points, vector files possess a relatively compact file size.

Raster images consist of pixels or small dots that use color and tone to generate the visual representation. When an image is magnified or scaled up, the individual pixels become visible and resemble small squares on a grid, akin to the appearance of squares on graph paper. The production of these images involves the usage of digital cameras, the process of scanning physical images into a computer, or the use of raster-based software. The resolution of an image is determined by the number of pixels it contains, with a fixed limit for each image.

This phenomenon is commonly referred to as resolution. Increasing the number of pixels yields enhanced quality when maintaining or enlarging the original dimensions. However, this augmentation concurrently amplifies the file size and the storage space required to accommodate the file. A decrease in pixel count corresponds to a decrease in resolution. The resolution of an image determines the maximum size at which it can be scaled up without pixelation becoming visible. Nevertheless, it is important to note that when a high-resolution image is printed at a reduced size, the pixels tend to become densely packed together, resulting in a visually unappealing outcome. This phenomenon is comparable to the lack of pixel density in a larger image, both of which can undermine the overall professionalism of the visual representation.

Raster vs. vector files: frequently asked questions

How do you know if an image is a vector?

To determine whether an image is a vector, one can examine the file extension and look for formats commonly associated with vector graphics, as mentioned earlier. An alternative approach involves resizing the image. If the resolution remains consistent upon scaling, the file in question is probably a vector file. If the image becomes pixelated, it is probably a raster file.

Is a Portable Document Format (PDF) classified as a raster or vector format?

The majority of PDFs are typically classified as vector files. The ability to save PDFs as raster files is contingent upon the specific software program used for document creation. As an illustration, it is worth noting that any PDF generated through the usage of Adobe Photoshop will be stored in the form of a raster file.

Is it possible to convert a JPEG image into a vector file?

Adobe Illustrator can be used to convert a JPEG image into a vector format.

- To begin, please access your JPEG image within the Adobe Illustrator software.
- Choose the JPEG file and navigate to the top bar, then click on the "**Image Trace**" option.
- Next, proceed to choose the option "**Expand**" to convert the image into a vector format.
- To separate the new vector image from its background, you can use the right-click function and select the "**Ungroup**" option.
- Proceed to make necessary edits to the image, and subsequently save and export it as a vector file.

Is Adobe Photoshop vector-based software?

No, Adobe Photoshop is a raster-based software application, which employs pixels to generate intricate images. One of the primary applications of Adobe Photoshop involves the manipulation and enhancement of digital photographs, typically stored as raster files. However, it is possible to access and modify vector files within Photoshop by using either a smart object or a rasterized file.

Image Size vs. Canvas Size

Canvas size and picture size may sound and seem similar in Photoshop, but they are not the same thing. Although both affect the final size of the file, the canvas size and image size selections affect distinct areas of your project. Since they are on the same menu, it is simple to mix them up.

What Is Photoshop Canvas Size?

Canvas symbolizes your workplace in Adobe's universe. This word does not refer to the picture you opened in Photoshop, but rather to the program's usable area. You may expand or reduce the size of the area you can work on by setting the canvas size.

Is the size of an artboard and a canvas the same?

In some ways, the artboard and canvas sizes are fairly comparable (more so than the canvas and picture sizes). These two, however, are not the same thing. In Photoshop, an artboard is a blank canvas on which you may place photos, objects, text, and other items. You can add several layers and layer groups to the project's artboard. In Photoshop, you can have many artboards active at the same time. The canvas represents the single workspace that you have open. Artboard and canvas sizes are the same in that they both modify your working area but not any components within them. When you change the size of the artboard or canvas, all images and information in the workspace will retain their previous proportions. However, artboards have numerous pages, while canvases only have one.

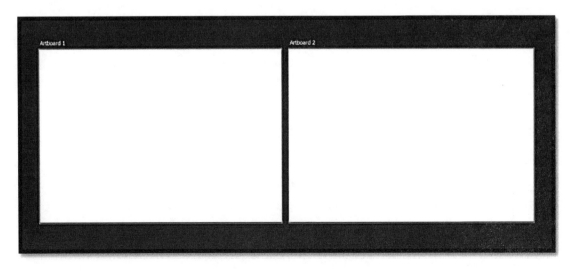

What is an Image Size?

The actual dimensions and resolution of the picture you've opened in Photoshop are affected by image size. When you want to print a picture, you can adjust the image to the precise size of the print you want to generate. Changing the picture size affects the image's quality since it either expands or shrinks the pixels in the photo. If you raise the picture size too much, the image may get pixelated. If you severely reduce the picture size, the image may look sharper because the pixels become more compressed and crushed.

What Is the Distinction Between Canvas and Image Size?

The primary distinction between these two words is the magnitude of the effect. Canvas size expands or contracts the usable area, while image size expands or contracts the actual size of the picture opened in the software. The first expands or shrinks the workspace (leaving the picture on the workspace alone), while the second stretches and shrinks the pixels in the image that has been opened. A nice way to see this in action is to compare what happens when you raise the canvas size to what occurs when you increase the picture size.

Let's look at this image, which is 4,480 pixels by 6,720 pixels in size.

Let's proceed to expand the canvas to 6,000 by 9,000 pixels, which is greater than the original picture size. The outcome will be that the picture now has blank margins around it. This demonstrates that the usable area has grown, but the picture itself has not been changed in any way.

 Let us go on to do the same thing with image size, increasing it to 6,000 pixels by 9,000 pixels. As a result, the image is stretched to meet the dimensions specified above.

As you can see, the size modification has a varied effect on canvas size and picture size. From the standpoint of a photographer, adjusting the canvas size allows you to add borders to your picture or crop it in. You can change the picture size if you need the photo to be larger or smaller to meet the resolution of a print or online upload.

Changing Image Size and Resolution

- To change the size of a picture, go to the **Menu Bar** and choose **Image > Resize > Image Size**.

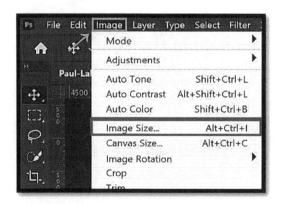

- The Image Size dialog box will then appear.

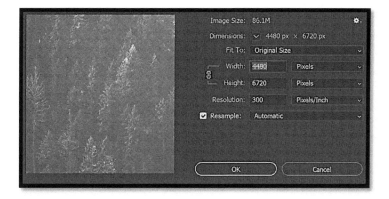

- Enter the updated image dimensions in the Document Size area of the dialogue box. Dimensions are shown in inches by default. To change the measurement to percent, centimeters, millimeters, points, picas, or columns, click the downward arrow to the right of Inches.
- Proceed to enter a new value in the box to adjust the resolution.
- If you want to resample the picture, check the box next to "**Resample Image**" and then choose a resampling technique from the dropdown menu. When you resample a picture, you can adjust both the size and the pixels. The advantage of resampling is that you receive the highest quality picture for the image size you choose without having an output file size that is too huge.

The resampling approaches are as follows:

- **Bicubic**: The standard resampling procedure. Produces a medium-quality picture. Unless you obtain considerably better results with another, this is the best resampling approach to use.
- **Bicubic Smoother**: Produces quality is higher than bicubic, although edges may be softened.
- **Bicubic Sharper**: Produces high-quality results. Image sharpening.
- **Nearest Neighbor**: The quickest resampling approach. Reduces the file size. Best suited for photos with vast regions of the same hue.
- **Bilinear**: Produces a medium-quality picture. It works well with grayscale and line art. When you're done, click **OK**.

Changing the Canvas Size

In addition to resizing photos, you can widen the canvas by adding blank space to either side of an image. Remember that this will not expand the picture. It simply increases the amount of space on the sides of your canvas. The canvas that you add shows in background layers as the background color. All other layers are translucent. **To change the canvas size, follow these steps:**

- Navigate to **Image > Resize > Canvas Size**. The Canvas Size dialog box will then appear.

You can now choose from the following options:

- Enter the new height and width in the height and width boxes. By selecting the dropdown box beside either the height or width box, you can input it in inches, picas, centimeters, percent, pixels, columns, or millimeters.
- The anchor can also be used. Select a location for the picture on the new canvas.
- When completed, click the **OK button**.

Selections

A selection is a defined section of a photograph. When you make a selection, the area around it becomes editable (for example, you may brighten one section of a photo without changing the rest). A selection may be made using either a selection tool or a selection command. The selection is surrounded by a selection border that you can hide. You can change, copy, or remove pixels inside the selection boundary, but you can't touch anything beyond the selection border until you deselect it. Adobe Photoshop Elements has selection tools for several types of selections. The Elliptical Marquee tool, for example, picks circular and elliptical areas, while the Magic Wand tool may choose an area of similar hues with a single click. With one of the Lasso tools, you can make more complicated selections. You can even use feathering and anti-aliasing to soften the edges of a selection.

Layers

A layer in Photoshop Elements is similar to a transparent sheet piled on top of other sheets. Each layer may include various visual components such as text, shapes, or changes. You can change, relocate, or hide particular areas of a picture without impacting the rest by grouping objects into layers.

Key Concepts

Background Layer

- Every new Photoshop Elements project normally begins with a background layer. This layer is often used to hold the primary picture or canvas.
- The background layer is often locked, which means it is initially secured to prevent unauthorized alterations. It may, however, be unlocked for altering.

Adding Layers

- In the Layers panel, click the "**New Layer**" button to add new layers to your project.
- Layers can be of several sorts, such as picture layers, text layers, adjustment layers, and so on.

Layer Visibility

- Layers can be made visible or invisible, enabling you to concentrate on certain aspects of your project while working on it.
- In the Layers panel, clicking the eye symbol next to a layer toggles its visibility.

Layer Opacity

- Adjust the opacity of each layer to make it more or less translucent. This is great for generating subtle effects or flawlessly mixing layers.

Layer Styles

- Layer styles like drop shadows and glows may be added to layers to improve the look of items on that layer.

Layer Mask

- Layer masks allow you to selectively conceal or show elements of a layer without erasing them. This is a really useful non-destructive editing option.

Blending Modes

- Layers can be blended in several ways, which change how they interact with the layers underneath them. Overlay, multiply, and Screen are examples of common blending modes.

Grouping Layers

- Layers can be organized into groups to keep your project well-structured. This is very useful when working on intricate designs with many pieces.

Usage

Photo Editing

- Layers are vital for picture editing and enhancement. Separate layers for adjustments, filters, and text allow for simple editing.

Graphic Design

- Layers are used by graphic designers to construct complicated designs using various components such as text, pictures, and shapes. Layers provide for more design flexibility and control.

Digital Art

- Layers are used by artists to build up digital paintings, enabling them to work on individual components separately and experiment with different effects.

Alpha

In Photoshop, an alpha channel is produced as an extra channel alongside the RGB color channels and enables you to store an image's or selection's transparency settings. To preserve selections for later use or to transfer selection information across editing applications, alpha channels are used. When you simplify the selection process, learning how to deal with alpha channels may enhance your productivity. You can use selections to isolate particular portions of your picture or to modify the opacity of specific sections. Creating an alpha channel allows you to save your selections for later use if necessary. This is particularly useful when dealing with difficult selections during a project.

What is an Alpha Channel?

An alpha channel is an additional channel that is added to a picture to enable you to alter certain components while leaving the rest of the image alone. It enables you to quickly generate translucent sections and preserve a selection for later usage. Simply described, an alpha channel is a form of mask that greatly simplifies picture editing. To understand how an alpha channel works, you must first grasp what normal channels are and how they operate on an image. By default, every image in Photoshop has three channels. RGB is made up of three channels: red, green, and blue. When you choose these channels, you can see how much of each hue is in the picture. You can also add a new channel, known as an alpha channel, to allow for more creative editing of the picture.

An alpha channel can be used for a variety of purposes, including:

- Adjust the opacity of certain parts in your picture.
- Separate picture components to create a translucent background.
- Save challenging options for later use.

Learning what alpha channels are and how to use them correctly can essentially make your workflow simpler, and quicker, and improve your editing talents. The biggest advantage of using an alpha channel is that it allows you to construct translucent sections that can be transferred to other applications that accept alpha channels. This is useful if you need to isolate a certain item in a picture for usage in other applications, such as video editing software. After you've made your choice, save it as an alpha channel. When you move the picture to another software, it will recognize the alpha channel and allow you to work with the selection.

How to create and edit an alpha channel

Making an alpha channel is easy. However, it opens up a slew of additional editing possibilities, allowing you to take your editing talents to the next level. You can isolate an item from the background in an alpha channel, allowing you to use the object on different backgrounds for different projects.

Creating an Alpha Channel

Navigate to the Channels panel, which is placed next to your layers, to create an entirely new alpha channel. If you don't see it, go to **Window > Channels** and it will show.

Select **New Channel** from the drop-down menu at the upper right of the Channels screen. On the pop-up window, give the channel a name.

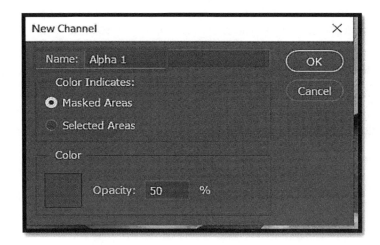

The brush tool can then be used by choosing it from the toolbar or pressing B on your keyboard. This allows you to draw areas you want to pick by subtracting from the alpha channel. Then, at the bottom of the Channels window, click "**Save selection as channel**" to make a selection from your marks. If you use any of the Adjustment tools, you can change the selected area as required. At 50% opacity, the alpha channel appears as crimson overlay. When you use the Brush tool, it eliminates bits of the overlay to reveal the location of your selection.

RGB Color

RGB stands for the main colors of light, red, green, and blue. Different colors are formed in the RGB color model by mixing differing intensities of these three hues. This model is additive, which means that when all three hues are merged at maximum intensity, white light is produced. When all hues are missing, the effect is black.

The following is an explanation of how RGB color works in Adobe Photoshop Elements:

Color Channels

- In Photoshop Elements, each RGB picture is made up of three color channels: red, green, and blue.
- The combination of these three channels produces the full-color spectrum seen by the human eye.

Color Picker

- In Photoshop Elements, use the Color Picker to choose colors. This tool lets you choose the strength of red, green, and blue to create a certain color.
- In addition, the Color Picker shows the final color as a hexadecimal value, which is a six-digit code that represents the combination of the three-color channels.

Color Modes

- Photoshop Elements supports a wide range of color modes, including RGB. RGB is the chosen color option for dealing with digital pictures for displays (such as online graphics).
- Other color modes, such as CMYK, are used for print, but RGB is essential for digital work because it closely matches how monitors display colors.

Adjustment Layers

- In Photoshop Elements, you can use adjustment layers to perform RGB modifications. These layers enable you to change the color, brightness, and contrast of a picture without affecting the original.
- Each RGB channel can be adjusted separately, providing exact control over the image's final look.

Blending Modes

- Photoshop Elements' blending modes allow you to mix layers in a variety of ways. Depending on the mixing mode used, RGB colors interact differently, allowing for more creative and complex results.

Color Correction

- RGB color correcting is a regular Photoshop Elements operation. This is changing the color balance of a picture to ensure that the colors seem natural and correct.
- The Levels and Curves adjustments, which enable you to fine-tune the intensity of each channel, are widely used for RGB color correction.

Exporting to the Web

- When producing photos for the web, keep RGB color in mind. Images intended for online usage should be in RGB color mode to guarantee correct display on displays.

The Tools Options Bin

The Editor window has a long, narrow strip at the bottom that changes to show various items based on what you're doing at the time. When you first open a picture, the picture Bin appears in this section, displaying all of your open files. When you click a tool in the toolbox on the left side of the Editor window, the Photo Bin is replaced by tool settings named (logically) the Tool Options. The Photo Bin/Tool Options section is set in place; you cannot move or resize it. You may, however, conceal it by clicking the down arrow at the right end of the light gray bar slightly above it. This provides you more room, but it also conceals the tool settings, making it difficult to perform any work with it hidden. Click the **Photo Bin or Tool Options button** at the bottom of the window to bring it back. The Photo Bin does a lot more than simply display which images are currently open. If you want to use the images in a project, you can rearrange the thumbnails by dragging them into the bin.

There are also two drop-down selections in the bin:

- **Show Open Files**: This option in the top left corner of the bin allows you to choose whether the Photo Bin shows the photos now open in the Editor, chosen photos from the Organizer, or any albums (Albums) you've created. You may even

transfer files from the Organizer to the bin without first opening them. Simply click photos in the Organizer to choose them, then return to the Editor and change this option to "**Show Files Selected in Organizer**"; the photos you chose in the Organizer will be waiting for you in the bin. Double-click one to make it editable.
- **Bin Actions**: This is where the Photo Bin comes in handy, although it's difficult to find: it's the small four-line square in the bin's top right. This option allows you to print the images in the bin or create an album without ever leaving the Photo Bin. If you don't use the Organizer, the Photo Bin is a very useful feature since it allows you to organize images into albums (Albums), and then choose the album's name from the bin's Show Open Files option to see those photos. If you like to keep things organized, the Show Grid menu choice adds a thin black line across each thumbnail.

What is a native PSD file?

In the field of photography, image editing is a critical step in the process. In the digital era, image manipulation has replaced darkroom techniques. Adobe Photoshop is one of the most popular image editing tools, and its native file type is called PSD (Photoshop Document). Photoshop has had a massive influence on the design and art worlds, and as a consequence, PSD files have their mythology and story. PSD files are flexible and widely used. It is used to embed pictures and layers in Adobe Illustrator, Adobe Premiere Pro, Adobe After Effects, Adobe InDesign, and many more third-party tools, in addition to Photoshop. If this powerful file format suddenly vanished, it would leave a huge hole.

Recognizing the PSD File Format

Adobe Photoshop Elements, the industry-leading image editing program, uses the PSD (Photoshop Document) file format as its native file type. Photoshop files have the file extension ".psd" at the end. Adobe (formerly Adobe Systems Incorporated) created the file format in 1988 and made it available to the public as part of Photoshop in 1990. It is the foundation of several Photoshop features, including masks, layers, adjustment layers, layer effects, blending modes, and more. PSD files enable the smooth saving of these characteristics while keeping high-quality, lossless, editable documents. PSD files hold photos as well as their layers, masks, effects, and other features, enabling photographers and designers to work on certain aspects of a composition without impacting the rest of the image. As previously stated, the PSD file format is built at its core to hold multiple image components non-destructively. This implies that any modifications made to the picture can be undone or adjusted without affecting the original data permanently.

PSD files are raster and vector graphics compatible, with editable text, paths, vector shapes, and masks, making them excellent for a broad variety of creative tasks. In terms of technical settings, the PSD format allows for a maximum file size of 2 gigabytes and a width and height of up to 30,000 pixels. Adobe, on the other hand, provides the PSB (Photoshop Big) format for bigger files or more complicated projects, which enables files up to 300,000 pixels in width and height and nearly infinite file size. PSD files are often not designed for final picture transmission because of their enormous size and proprietary nature, which limits compatibility with other tools and platforms. Instead, they are used as a working format for heavy modification, with final photos transferred to more commonly recognized formats like JPEG, TIFF, or PNG.

Different Types of Layers

Photoshop has many layer types that can be used for a variety of reasons in a project.

The following are some of the most popular types of layers:

1. **Pixel layers**: These are the standard layer types that hold pixel data. When you paint, paste, or insert an image into the document, they are generated.
2. **Adjustment layers**: These layers are used to make non-destructive changes to the layers below them. **Typical adjustment layers include:**
    - Brightness/Contrast
    - Levels
    - Curves
    - Exposure
    - Vibrance
    - Hue/Saturation
    - Color Balance
    - Channel Mixer
    - Photo Filter
    - Black and White
    - Threshold
    - Invert
    - Posterize
    - Gradient Map

- Selective Color

3. **Text layers**: Text layers are used to include text in your design. They are made by using the Text tool and are completely customizable, enabling you to modify the font, size, color, and other text attributes.
4. **Shape layers:** They are generated using the Shape tool and are made up of vector shapes such as rectangles, ellipses, or custom pathways. These layers may be scaled and altered without sacrificing quality.
5. **Smart object layers:** Layers with Smart Objects enable you to include raster or vector images in a Photoshop project. When scaled or changed, they retain their original quality and may be modified non-destructively.
6. **Layer groups:** Layer groups aid in layer organization by grouping layers in a folder-like manner. This makes complicated projects with several levels simpler to handle.
7. **Fill layers:** Use fill layers to add a solid color, gradient, or pattern to your design. They are produced by selecting **"Layer" > "New Fill Layer"** from the menu and may be changed at any moment.
8. **Video layers** enable you to import and edit video clips from inside your Photoshop project. They can be made by either importing a video file or transforming an existing layer into a video layer. These many layer types open up a world of creative possibilities in Photoshop, enabling you to create sophisticated designs, picture manipulations, and digital art.

PSD Files in the Photographic Process

Most photographs begin as RAW or JPEG files in the camera. Many are saved straight as TIFFs or JPGs from a RAW editor like Lightroom or Capture One Pro, while others are exported as PSDs so that the photographer has complete control over the editing process.

The PSD file type is essential in the photographic workflow, particularly for post-processing and editing. Here are some examples of how photographers use PSD files:

- **Retouching**: PSD files allow photographers to retouch images non-destructively, making it simple to eliminate undesired components, improve skin texture, and repair imperfections without causing damage to the original image.
- **Compositing**: Photographers use layers in PSD files to merge several pictures, create realistic effects, and blend various components flawlessly.

- **Color Grading:** Adjustment layers in PSD files enable photographers to apply color grading methods to their photographs, giving them a distinct and consistent appearance.
- **Adding Text and Graphics:** Since text and shape layers are supported, photographers may add titles, captions, and graphics to their photographs right inside the PSD file.
- **Image Preparation for Print**: PSD images may be readily converted to other formats, such as TIFF or JPEG, that are more suited for printing.

The influence that these files have on the whole process of picture editing and retouching is difficult to express in language. To understand the PSDs flexibility and variety, one must first work with less adaptable file types.

PSD File Conversion to Other Formats

You may need to convert your photos after altering them in a PSD file to another format for sharing, printing, or archiving.

PSD files may be converted to the following formats:

- **JPEG**: A popular compressed picture format for sharing photos on the internet or showing them on displays.
- **TIFF**: A lossless, high-quality picture format often used for printing or archiving.
- **PNG**: A lossless format with transparency capability, making it ideal for online graphics or pictures with translucent backgrounds.

Photoshop or any other program that supports PSD files may be used to convert a PSD file to another format. Simply open the PSD file and save the picture in the preferred format using the "**Save As**" or "**Export**" functions.

PSD File Alternatives

PSD files have no true alternatives since they represent Adobe's original Photoshop file format. While PSD files have numerous benefits, alternative file types with certain limitations may also be used in photography.

Among the most prominent possibilities are:

- **TIFF (Tagged Image File Format):** TIFF files are high-quality, lossless image files that also enable layers, making them a viable editing and archiving alternative to PSD files.
- **JPEG (Joint Photographic Experts Group):** Although JPEG is a lossy, compressed format; it is commonly used for picture sharing and can be used for editing activities that do not need the extra functionality provided by PSD files.
- **PNG (Portable Network Graphics):** PNG is a lossless picture format that allows for transparency, making it an excellent choice for online graphics or easy editing jobs.
- **RAW Files**: Some photographers prefer to work directly with RAW files from their cameras, which provide more freedom and control over picture quality, exposure, and color. Adobe Lightroom, Capture One, and DxO PhotoLab may all be used to edit RAW files.

PSD File Benefits and Drawbacks

Understanding the PSD format's strengths and limitations might help users make the most of it.

Pros

- **Layer Preservation**: Individual changes are kept separate, making subsequent revisions simple.
- **High-Quality**: The format preserves the original quality of photos.
- **Compatibility**: Works well with other Adobe suite products.
- **Flexibility**: Supports several image modalities, including RGB, CMYK, and grayscale.

Cons

- **File Size**: Due to their comprehensive nature, PSD files may grow huge and take up a lot of storage space.
- **Specialized Software**: To completely read and modify a PSD file, Adobe Photoshop or comparable software is often required.
- **Not Directly Web-Friendly**: PSD files must often be transformed to a more widely accessible format before being shared or used online.

How to Open PSD Files

While PSD files are unique Adobe Photoshop documents, they are simple to open if you have the correct tools. Of course, Adobe Photoshop is the most apparent choice. Simply double-click the PSD to open it in Photoshop if you have it installed. This is true for both Windows and Mac. However, even if you don't have Photoshop, you can open PSD files. Adobe Photoshop Elements, CorelDraw, PaintShop Pro, and Adobe Illustrator can all open PSD files without difficulty.

How to Create and Edit a PSD File

Starting from the beginning with a PSD file or modifying an existing one? It's quite simple. To begin your creative adventure, launch Adobe Photoshop Elements and create a new document. Once you've completed your design or picture, save it as a PSD to save all of its layers and features. You can always go back and make changes, add layers, or adjust the effects this way. Changing anything in an existing PSD file? Simply open it in Photoshop, and all of the layers and components are there for you to make whatever alterations you like.

PSD File FAQs

How can I open a PSD file if I don't have Photoshop?

There are various ways to open PSD files without Photoshop. Popular options include GIMP, Photopea, and IrfanView. These apps can read Photoshop documents and show their contents, allowing for picture manipulation and layer viewing.

Is a PSD identical to a PNG?

No, they're not the same file format. A PSD file is an Adobe Photoshop layered Photoshop document. A PNG (Portable Network Graphics) file, on the other hand, is a widely recognized picture file format that enables transparency but does not retain layers like a PSD file.

Is it possible to edit PSD files without Photoshop?

Yes! While Photoshop is the industry standard for image editing, there are alternatives such as GIMP, Canva, and Photopea that can read PSD files and enable modifications, including layer manipulation.

System Requirements

System requirements for running Adobe Photoshop Elements 2024 in the best possible way:

Windows

- Intel 6th Generation or newer CPU with SSE4.1 capability, or AMD equivalent.
- Only 64-bit versions of Microsoft Windows 10 (version 22H2) or Windows 11 (version 22H2) are supported; Windows 7, and Windows 8.1 are not supported.
- 8 GB RAM
- 8GB of free hard disk space is needed to install the program.
- Display resolution of 1280x800 (at 100% scale factor)
- Display driver for Microsoft DirectX 12
- Internet access is essential for product activation as well as the download of features and online content.

macOS

- Intel processor 6th Generation or newer; Apple silicon M1 or newer processor
- macOS 12 (13.4 or later), macOS 13 (13.4 or later)
- 8 GB RAM
- 6GB of hard-disk space is needed to install the program; extra space is necessary for downloading online content and temporary files during product installation and operation (cannot install on a volume that employs a case-sensitive file system or on portable flash storage devices).
- Display resolution of 1280x800 (at 100% scale factor)
- Internet access is essential for product activation as well as the download of features and online content.

How to download and install Adobe Photoshop Elements 2024

Make your images appear magical using Photoshop Elements. You can install several versions of Photoshop Elements on your PC. As a result, there is no need to remove previous versions.

Before you start, here are some things you need to check out:

- Confirm that the account you're using has administrator access.

- Make sure you're using the most recent version of Internet Explorer, Firefox, Chrome, or Safari.
- Confirm that you have a valid Adobe ID.
- Turn off pop-up blockers in your browser.
- Disable firewalls, antivirus software, and third-party security software temporarily. Disabling them expedites the installation.
- Check that Photoshop Elements has a valid serial number.
- Maintain an Internet connection until the installation is complete.

Here are the steps:

1. In your web browser, go to the Adobe Photoshop Elements download website.
2. Log in with your Adobe ID. If you do not already have an Adobe ID, you need to create one.
3. Choose a platform and language for download.
4. Click **Download**.

Install Photoshop Elements

1. Double-click the Adobe Photoshop Elements installation file you got from the Adobe website.
2. Log in using your Adobe ID (typically your email address) and password.
3. On the next screen, click **Continue**.
4. On the Installation Options page, complete the following steps and click **Continue**:
- Choose a language
- Indicate the installation site

5. While the installation is running, you can learn about the new features in Photoshop Elements 2024 by clicking on the picture carousel at the bottom of the installer.

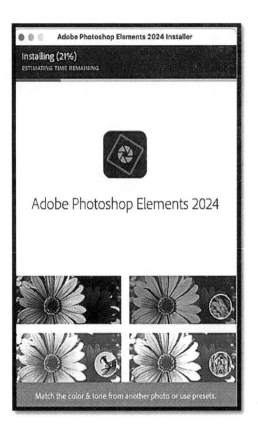

6. Select **Photo Editor** from the menu that displays.

7. Proceed to sign in with your email and password.

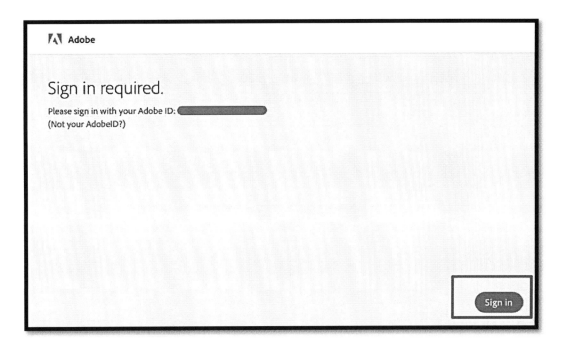

8. On the Welcome screen, click the **Activate Now button**.

9. On the following page, enter the serial number and click **Next**.

Frequently Asked Questions

1. How do you download and install Photoshop Elements 2024?
2. What is the difference between Image Size and Canvas Size?
3. What is the difference between Raster and Vector graphics?
4. How do you explain pixels and resolution?
5. How do you explain alpha, selections and PSD files in Photoshop Elements?
6. What's new in Photoshop Elements 2024?

CHAPTER TWO

GET TO KNOW PHOTOSHOP ELEMENTS 2024

Overview

Chapter two introduces us to learning about Photoshop Elements 2024 including the editor workspace, the toolbox, the panel bin, the photo bin, and so much more.

The Elements Hub

Adobe Photoshop Elements' Elements Hub

Accessing the Hub:
- When users run Adobe Photoshop Elements, they are welcomed with the Elements Hub. This is effectively the application's starting point.
- The Hub is intended to simplify the user experience, particularly for people unfamiliar with the more technical capabilities of professional-grade Adobe Photoshop.

Guided Edits:
- The **'Guided Edits'** area is a significant component inside the Elements Hub. This tool gives detailed instructions for a variety of picture editing activities.
- With simple instructions, users may experiment with a variety of creative effects, repairs, and additions, making it accessible to users of various levels of competence.

Quick Edits:
- The Hub contains a **'Quick Edits'** area that allows users to make quick changes to their photos. Cropping, straightening, rotating, or performing fast repairs to improve the overall quality of the picture may be included.

Photo Creations:
- Users can discover tools to convert their images into customized masterpieces in the **'Photo masterpieces'** area. Making picture albums, calendars, greeting cards, or collages is one example.
- The Hub simplifies these procedures, allowing users to create visually attractive and personalized projects without having to go into complicated design tools.

Organizer:
- The **'Organizer**,' a tool for managing and arranging images, is integrated with the Elements Hub. Users can tag, rank, and classify their photographs to make them easier to find.
- The Organizer also allows users to easily navigate through their picture collection, allowing them to swiftly find and work on the photographs they desire.

Learn and Support:
- Adobe understands the value of lifelong learning. The **'Learn & Support'** part of the Elements Hub contains lessons, tips, and tools to assist users in improving their abilities and making the most of the program.

Community and Updates:
- The Elements Hub keeps users up to speed on the newest upgrades, features, and announcements. It also connects users to the Adobe community, where they can interact with other enthusiasts, exchange experiences, and seek help.

User-Friendly Interface:
- The Elements Hub has a user-friendly layout with straightforward iconography and simple navigation. As a result, it is appropriate for both novices and people with more advanced editing abilities.

Other Adobe Services Integration:
- Elements Hub can integrate with other Adobe services, improving the user experience overall. Cloud storage options or access to Adobe Stock for more materials might be included.

The Editor workspace

The Adobe Photoshop Elements workspace has a simple interface that allows you to edit your photographs the way you desire. You can work in Quick, Guided, or Expert settings depending on your degree of Photoshop Elements proficiency.

Home Screen

The Home screen is the first screen you see when you run Adobe Photoshop Elements. You may launch your selected program, see multiple feature tutorials, access resources for the newest features, and view Auto Creations and more from this page.

Begin with the Home screen

When you run the most recent version of an Elements app for the first time, the Last Used Version section appears on the Home screen.

You can perform one of the following in this section:

- In Adobe Photoshop Elements, choose your previously used version from the choose Version drop-down box and click **Confirm**.

Explore and customize Auto Creations

Auto Creations, often known as auto-generated creations, are accessible on the Home screen. You can browse auto-created image collages, slideshows, video collages, and Candid Moments in the Auto Creations area. To see all of the auto-created projects, click **See All** or use the number icons below the Auto Creations thumbnail. Auto Creations are made using imported media (photos or videos). If you haven't already, go to the Home screen and choose **Add media** under Auto Creations to add images and videos. Relaunch the app after a while to see Auto Creations on the Home screen.

The Welcome Screen

The Welcome screen is shown by default when you launch Photoshop Elements. The Welcome screen serves as a useful beginning point, or hub, for key activities.

Select the following on the welcome screen:

- **Photo Editor**, for enhancing photos and adding unique effects.
  - Double-click the Photo Editor icon to launch the editor in its default mode.
  - Select the Photo Editor drop-down menu to launch the editor with one of the previously opened files, a new file, or a file to open.
- **Organizer**, which allows you to import, tag, and organize your photos.
- **Video Editor**, for artistically editing and creating interesting videos from your videos.

Note:

Video Editor is not included in the Windows Application Store edition of Photoshop Elements.

- Click the **Close button (X)** in the upper-right corner of the Welcome screen to close it. You don't have to return to the Welcome page to open additional workspaces; you may do so from inside any other workspace.
- The **Settings icon (next to the Close button)** allows you to choose which application is launched when you launch the program.

Quick Mode

Allows you to edit photos in Quick mode. Use this mode to quickly and easily edit your photos, such as adjusting the exposure, color, sharpness, and other characteristics.

Guided Mode

Allows you to edit photos in Guided mode. The Guided mode is a wizard-like interface that lets you perform predetermined effects. When you hover the mouse cursor over an attached picture, the applied effect is shown.

Advanced Mode

Allows you to edit photos in Advanced Mode. The Advanced Mode includes tools for correcting color issues, creating special effects, and enhancing photographs. The Quick mode includes easy tools for color and lighting correction, as well as instructions for swiftly resolving common issues like red eye. The Guided mode includes basic picture editing tools, guided exercises, and photographic effects. If you're new to digital photography, the Quick or Guided modes are a fantastic place to start. If you've used image-editing software previously, you'll see that the Advanced Mode offers a versatile and sophisticated image-correction environment. It includes lighting and color-correction capabilities, as well as tools for repairing picture flaws, creating selections, adding text, and painting your photos. You can rearrange the Expert workspace to meet your requirements. Panels in the Panel Bin can be moved, hidden, and shown, as well as arranged. You can also zoom in and out of the image, move the document window around, and create several windows and views.

Customize workspace

- To fit your requirements, you can hide or expose various areas of the workplace.
- Toggle the corresponding icons at the bottom of the screen to hide or display the picture bin or the Tool Options.
- Use Quick mode and then pick one of the View options to work split-screen with the original picture on one side and the altered photo on the other.

Use Context Menus

Context menus are available in both the Photo Editor and Organizer workspaces. Context-sensitive menus show commands that are relevant to the currently selected tool, selection, or panel. These menus are often used to access commands from the main menus.

1. Place the cursor on an image or panel item. Note that context menus are not available in all panels.
2. Select a command from the menu by right-clicking.

Use keyboard commands and modifier keys

Keyboard shortcuts are available in both the Photo Editor and Organizer workspaces. Keyboard commands allow you to perform instructions without using a menu; modifier keys allow you to change how a tool works. When accessible, the keyboard command displays in the menu to the right of the command name.

Exit Photoshop Elements

Exit both the Photo Editor and Organizer workspaces to leave Photoshop Elements—closing one does not immediately shut the other.

1. **Do one of the following from any workspace:**
- Select **File > Exit (Ctrl + Q) on Windows.** Select **Photoshop Elements > Quit Photoshop Elements (Cmd + Q)** on the Mac.
- In the top right hand side of the workspace, select the **Close button (X).**
2. Select if to save any open files that you have edited when you close Photoshop Elements.

Light or Dark Interface?

The desire for a bright or dark interface in Adobe Photoshop Elements (PSE) 2024 is determined by your own preferences and working environment. Some individuals like dark interfaces because they are less taxing on the eyes, particularly while working for long periods. Others choose a light interface because it seems more comfortable and is simpler to read.

In Adobe Photoshop Elements, you can toggle between bright and dark interfaces by doing the following:

1. Launch Adobe Photoshop Elements 2024.
2. **Navigate to Preferences:**
- On Windows, select "**Edit**" from the top menu, then **"Preferences" > "Interface."**
- On a Mac, click **"Photoshop Elements"** from the top menu, then **"Preferences" > "Interface."**
3. In the Interface options, search for an option such as "**Interface Color**" or "**UI Theme**." You can find possibilities such as **"Dark," "Medium Gray,"** or **"Light."** Select the one that most meets your needs.

4. After you've chosen your favorite interface color, click "**OK**" or "**Apply**" to finalize the changes. The color change to the interface should take effect instantly, and you should see the interface in the color scheme you choose.

Guides and Rulers

In Advanced Mode, rulers, grids, and guides assist you in accurately positioning elements (such as selections, layers, and shapes) across an image's width or length. Only grids are accessible in Quick mode. When rulers are enabled, they show along the top and left sides of the current window. When you move the pointer, the ruler's markers reflect its location. You can measure from a particular place on the picture by changing the ruler origin (the 0, 0 mark on the top and left rulers). The point of origin of the grid is also determined by the ruler's origin. To display or hide the rulers (Advanced Mode only), grid, or guide, use the View menu. You can also use the View menu to activate or disable item snapping to the grid or guide. Guides are non-printing lines that may be placed anywhere on your page to help you precisely position items. They serve as visual assistance, helping you to establish an organized layout and preserve design consistency.

Types of Guides

They include the following

- **Horizontal Guides:** These go across the breadth of the canvas and help with vertical alignment.
- **Vertical Guides:** These run from the top of the canvas to the bottom, assisting in horizontal alignment.
- **Custom guidelines:** Users can construct custom guidelines by dragging them from the rulers.

Adding Guides

- To add a guide, click and drag it onto the canvas from the horizontal or vertical ruler.
- Go to the "**View**" menu and choose "**New Guide**" for accurate placement.

Rulers in Photoshop items are used to visually measure and align-items on the canvas. They can be found on the workspace's top and left borders and are essential for proper design work.

Types of Rulers

- **Horizontal Ruler**: Displays measures along the canvas's top edge.
- **Vertical Ruler**: Appearance on the canvas's left side.

Measuring Units

Users can tailor the measuring units (pixels, inches, centimeters, etc.) to their own project needs.

Using Rulers for Accuracy

- Dragging ruler guidelines enable exact element positioning.
- Rulers are useful for establishing the size and spacing of things on the canvas.

Change the rulers' zero origin and settings

1. **Perform one of the following in Advanced Mode:**
- To modify the zero origin of the rulers, place the cursor above the intersection of the rulers in the upper-left corner of the window and drag diagonally down onto the picture. A set of cross hairs emerges, indicating the rulers' new origin. The new zero origin will be established when you let go of the mouse button.

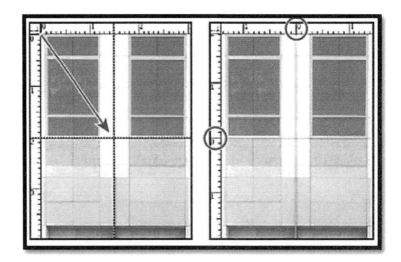

Note: Double-click the upper-left corner of the rulers to reset the ruler's origin to its default setting.

- To adjust the settings of the rulers, double-click one of them or go to **Edit > Preferences > Units & Rulers**. Select a unit of measurement for Rulers. Select **OK**.

When you change the units on the Info panel, the units on the rulers change as well.

Change the guides and grid settings

The steps:

1. Navigate to **Edit > Preferences > Guides & Grid**.
2. **In the Guides or Grids section:**
- Select a predefined color or click the color swatch to select a new color.
- Select the grid's line style. Select Lines for solid lines and Dashed lines or Dots for broken lines.
3. Enter a numerical value for Gridline every, and then choose the unit of measurement to set the spacing of the main grid lines.
4. Enter a numeric value to determine the frequency of minor grid lines in Subdivisions, then click OK.

The Toolbox

Photoshop Elements has a toolkit in Quick and Advanced Modes to assist you in working with your photographs. The toolbox contains tools for selecting, enhancing, drawing, and viewing pictures.

Toolbox in the Quick mode

In Quick mode, the toolbox offers a minimal collection of simple tools. Zoom, Hand, Quick Selection, Eye, Whiten Teeth, Straighten, Type, Spot Healing Brush, Crop, and Move are the tools accessible in this mode.

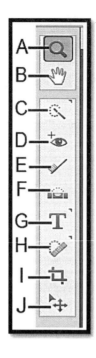

A. Zoom Tool
B. Hand Tool
C. Quick Selection Tool
D. Eye Tool
E. Whiten Teeth Tool
F. Straighten Tool
G. Type Tool
H. Spot Healing Brush Tool
I. Crop Tool
J. Move Tool

Toolbox in the Advanced Mode

The toolbox in Advanced Mode is more extensive than the toolbox in Quick mode. The tools are divided into the following logical categories:

- View
- Select
- Enhance
- Draw

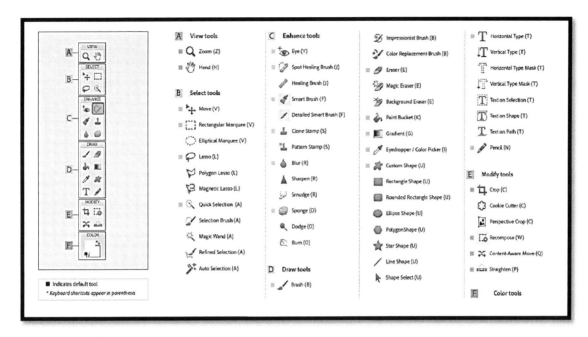

- Modify

Tools in the Advanced Mode toolbox's View group

Zoom (Z) tool

Zooms your picture in or out. Zoom In and Zoom Out are the related tools shown in the Tool Options bar.

Hand Tool (H)

The picture is moved in the Photoshop Elements workspace. You can use this tool to drag your picture.

Tools in the Advanced Mode toolbox's Select group

Move tool (V)

Selective or layer movement.

Rectangular Marquee (M) tool

In a rectangle box, choose an area in your image. To make the selection a square, hold down the Shift key.

Elliptical Marquee (M) tool

Select an ellipse area in your picture. To make the selection a circle, hold down the Shift key.

Lasso (L) tool

Choose a free-form shape from your photo.

Magnetic Lasso (L) tool

Selects a part of a picture by highlighting the high-contrast edges of a form.

Polygonal Lasso Tool (L)

Draws straight-edged selection border segments.

Quick Selection Tool (A)

Clicking or clicking and dragging an area will make the selection based on color.

Selection Brush tool (A)

Select the area to be painted using the brush.

Magic Wand tool (A)

In a single click, select pixels with comparable colors.

Refine Selection Brush tool (A)

By automatically recognizing the edges, this function adds and removes sections from a selection.

Auto Selection tool (A)

When you draw a shape around the item you wish to choose, it automatically selects it.

Tools in the Advanced Mode toolbox's Enhance Group

Eye tool (Y)

Removes the red eye, pet eye, and closed eye effects from your images.

(Spot Healing Brush tool (J)

Removes blemishes/spots from your photos.

Healing Brush tool (J)

Removes spots from your image by selecting a part of the image as the reference point.

Smart Brush tool (F)

Tonal and color changes are applied to particular parts of a photograph.

Detail Smart Brush tool (F)

Just like a painting tool, it paints the modification to particular areas of a picture.

Clone Stamp tool (S)

Paints with an image sample that you can use to reproduce things, repair picture flaws, or paint over objects in your photo. You can also clone a part of one picture to another.

Pattern Stamp tool (S)

Paint a pattern from your picture, another image, or a predefined pattern.

Blur tool (R)

Reduces details to soften rough edges or areas in a picture.

Sharpen tool (R)

Sharpens a picture by concentrating on the photo's soft edges to boost clarity or focus.

Smudge tool (R)

The movements of dragging a finger across wet paint are simulated. Color is picked up where the stroke starts and pushed in the direction you drag.

Sponge tool (O)

Adjusts the color saturation of a specific area.

Dodge tool (O)

Image parts are lightened. The tool can be used to bring out details in shadows.

Burn tool (O)

The image parts are darkened. The tool can be used to bring out details in highlights.

Tools in the Advanced Mode toolbox's Draw Group

(Brush tool (B)

Color strokes might be gentle or harsh. It can be used to mimic airbrush methods.

Impressionist Brush tool (B)

Change the current colors and details in your picture so that it seems to have been painted with stylized brush strokes.

Color Replacement tool (B)

Replace certain colors in your picture more easily.

Eraser tool (E)

As you drag across the pixels in the picture, they get erased.

Background Eraser tool (E)

Color pixels are converted to transparent pixels, allowing you to quickly detach an item from its background.

Magic Eraser tool (E)

When you drag inside a picture, it changes all related pixels.

Paint Bucket tool (K)

Fills an area with the same color value as the pixels you clicked.

Pattern tool (K)

Instead of using a brush tool, apply a fill or a pattern to your picture.

Gradient tool (G)

A gradient is used to fill up an area of a picture.

Color Picker tool (I)

To establish a new foreground or background color, copy or sample the color of an area in your picture.

Custom Shape tool (U)

You can design many shapes using this tool. These forms are available in the Tool Options bar when you pick the Custom Shape tool.

The following shape-related tools are accessible in the Tool Options bar:

- Rectangular
- Ellipse
- Rounded Rectangle
- Line
- Star
- Polygon
- Selection

Type tool (T)

Allows you to create and edit text on your photo.

Other type-related tools in the Tool Options tab include:

- Text Vertical Type
- Vertical Type Mask
- Horizontal Type Mask
- on Shape

- Text on Selection
- Text on Custom Path

Pencil tool (N)

Freehand lines with strong edges are created.

Tools in the Advanced Mode toolbox's Modify Group

Cropping tool (C)

Trims a part or an area of a picture based on the chosen.

Cookie Cutter tool (C)

Crops a picture into the form you choose.

Perspective Crop tool (C)

Crops a photo while changing its viewpoint.

Recompose tool (W)

Intelligently resizes photos without affecting vital visual material like people, buildings, animals, and more.

Content-Aware Move tool (Q)

Select an item in your shot and move or extend it to a new spot.

Straighten tool (P)

Vertically or horizontally realigns a picture.

Use a tool

To use a tool in Quick or Advanced Mode, choose it from the toolbox. Then, to complete your work, use the numerous selections in the Tool selections bar.

Choose a tool

Perform one of the following:

- Select a tool from the toolbox.
- Enter the tool's keyboard shortcut. To pick the Brush tool, for example, press B. A tool's keyboard shortcut is indicated in the tooltip.

Note:

You cannot deselect a tool; once picked, it stays selected until a new tool is selected. If you've used the Lasso tool and wish to click your picture without choosing anything, choose the Hand tool.

Select options from the Tool Options bar

In the Photoshop Elements window, the Tool Options bar is located at the bottom. It provides the selections for the currently chosen tool. For example, if you select the Crop tool from the toolbox, the Tool possibilities bar displays related tools (Cookie Cutter tool and Perspective Crop tool) as well as other possibilities.

Change the tool preferences

Change the default tool settings. For example, you can hide tooltips or modify the look of a tool pointer.

Change your general preferences

1. **Perform one of the following:**
- Select **Edit > Preferences > General on Windows**.
- On a Mac, go to **Photoshop Elements > Preferences > General**.
2. Choose one or more of the following:
- To display tooltips, choose **Show Tool Tips**.
- Choose **Use Shift Key for Tool Switch** to cycle among a collection of hidden tools while holding down the Shift key. When this option is off, you can cycle between a set of tool selections by using the keyboard shortcut (without holding Shift down). Pressing B on your keyboard, for example, cycles through all of the Brush tool selections (Brush, Impressionist Brush, and Color Replacement tools).
- Choose **Select Move Tool After Committing Text** to use the Move tool after adding text to your picture using the Type tool.
3. Select **OK**.

Set the appearance of a pointer

The steps:

1. **Perform one of the following:**
- Select **Edit > Preferences > Display & Cursors in Windows**.
- On the Mac, go to **Photoshop Elements > Preferences > Display & Cursors**.
2. **Choose an option for the painting cursors:**
- **Standard**: Shows pointers as tool icons.
- **Precise**: Pointers are shown as cross-hairs.
- **Normal Brush Tip**: Shows pointers as circles at 50% of the brush size you set.
- **Full-Size Brush Tip:** Shows pointers as circles at the brush's full size.
- **Show Crosshair In Brush Tip**: Shows crosshairs in the circles when either the Normal Brush Tip or the Full Size Brush Tip is selected.
3. Choose an option for other cursors:
- **Standard**: Pointers are shown as tool icons.
- **Precise**: Pointers are shown as cross-hairs.
4. Select **OK**.

Drag to resize or modify the sharpness of painting cursors (Windows only)

By moving the picture, you can resize or adjust the roughness of a painting cursor. You can see the size and hardness of the painting tool as you drag.

- To resize a cursor, **right-click + Alt-drag** to the left or right.
- To adjust the opacity of a cursor, right-click + hit Alt, then drag up or down.

Restore the tool's default settings

You can reset the default settings of one or more tools.

1. Choose a tool from the toolbox. Alternatively, use the tool's keyboard shortcut.

2. Click ▤ to access the Tool Options bar's pop-up menu and choose one of the following options:
- Click **Reset Tool** to reset the chosen tool.
- Click **Reset All Tools** to reset all tools.

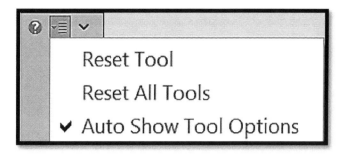

The Panel Bin

Panels are present in both Photoshop Elements and Elements Organizer, although their behavior varies. Panels assist you in managing, monitoring, and modifying photos. Menus on several panels give extra commands and settings. In Advanced Mode, you can arrange panels in the basic and custom workspaces. Panels can be stored in the Panel Bin to keep them out of the way yet conveniently accessible.

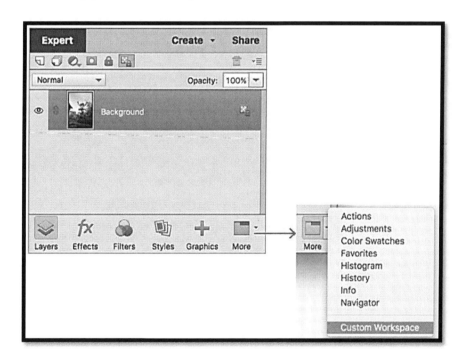

Panel menus

Some commands are available from both the panel menu and the menu bar. Other commands are only available in panel menus. To see the many commands in each panel, click the panel menu.

Pop-up sliders within panels

Some panels and dialog boxes include pop-up slider settings (for example, the Opacity option in the Layers panel). You can activate the pop-up slider by clicking the triangle that appears next to the text field. Place the cursor on the triangle adjacent to the setting, then move the slider or angle radius to the appropriate value while holding down the mouse button. To close the slider box, click outside it or press Enter. Press **Esc** to cancel changes. When the pop-up slider box is open, hold Shift and hit the **Up or Down arrow keys** to raise or decrease values in 10% increments.

Work with Panels

Panels gather together features, information, or functionality for quick and simple access. Photoshop Elements' Panel Bin is located on the right side. Depending on the mode you're in or the kind of items you want to work with, it shows tabs and panels.

The Panel Bin shows:

- **Quick mode**: Displays a list of the quick-mode effects that may be applied to a photo.
- **Guided mode:** Displays a list of all the guided-mode adjustments available for a picture.
- **Advanced Mode:** Displays the available selections for a certain panel (Layers, Effects, Graphics, or Favorites).

Panels in the Advanced Mode

Panels can be shown in two ways in Advanced Mode: Basic Workspace and Custom Workspace.

Basic Workspace

The Basic Workspace is the default workspace that is presented. The taskbar has buttons for the most commonly used panels in this view. Layers, Effects, Graphics, and Favorites are the buttons in this workspace. For example, choosing the Layers button exposes all options related to layers. Select **More** to see all of the other available tabs or to dismiss any open tabs.

Custom Workspace

To display panels in the Panel Bin in a tabbed arrangement, click the arrow next to More and then Custom Workspace. Click **More** to get a list of all possible tabs, then choose one from the drop-down menu. The chosen tab is shown. In the personalized workspace, you may keep commonly used panels open. Dock one panel at the bottom of another or group panels together. You can drag and drop the tab's title bar into the tabbed layout, or drag and drop the tab dialog into the tabbed layout.

Note: If you want to remove a panel from the Panel Bin while keeping it open, drag it out.

The steps to use a custom workspace:

1. Select **Window > Panel Bin** to see or hide the Panel Bin.
2. In the Custom Workspace Panel Bin, carry out any of the following:

- Drag the panel's title bar out of the Panel Bin to remove it from the Panel Bin.
- Drag the panel's title bar into the Panel Bin to add it to the Panel Bin.
- To reposition panels in the Panel Bin, drag the panel's title bar to a new spot.
- Double-click the name of a panel in the Panel Bin to expand or collapse it.
3. In the Custom Workspace view, perform any of the following to use panels that are not in the Panel Bin:
- To open a panel, select it from the Window menu, or click the arrow next to the **More icon** in the taskbar and choose a panel.
- To shut a panel, choose the panel's name from the Window menu. Alternatively, click the Close button in the panel's title bar.
- To modify the size of a panel, drag any of its corners.
- To group panels (one panel with several tabs), drag the panel onto the target panel's body. When the cursor is above the right region for grouping, a thick line appears around the body of the target panel. To relocate a panel to another group, drag the panel's tab to that group. Drag the panel's tab outside the group to detach it from the group.
- Drag the title bar to shift a panel group.
- To expand or collapse a panel or panel group, double-click the panel's or title bar's tab.
- Drag a panel tab or the title bar to the bottom of another panel to dock them together (stacked panels). When the pointer is over the proper location, a double line appears at the bottom of the target panel.
- Select **Window > Reset Panels** to return panels to their default locations.

Use the taskbar

The taskbar, located at the bottom of Photoshop Elements, shows buttons for the most commonly used panels and activities done when editing and changing photos. Toggle between viewing thumbnails and tool selections by using the Photo Bin and Tool selections buttons. You can undo and redo tasks fast, rotate photos, and adjust the layout. You can also launch Photoshop Elements Organizer by clicking the **Organizer icon**. The Home Screen button allows you to return to the home screen. To switch between Basic and Custom workspaces in Advanced Mode, click the arrow next to the **More icon**.

The Photo Bin

The Photo Bin located toward the bottom of the Photoshop Elements window, above the taskbar, shows thumbnails of open photos. It comes in handy while flipping between numerous open photographs in your workstation. The Photo Bin has options for opening and closing photographs, hiding images, navigating between open images, making a particular image the frontmost image, duplicating an image, rotating an image, and seeing file metadata. Open photos may be simply brought into Quick mode for editing. In the Create panel, multipage projects created using the Create tab are open.

1. **Perform any of the following:**

- (Windows only) Drag a file into the Photo Bin from any location on your computer to open an image.
- Click a thumbnail to make an opened image the frontmost image.
- Drag thumbnails in the Photo Bin to rearrange them. The order here does not affect the order of the photo in the Elements Organizer.
- To close an image, right-click it in the Photo Bin and select **Close**.

Note: To restore an image after it has been hidden, double-click its thumbnail in the Photo Bin, or right-click the thumbnail and select **Restore** from the context menu.

- To view the file information for a photo, right-click a thumbnail and select **File** Info from the context menu.
- To duplicate an image, right-click it, select **Duplicate** from the context menu, and then name the file.
- To rotate an image, right-click it and select **Rotate 90° Left** or **Rotate 90° Right** from the context menu.
- To display filenames, right-click the **Photo Bin** and select **Show Filenames** from the context menu.

The Photo Bin flyout menu contains additional options for working with the images in the Photo Bin:

- **Print Bin Files**: Launches the Photoshop Elements Print dialog box, which includes options for printing the photos currently in the Photo Bin.
- **Save Bin as an Album**. Allows you to name and save an album that contains the images from the Photo Bin. The new album has been added to Organizer.
- **Show Grid:** A grid is displayed around images in the Photo bin.

What do these panels do?

Photoshop Elements includes a plethora of panels, each of which aids in the editing process. Some only appear in the Advanced Mode (such as the Info panel), while others only appear in the Quick edit mode (such as Adjustments).

Here's a rundown of what each panel has to offer:

- **Adjustments**: This section contains sliders for adjusting the Exposure, Lighting (contrast), Color, Balance, and Sharpness.
- **Effects**: This section offers the user a wide variety of looks, automated colors, and special effects; in essence, these are recipes that can be applied to an image with a single click.
- **Textures**: Elements include a plethora of creative assets, such as surface textures, which, when clicked, apply as a textured overlay to the opened image. These are suitable for backgrounds, web pages, and other applications.
- **Frames**: These are used to display graphic artwork. When you click on a frame thumbnail in the panel, it downloads it from www.adobe.com and then automatically resizes and applies it to the image if it has never been used before.
- **Layers**: Probably the most important panel for advanced projects, where text, multiple images, or other assets are added to different layers in the document, allowing for editability throughout the production process.
- **Filter**: The small thumbnails for each FX filter attempt to demonstrate its effect. You can apply the effect by clicking on the thumbnail. You can also adjust the

intensity of each effect using the associated slider. There are 98 different filters to choose from, with billions of possible combinations.

- o **Styles**: Styles, like filters, are one-click presets used to change the image—most notably by adding an effect to the entire layer. Whereas Filters and Effects presets are used to change the appearance of the image's surface, Styles are used to add more esoteric features such as drop shadows, bevels, glows, patterns, and glass button effects. Though there is a small photographic subset in Styles, the majority are used for design rather than image enhancement. This panel contains 176 different styles.
- o **Graphics**: This panel provides several (downloadable) clip art, text effects, scalable vector shapes, and picture frame styles, all of which may be applied to an image by just clicking on the thumbnail. Since this panel contains so many objects, you can filter or sort them by Type, Activity, Mood, Event, Object, Season, and other criteria.

Other Panels

Once you begin editing, you will realize that there are even more panels lying in the rear of the Panel Bin. While still extremely beneficial, these panels give somewhat more specialized editing aid and should be avoided until you have achieved a fair skill level.

These panels consist of the following:

- o **Actions**: Essentially, this is a watered-down version of Photoshop's preset tool. The provided Actions may be played back on photographs to do tasks such as adding a photo border, resizing, and cropping. An Action is just a short file containing instructions; you may locate additional Actions online, download them, and import them into Elements to supplement the limited variety provided by default.
- o **Color Swatches:** These are used to choose colors for a variety of elements, such as font, pencil, paintbrush, and background colors. You can create your own unique Swatch for certain projects using the panel.
- o **Histogram**: This shows the range of tones in a picture and, more precisely, where those tones fall in the brightness range (such as mid-tone, highlights, whites, blacks, underexposed, and overexposed).
- o **History**: This is a helpful window that shows your editing actions, from viewing the picture to saving the new work. You can move back in time to a prior state by

clicking on one of the stages listed in the panel, mouse click by mouse click. This is useful if you feel you've over-edited the picture; just go back a few steps to a prior version.

- **Favorites**: This is a huge time saving; drag the appropriate thumbnail into the Favorites panel to save your often-used Styles and Graphics in one spot.

Save files to the Cloud

When you save an Elements 2024 file after editing it, you can save it in the same file format or change the format to meet the standards of your photo service center or to guarantee that your picture downloads fast on a website.

The Save/Save As dialog box and how to use it

Elements 2024 provides a new choice for where you wish to store your work before you save it. When you choose **File > Save or File > Save As**, the Save As dialog box appears, as shown.

This dialog box provides options such as storing your data in the cloud. When you sign in to Adobe Creative Cloud, you may opt to store files on Adobe's servers and access them from any computer. Alternatively, you may store files directly on your PC. To prevent this dialog box from appearing every time you save a file, tick the box at the bottom of the dialog window. The Save (or Save As) dialog box is a common spot in practically every software where you make selections concerning the file to be saved. You can use **Save As** to save a duplicate copy of your picture or to save a modified copy while keeping the original file. If you want to submit your finished picture to the web, skip the typical Save (or Save As) dialog box and go to the next section, "**Saving files for the web**." To open the Save (or Save As) dialog box, choose **File > Save for files** to be saved for the first time, or **File > Save As** for a copy of an open file, and a dialog box will appear.

When you open a picture, you should always click **File > Save As** as your first step in modifying it. Make a copy by saving it with a different filename and then editing the picture. If you don't like the results of your editing, you may go back to the original, unedited picture and create another copy for editing. The Elements Save/Save As dialog box includes the basic navigational features seen in any Save dialog box.

In the Elements Save/Save As dialog box, there are two typical options:

- **Filename**: This setting is shared by all Save (Windows) and Save As (Mac) dialog boxes. In the text box, give your file a name.
- **Format**: Select a file format from the drop-down menu.

A few options distinguish the Photoshop Elements Save/Save As dialog box from other Save dialog boxes you may be familiar with.

The Save Options section of the Save As dialog box includes the following options:

- **Include in the Elements Organizer:** Check this option if you want the file to be included in the Organizer.
- **Save in Version Set with Original:** This is an unusual option. Version Set will not be accessible for any picture you open in Quick or Advanced Mode by selecting **File > Open**. You must load the file into the Organizer and then open it in the Photo Editor; then, when you save the photo in any mode, Version Set appears. This option allows you to make many changes to a file and save them as separate versions all inside the same file.
- **Layers**: If your file contains layers, checking this box will keep them.
- **As a Copy:** Use this option to save a duplicate file without overwriting the original.
- **Color**: Color profiles help you retain the correct color, and this box regulates the color profile for your picture. Check the ICC (International Color Consortium) Profile box. Depending on the profile, the choice for sRGB or Adobe RGB (1998) shows. When this option is checked, the profile is incorporated into the picture.

- **Thumbnail (Windows only):** When you save a file with a thumbnail, a small version of your picture appears when you view it in folders or on the desktop. The check box **Ask When Saving** can be activated or removed in the Saving Files options. This box is enabled or hidden (grayed out) for you if you select **Never Save or Always Save** in the Preferences dialog box. If you want to change the setting, you must return to the Preferences dialog box.

How to save files for the web

The Save for Web function assists you in preparing photos for display on the web or merely onscreen. Select **File > Save for Web**. In the Save for Web dialog box that appears (see figure), you can see your original picture on the left and the outcome of changing the file format and quality options on the right. The general guideline for online graphics is to obtain the minimum file size that produces an acceptable picture look. There are many options for minimizing file size in the Save for Web dialog box. The original picture is shown in the accompanying figure, with the file size provided below the image on the left. When you choose JPEG as the file format, you can see that the picture size has decreased from 12.8MB to 733.5K.

You can also change the final quality of the saved file by using the Quality option, which displays to the right of the drop-down list. Here, you must strike a compromise between fast download speeds and picture appearance. Just keep an eye on the preview picture and the download time for your optimized file. Set the zoom setting to 100 percent for the most precise viewing. Choose zoom levels from the drop-down list in the lower-left corner of the dialog box, or simply input a value in the field box. If your selected settings impair your picture quality substantially, you can readily see the loss while viewing at 100%. Making selections and evaluating the outcomes is how you work with the Save for Web dialog box. Toggle the various file type options and make quality changes. If you notice picture deterioration, modify the quality setting or file format. Always check the file-size item provided below the picture on the right to determine the smallest file size that provides a good-looking image.

Supported file formats for saving

Photoshop Elements supports the following image file formats:

BMP

A common Windows picture format. Select whether the picture should be in Windows or OS/2 format, as well as its bit depth. RLE compression can be specified for 4-bit and 8-bit pictures in Windows format.

GIF (Graphics Interchange Format) on CompuServe

Graphics and short animations are often used on websites. GIF is a compressed format that is intended to reduce file size and transport time. GIF only accepts 8-bit color pictures (256 or less colors). You can also use the **Save For Web command** to save a picture as a GIF file.

JPEG (Joint Photographic Experts Group)

JPEG format, which is used to store images, keeps all color information in an image while compressing file size by selectively eliminating data. The degree of compression is adjustable. Lower compression leads to greater picture quality and a bigger file size; higher compression results in poor image quality and a smaller file size. JPEG is a common format for presenting photos on the internet.

Adobe Photoshop (PSD)

The picture format used by Photoshop Elements. To save your work and maintain all of your picture data and layers in a single-page file, use this format for altered photos.

PSE (Photo Creations Format)

The typical Photoshop Elements format for creating many pages. For picture projects, utilize this format to save your work and maintain all of your image data and layers in a multi-page file.

Photoshop PDF (Portable Document Format)

A file format that works across platforms and applications. Fonts, page layouts, and vector and bitmap images are all faithfully shown and preserved in PDF files.

Pixar

Used for file exchange with Pixar image computers. Pixar workstations are intended for high-end graphics applications including three-dimensional imagery and animation. RGB and grayscale pictures are supported by the Pixar format.

PNG (Portable Network Graphics)

Used for lossless image compression and online picture presentation. PNG, unlike GIF, provides 24-bit images and generates background transparency without jagged edges; nevertheless, PNG images are not supported by all web browsers. In grayscale and RGB pictures, PNG retains transparency.

TIFF (Tagged-Image File Format)

Files are exchanged between programs and computer systems via this protocol. TIFF is a versatile bitmap image format that is supported by the majority of paint, image editing, and page-layout software. TIFF files can be created by the majority of desktop scanners. Photoshop Elements also supports the following older file formats: Pixel Paint, Portable Bitmap, SGI RGB, Soft Image, Wavefront RLA, and Electric Image.

File Compression

To minimize file size, several picture file formats compress image data. Lossless compression maintains all picture data while losing some detail; lossy compression eliminates image data while retaining some detail.

Compression methods that are regularly used include:

RLE (Run Length Encoding)

A lossless compression method that compresses the transparent areas of each layer in photos that feature transparency on many levels.

LZW (Lemple-Zif-Welch)

Lossless compression yields the greatest results when compressing photos with huge portions of a single color.

JPEG

Lossy compression yields the greatest photographic images.

CCITT

A class of lossless black-and-white picture compression algorithms.

ZIP

A lossless compression method that works well for photos with huge parts of a single color.

Frequently Asked Questions

1. How do you save files to the cloud?
2. How do you access the toolbox in Photoshop Elements?
3. How do you use guides and rulers?
4. How do you access and use the photo bin in Photoshop Elements?
5. How do you access the editor workspace?

PART II
QUICK AND GUIDED PHOTO EDITING

CHAPTER THREE

QUICK FIXES AND EFFECTS

Overview

In this chapter, you will learn how to easily touch up your photos using quick fixes and effects and a quick fix toolbox.

The Quick Fix Toolbox

A subset of the tools that are accessible in Advanced Mode is included inside the toolbox of the Quick Fix window, which is simple to browse. Each of the tools functions in the same manner regardless of the mode, and you may transition between tools by using the same keystrokes. Additionally, when you select a tool, the Tool Options replace the Photo Bin, exactly as they do when you are in Advanced Mode. The Photo Bin may be brought back into display by simply clicking the button labeled "**Photo Bin**" which is located at the bottom of the screen.

From the very top to the very bottom, this is what you get:

- By using the **Zoom tool**, you can zoom in and out of your image, which is ideal for getting a nice, close look at details or pulling back to examine the whole picture. The Zoom slider, which is located in the upper-right corner of the picture preview area, also allows you to zoom in and out of the image.
- It is possible to move your picture about in the image window by using the **Hand tool**, which functions in the same way as if you were to take it and move it with your own five fingers.
- Apply Quick Fix instructions to certain areas of the picture by using the **Quick Selection tool.** The instructions that you use with this tool will only affect the region that you have chosen, and not the whole photo, after you have made a selection with it. You can also use the ordinary Selection Brush in Quick Fix; all you need to do is activate the Quick Selection tool and then select the icon named Selection Brush which is located in the Tool Options section. This is the brush that is pointing down, creating the impression that it is painting.

To what extent are the two tools distinct from one another? The Selection Brush gives you the ability to paint a selection precisely where you want it to be (or to mask off a portion of your photograph so that it does not change), whilst the Quick Selection tool allows Elements to determine the limits of your selection based on markings you make on the picture (which do not have to be accurate). Additionally, in comparison to the standard Selection Brush, the Quick Selection tool is far more automated.

- Using the **Red Eye Removal tool**, you can reduce the appearance of those red flash reflections in people's eyes that have a demonic appearance.
- The **Teeth Whitening Tool** is available. Using this convenient tool, you can easily bring out the natural brilliance of your subject's radiant smile.
- **The Type Tool**. Using this tool, you only need to click on your picture and then begin typing to add text. Making changes to the size and color of the text, as well as selecting a new font, is made simple by the Tool Options that are located at the bottom of the window. You can do any action that does not need access to the Layers panel inside the Quick Fix window. This includes the ability to bend and distort text for example.
- **The Healing Brushes.** The Spot Healing Brush enables you to make completely undetectable adjustments, allowing you to quickly heal imperfections. The Spot Healing Brush: Fixing Small Areas provides comprehensive instructions on how to make use of this useful tool. For the time being, if you are just starting, you should first zoom in so that you can see what you are doing. After that, use the slider in the Tool Options to choose a brush size that just barely covers the area that you want to correct. You can make it blend in with the surrounding area by clicking on that location, and Elements will correct it immediately.

You can also use the conventional Healing Brush in Quick Fix; all you have to do is click its icon in the Tools Options box, which is shaped like a Band-Aid but does not have a dotted semicircle next to it.

- With the **Crop tool**, you can change the dimensions and contours of a photograph by removing the parts that you do not want.

Adjustments, Effects, Textures, and Frames

Effects

The Effects panel can be used as a central place from which you can apply various effects to your photographs. You can find the Effects panel on the taskbar while you are in either the Quick or Advanced mode. This feature provides a thumbnail representation of the artwork or effects that are applied to a photo or added to it. Almost all of the sections include a menu of category selections and subcategories that correlate to those options. Within the realm of effects, you have the option of selecting from three distinct categories: artistic, classic, and color match.

Artistic Effects

Use effects that are influenced by well-known works of art or popular art styles to alter your photos with just a single click. You can choose from a wide variety of incredible artistic effects that you can apply to all or a part of your shot, and you can quickly modify the results to get the precise appearance that you like. These creative effects are accessible in both the Quick and Advanced modes of the game.

Note: You will find 5 new artistic effects in the new Photoshop Elements update.

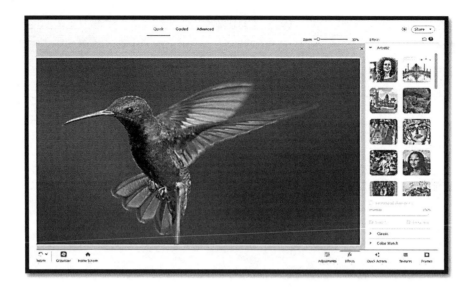

Classic Effects

Black and white, vintage styles, and cross-process presets are just some of the effects that are included in the 55 Classic effects. To examine the possible variants inside the preset, choose a Classic effect from the drop-down menu.

Textures

Use the Textures section to choose from 10 different textures that you may add to your photo. There are a variety of surfaces or backgrounds that the photograph might be printed on, and textures emulate them. For instance, the appearance of worn paper, the texture of chipped paint, the rough blue grid, and the chrome feel.

To apply textures, a new layer is created, and a layer mask is used. In Advanced mode, you can change the layer mask to remove or lessen the amount of texture in certain places (facial or skin).

Frames

Through the use of the Frames panel, you may choose and apply frames from the various options for your camera. The frame is automatically designed to fit in the most effective manner possible. You can also move or change the frame and the picture. To do this, use the move tool and then double-click the frame to make the change. By making adjustments to the Color Fill layer, you can alter the background color from white to any other color you like while you are in Advanced mode.

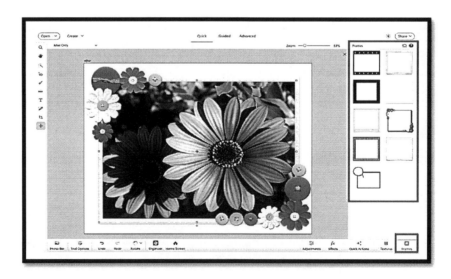

Apply an Effect, Texture, or Frame

The steps:

1. The first step is to open a picture in Photoshop Elements Editor and then switch to Quick mode.
2. In addition to the Adjustments panel, there are three more panels; these are the Effects panel, the Textures panel, and the Frames panel. Choose the icon that corresponds to any of the panels.
3. Live preview thumbnails of the picture that is now open are shown in the Panel bar. After clicking on a thumbnail, the Effect, Texture, or Frame will be applied.
4. Change the effect, texture, or frame that you applied to the picture by switching to the Advanced mode and making the necessary adjustments. The adjustment that was done in the Quick mode is accessible in a layer that is dedicated to it.

Frequently Asked Questions

1. How do you make quick adjustments in Photoshop Elements?
2. How do you access the Quick Fix toolbox?
3. How do you add quick frames?
4. How do you apply quick effects?
5. How do you apply quick actions in Photoshop Elements?

CHAPTER FOUR
GUIDED EDITS

Overview

Chapter four talks about guided edits in Adobe Photoshop 2024. Furthermore, you will also learn how to adjust photos one step at a time and also get to know how to use the different guided edit options.

Guided mode and Guided Edits

Guided Edits - a wizard-like interface for achieving several predetermined effects - are available in Guided mode. When you hover the cursor over a Guided Edit, it shows the effect that was applied. Guided Edits are divided into six categories on the Guided mode panel. Open the picture you want to improve and click the thumbnail for a category to learn more. In Photoshop Elements, the Guided Edit mode allows you to make simple selections and have the software perform the rest. Click "**Guided**" in the Shortcuts Bar to activate Guided Edit mode in Photoshop Elements. Select the picture to be used in Photoshop Elements' Guided Edit mode. You can choose a picture from the "**Photo Bin**" located underneath the work area. To find photos, use the dropdown menu above the Photo Bin. After you've decided which photos will be displayed in the Photo Bin, click a photo to choose it from the Photo Bin. Then, to begin modifying your picture, choose one of the six categories provided below the Shortcuts Bar.

The Guided Edit mode categories are located just below the Shortcut Bar. The "**Basics**" menu allows you to perform simple picture modifications. This contains, for example, the "**Brightness and Contrast**" **and** "**Sharpen**" capabilities. You can modify the color of your picture using the "**Color**" category. This contains, for example, the "**Remove a Color Cast**" feature. Choosing "**Black & White**" allows you to convert all or part of the picture to black and white. For example, the "**B&W Color Pop**" function is included in this category. The "**Fun Edits**" section enhances images with effects such as "**Puzzle Effect**," which transforms an image into a jigsaw puzzle. The "**Special Edits**" category includes creative effects such as the "**Orton Effect**" and a restoration feature called "**Restore Old Photo**." The "**Photomerge**" option in the category list allows you to combine several photographs to produce a new image. Each category has at least four separate capabilities that allow you to customize the picture. Simply choose the function you wish to use within the category to open the chosen picture in the guided edit mode for that function.

All of the functions in Guided Edit mode allow you to choose from a list of options. You will next be directed through the process of modifying your chosen picture. A panel on the right side of the program window then appears to guide you through the picture editing process. To finish the guided editing process, just follow the directions indicated in the window. The Guided Edit option in Photoshop Elements allows you to generate professional-looking photographs without any photo-editing experience.

How to Use the Guided Edit Mode in Photoshop Elements

The steps:

1. Click "**Guided**" in the Shortcuts Bar to activate Guided Edit mode in Photoshop Elements.
2. Choose a picture to use, and then choose one of the six categories given below the Shortcuts Bar.
3. After choosing a category, select a function to apply to your picture.
4. In the window that displays, follow the directions to change your picture.

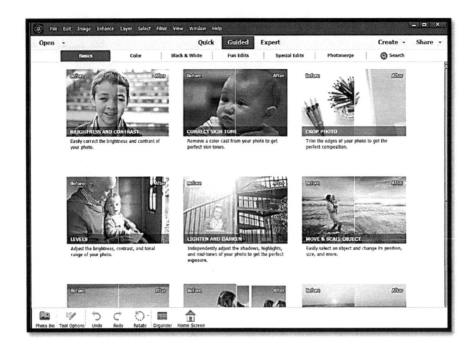

Search Guided Edits

The Guided Edit Search box in Photoshop Elements helps you to locate the appropriate Guided Edit. By searching for - you can quickly and simply locate what you want to do or discover new things to try.

- **Text** - If you're positive about a Guided Edit, put its name or related text into the search box to discover it fast.
- **Keywords** - Click on the keywords to view a list of Guided Edits that are related to them.
- **Explore** - In the Explore area, you'll find some hidden jewels.

To use this functionality, open the **Search window** by clicking the **Search icon** in the Guided workspace.

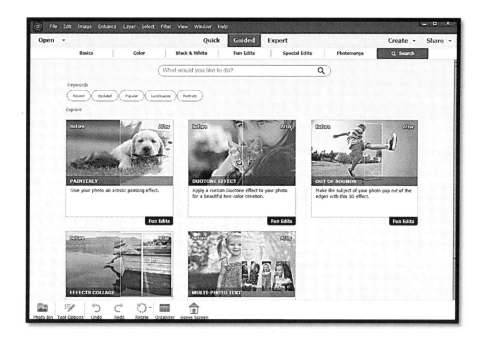

Basics

Add Text guided edit

Using the **Add Text** guided edit; you can create stylish text for shareable postings. Text can be aligned horizontally, vertically, or on a route or form. Warp it and add gradients and patterns to it.

To use this guided edit, follow these steps:

1. Perform one of the following:
- Launch **Photoshop Elements** and open a picture.

- From the Photo Bin, choose a photo.
2. Navigate to **Guided mode > Basics > Add Text**.
3. Choose one of the Type tools from the right panel:
- **Horizontal Type Tool -** This tool lets you type text horizontally.
- **Vertical Type Tool** - This tool lets you type text vertically.
- **Text on Selection Tool** - Allows you to do a quick selection and input text around the quick selection's boundaries.
- **Text on Shape Tool** - This tool lets you put text around the boundaries of a custom shape created over an image.
- **Text on Path Tool** - This lets you input text around the perimeter of a custom path created over a picture.

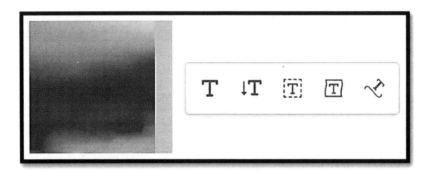

Note: Within the Tool selections panel, you can experiment with numerous formatting selections such as fonts, font styles, sizes, colors, leading, tracking, and text alignment.

4. Warp text by choosing the Create warped text icon from the action bar and then customizing it using the Warp Text dialog box's Style, Bend, Horizontal Distortion, and Vertical Distortion settings.
5. Create a text style with shadow, bevel, and stroke.

Note: When you choose the Advanced option, you can further change the text style in the Style Settings panel based on your unique needs.

6. To make your text more attractive, use a gradient or a pattern.
7. After you've obtained the required result, click Next to pick how you want to proceed:
   - **Save - Save/Save As**: Save the freshly made picture with styled text in any of the formats provided.
   - **Continue editing - In Quick/Advanced mode**: Choose whether you want to work on the picture with styled text in Quick or Advanced mode.
   - **Share - Flickr:** Choose to share your picture with styled text online using one of Photoshop Elements' social or sharing sites.

Advanced Type Tools

Use the Text on the Selection tool

Allows you to do a quick selection and insert text around the quick selection's boundaries.

To use the Text on Selection tool, follow these steps:

1. Choose the Text on Selection tool.
2. Drag the pointer over the picture to pick the area where you want the text to appear.

Note: To change the size of the selection tool, use square brackets.

3. To confirm your option, click the **Commit current operation button**.
4. Hover the mouse cursor over the chosen area's border until the Text on Selection type tool icon changes to the Type tool icon, then click to obtain the reference text over the selected area. Begin typing to enter the required text. You can further customize the reference text to meet your needs.
5. To save the text, click the **Commit current action button**, and to cancel the changes, click the **Cancel current operation button**.

Use the Text on Shape Tool

Allows you to add text around the perimeter of a custom shape created over an image.

To use the Text on Shape tool, follow these steps:

1. Choose the **Text on Shape** type tool.
2. Select the required custom shape from the Tool Options to use to add the text. To make the form, move the pointer over the picture.

3. Hover the mouse cursor over the selected shape's boundary until the Text on Shape type tool icon changes to the Type tool icon, and then click over the selected shape's boundary to obtain the reference text over the selected shape. Begin typing to enter the required text. You can further customize the reference text to meet your needs.
4. To save the text, click the **Commit current operation button**, and to cancel the changes, click the **Cancel current operation button**.

Use the Text on Path tool

It lets you input text around the perimeter of a custom route created over an image.

To use the Text on Path tool, follow these steps:

1. Choose the Text on Path tool.
2. Draw a path on the picture where you want the words to go.
3. To confirm the route, click the **Commit current operation button**.
4. Hover the mouse cursor over the drawn path until the Text on Path type tool icon changes to the Type tool icon, and then click over the path's border to display the reference text across the specified region. Begin typing to enter the required text.
5. To save the text, click the **Commit current operation button**, and to cancel the changes, click the **Cancel current operation button**.

The Move & Scale Object Guided Edit

Move and Scale Object guided edit allows you to choose an object and modify its location, size, and more—allowing you to customize the appearance of your design.

Object Removal Guided Edit

Delete undesirable information from your images with the object removal guided edit.

Here's how it's done:

1. **Perform one of the following:**
   - Launch **Photoshop Elements** and open a picture.
   - From the Photo Bin, choose a photo.
2. Select **Guided mode > Basics > Object Removal** from the menu.
3. Choose one of the following Selection tools from the right panel:

- **Brush** - Paint over the item you want to eliminate using the Selection Brush tool. The Brush Size slider allows you to change the size of the brush.
- **Lasso** - Draw a free-form selection around the item you want to delete using the Lasso tool.
- **Auto** - When you draw a shape around the item you want to delete, the Auto Selection tool will automatically produce a selection.
- **Quick** -When you choose or select-drag the item you want to delete, use the Quick Selection tool to create a selection based on its edges. The Brush Size slider may be used to change the size of the Quick Selection tool.

4. **To change your option, click one of the following buttons:**
- **Add** allows you to add additional photos to your selection.
- **Subtract** allows you to delete or delete a portion of the selection.

5. Choose **Remove Object** to remove the chosen object from your shot.
6. (Optional) Choose one of the following options to fine-tune your result:
- **Spot Healing Brush** - This tool is useful for editing a small area. Simply pick or drag this tool over the regions to be removed. The Brush Size slider allows you to modify the size of the brush. Use a tiny brush size for the best effects.
- **Clone Stamp Tool** - Use this tool to alter a wide area at once. After selecting this tool, hover over the area of the picture where you wish to cover the item using **Alt+click (Windows)/Option+click (MacOS)**. Drag the tool over the item to select it. The Brush Size slider allows you to change the size of the brush.

7. **After you've obtained the desired result, click Next and then pick how you want to proceed:**
- Select **Save or Save As** to save the freshly made picture in any of the supported formats.
- Return to Quick or Advanced editing mode.
- Upload to Flickr or Twitter.

Resize Guided Edit

To quickly generate a version of your image that meets specified size criteria - pixels, inches, or bytes - use the resize your photo guided edit.

1. Choose a picture from the picture Bin and go to **Guided > Basics > Resize Your Photo**.
2. Determine the function of the resized picture. Choose whether you want to use it online or print it.

Web output: Choose a size from the drop-down menu.

- **Long Edge:** Enter the image's width. To retain the aspect ratio, the height is automatically changed.
- **Short Edge**: Enter the image's height. To preserve the aspect ratio, the width is automatically changed.
- **Width and Height:** Enter your width and height. A crop window highlights a section of the picture. Drag the crop window over the picture with the mouse to pick which area will be saved.
- **File Size**: Enter the maximum file size in kilobytes. The generated result has a file size that is less than the number you provided.

Print output: Choose a dimension from the drop-down menu.

- **Long Edge**: Enter the image's width. To retain the aspect ratio, the height is automatically changed.
- **Short Edge**: Enter the image's height. To preserve the aspect ratio, the width is automatically changed.
- **Width and Height:** Enter a custom width and height, and then click **Preview/Apply**. A crop window highlights a section of the picture. Drag the crop window over the picture with the mouse to pick which area will be saved. When you click the **Shrink to Fit box**, the whole picture is reduced to fit one of the two dimensions (this may result in white borders at the photo's top/bottom or left/right corners).
- **Predefined sizes (for example, 4 x 6):** Select **Preview/Apply** from the available sizes. A crop window highlights a section of the picture. Drag the crop window over the picture with the mouse to pick which area will be saved. When you click the **Shrink to Fit box**, the whole picture is reduced to fit one of the two dimensions (this may result in white borders at the photo's top/bottom or left/right corners).
3. Choose **Next**, and then decide what to do with the result.

If you choose Web output in the previous phase, you are provided with the following options:

- **Save/Save As** - Save the freshly scaled picture in any of the formats provided.
- **Continue editing - Quick/Advanced:** Choose whether you want to work on the scaled picture in Quick mode or Advanced mode.

- **Share - Flickr/Twitter:** Choose to share your resized picture online using one of Photoshop Elements' social or sharing sites.

If you choose Print output in the previous step, you will be provided with the following options:

- **Save/Save As:** Save the freshly scaled picture in any of the formats provided.
- **Continue editing - Quick/Advanced**: Choose whether you want to work on the picture in Quick mode or Advanced mode.
- **Print - Local Printer/Order Prints:** Choose to print the picture outline to a printer that is locally (on this computer) installed. Alternatively, you can get prints from Adobe Photoshop Services.
4. Choose **Done**.

Vignette Effect Guided Edit

Use the vignette effect to accentuate the prominence of a person, group, or item in the center of your shot.

The steps:

1. Open the chosen image. Choose **Guided Mode > Basics > Vignette Effect** from the menu.
2. To determine the color of the vignette, choose between **Black or White**.
3. The Intensity slider determines how strong (dark or light) the vignette should be.

4. Select **Refine Shape** to fine-tune the vignette's edge (Feather slider) and size (Roundness). A lower pixel value for the Feather slider suggests a harder, sharper edge, while a higher value represents a softer, thicker edge. Negative values for the Roundness slider result in an enhanced vignette effect, while positive values result in a less noticeable vignette.
5. **After you've obtained the required result, click Next to select how you want to proceed:**
   - **Save - Save/Save As:** Save the newly produced picture in any of the formats provided.
   - **Continue editing - Quick/Advanced mode**: Choose whether you want to work on the picture in Quick or Advanced mode.
   - **Share - Flickr / Twitter:** Choose to upload your picture to one of Photoshop Elements' social or sharing platforms.

Color Guided Edits

Enhance Colors guided edit

To improve an image's color, saturation, and brightness, uses the **Enhance Colors Guided Edit**. You can see simply the after picture or both the before and after images vertically or horizontally.

Editing using the Lomo Camera Effect

Apply the Lomo camera effect in Guided Edit.

The steps:

1. Choose the **Lomo Camera Effect**. The Lomo Effect window on the right lets you apply the desired effects.
2. Select the **Lomo Camera Effect**.
3. Click the **Apply Vignette button**.
4. Open a picture and choose the Lomo Camera Effect from the Guided Edits tab. The Lomo Effect window on the right lets you apply the desired effects.
5. Select the **Lomo Camera Effect**.
6. Click the **Apply Vignette button**.

Note: Photoshop Elements enhances the previous effect you applied by clicking Lomo Camera Effect or Apply Vignette. You may click Reset at any time to erase all applied effects and restore the original picture.

7. After you've obtained the required result, click **Next** to choose how you want to proceed:
   - **Save - Save / Save As**: Save the newly created image in any of the formats provided.
   - **Continue editing - Quick / Expert**: Select whether you want to work on the picture in Quick mode or Advanced Mode.
   - **Share - Flickr / Twitter**: Select one of the social or sharing platforms available in Photoshop Elements to publish your picture online.

Remove a Color Cast guided edit

To remove color casts from a picture, use the Remove a Color Cast Guided Edit. You can see simply the after picture or both the before and after images vertically or horizontally. A color cast is an unfavorable color shift in a photograph. A shot taken inside without a flash, for example, may have too much yellow. To remove color casts from a picture, use the **Remove Color Cast command** to adjust the overall color composition.

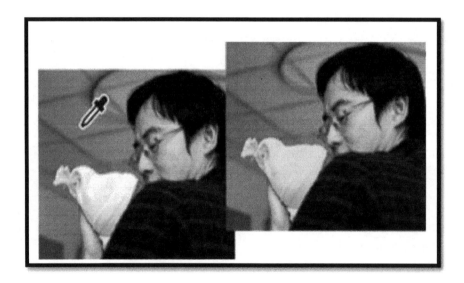

The steps:

1. Select **Enhance > Color Adjustment > Remove Color Cast**.
2. Click an area in your picture that should be white, black, or neutral gray. The picture varies depending on the color you choose.
3. Click **Reset** to start again and undo the modifications you've made to the picture.
4. To accept the color change, click **OK**.

Remove a color cast using Levels

Color correcting skills and understanding of the RGB color wheel are required for this procedure.

1. **Perform one of the following:**
- Select **Enhance > Lighting Adjustment > Levels**.
- Select **Layer > New Adjustment Layer > Levels,** or open a previously opened Levels adjustment layer.
2. Select a color channel to modify from the Channel pop-up menu:
- **Red** to make the picture red or cyan.
- **Green** to make the picture green or magenta.
- **Blue** to add a splash of blue or yellow to the picture.
3. To add or remove color, move the center input slider left or right.
4. When you're happy with the overall color, click OK.

Adjust color curves

The Adjust Color Curves command enhances a photo's color tones by changing the highlights, mid-tones, and shadows in each color channel. This command, for example, may repair shots with silhouetted images caused by intense backlighting or somewhat washed-out objects caused by being too near to the camera's flash. Adjust the highlights, mid-tone brightness and contrast, and shadows to fine-tune the adjustment.

Here are the steps:

1. Open an image in Photoshop Elements.
2. Select an image region or layer using one of the selection tools to make changes to it. (If there is no selection, the modification is applied to the whole picture.)

Note: Adjust the color curves on a duplicate layer to maintain the original shot while experimenting with tonal tweaks.

3. Select **Enhance > Color Adjustment > Color Curves**.
4. Choose a style (such as Backlight or Solarize).
5. Highlights, Midtone Brightness, Midtone Contrast, and Shadows sliders can be adjusted.
6. Click OK to modify your picture. Click **Reset** to cancel the modification and start afresh. Click **Cancel** to exit the Adjust Color Curves dialog box.

Black & White Edits

To make black-and-white photos from colorful images, use the Black and White Guided Edit on your photos. You can use a variety of black-and-white settings to make a sharp black-and-white shot, or you can add a diffuse light effect to the photographs to get a strange, dreamlike feel.

The steps:

1. Select **Black and White** in the Guided mode while an image is open. On the chosen image, choose a preset with which to operate.

Note: If you don't like the effect of one setting, try another. Photoshop Elements does not put one preset on top of another in this stage. When you choose a preset, the chosen picture is restored to its original condition, and the preset is applied again.

(Optional) A diffused glow may be utilized to emphasize a primary subject or an element of your photograph. To add a subtle light to the picture, click the **Diffuse Glow option**.

To apply the diffused light effect to particular areas of the image:

2. Click **Add** (to apply the diffused light effect) or **Remove** (to remove it).
3. Select the brush size that will be used to apply the action.

4. Slide the Opacity lever to choose how harsh or gentle the illumination should be.
5. Paint over parts of the photos.

6. (Optional) Click the **Increase Contrast option** to boost the contrast between the highlighted areas and the rest of the image.

Note: To improve the contrast, click the improve Contrast button many times.

7. **After you've obtained the required result, click Next to choose how you want to proceed:**
- **Save**: Save the new image in any of the formats provided.
- **Continue editing - Quick / Expert**: Select if you want to work on the picture in Quick mode or Advanced Mode.

B&W Color Pop guided edit

To emphasize one color in a photo while de-saturating the others, use the B&W Color Pop Guided Edit. You can choose a preset color (Red, Yellow, Blue, or Green) or use the available settings to fine-tune the effect.

The steps:

1. Select **B&W Color Pop** in Guided mode while an image is open.

2. Choose a color that you want to keep in the image. If you detect numerous color tones in this picture, Choose **Custom Color** and proceed to use the color picker to select a sample in the photo.

3. When you finish this stage, sections of the picture that are the same hue as the one you choose seem saturated. The remainder of the image begins to resemble a black-and-white photo.
4. Move the Fuzziness slider to the left or right to include fewer or more tones of the chosen color.

5. (Optional) Select **Refine Effect**, and then add or remove the **B&W Color Pop effect** from selected areas of the image. The Size slider allows you to change the size of the brush, while the Opacity slider controls the severity of the effect.
6. Increase Saturation to make the color you've picked stand out. This draws attention to the things of that hue in the otherwise flat black-and-white photo.

7. After you've obtained the required result, click **Next** to choose how you want to proceed:
- **Save:** Save the new image in any of the formats provided.
- **Continue editing - Quick / Expert:** Select if you would like to work on the picture in Quick mode or Advanced Mode.

B&W Selection guided edit

To desaturate the colors of a part of an image, use the Selective Black and White Guided Edit. When you desaturate parts of an image, the other parts of the photo get accentuated. After you've made your options, you can fine-tune them.

The steps:

1. Select **B&W Selection** in Guided mode when an image is open.

2. Select the **B&W Selection Brush** by clicking it. Choose whether to Add or Subtract regions to convert to black and white from the available selections. To select how much area is impacted in strokes over the shot, use the Brush Size slider.

Note: If you're using this effect on an item with several, delicate edges (like hair), select the **Refine Edge button** to fine-tune your selection.

3. To carefully apply or remove the black and white effect to additional areas of the shot, click **B&W Detail Brush**, choose an action and brush size, and then paint on the effect.

4. Choose **Invert Effect** to create the polar opposite of the effect you've created already.

5. After you've obtained the required result, select **Next** to choose how you want to proceed:
   - **Save / Save As:** Save the new image in any of the formats provided.
   - **Continue editing - Quick / Expert:** Select if you would like to work on the image in Quick mode or Advanced Mode.

High Key guided edit

To give your images an uplifting and pleasant tone, use an ethereal, dreamy effect.

1. Open a picture and choose **High Key** from the **Guided Edits room > Black and White menu**.

Note: When the High Key effect is applied to photos shot in bright light or that have been over-exposed, they will seem bleached out. Little darker images will provide better outcomes.

2. Select if you want to work with a color or black and white high key effect by clicking **Color or B&W**. The high key effect has been applied.
3. To reinforce the high key effect, use the give Diffuse Glow option to give a glow to the image's brighter areas. Click this button again and again to create a diffused light over the image.
4. After you've obtained the required result, select **Next** to choose how you want to proceed:
- **Save / Save As:** Save the newly created image in any of the formats available.
- **Continue editing - Quick / Expert:** Select if you would like to work on the image in Quick mode or Advanced Mode.

Low Key guided edit

By using the low-key effect, you can emphasize shadows, highlight edges, and provide a dramatic finish to your images.

Here are the steps:

1. Open a picture and choose **Low Key** from the **Guided Edits room > Black and White menu**.
2. Select if you want to work with a color or black-and-white low-key effect by clicking Color or B&W. The low-key effect has been introduced. Darker colors seem to be pushed darker, while brighter things appear to be somewhat overexposed. The contrast is excellent.
3. To locate the precise effect you want to add to your picture, use the Background Brush and Reduce Effect buttons.
4. **After you have gotten the required result, select Next to choose how you want to proceed:**
- **Save / Save As:** Save the new image in any of the formats available.
- **Continue editing - Quick / Expert:** Select if you would like to work on the picture in Quick mode or Advanced Mode.

Fun Edits

The Meme Maker Guided Edit

Photoshop Elements can instantly convert any picture into an interesting meme. The Meme Maker guided edit lets you create a meme out of a picture and text.

The steps:

1. Launch **Photoshop Elements** and open an image.
2. Navigate to **Guided > Fun Edits > Meme Maker**.

3. To use the default meme template, select **Create Meme Template**. The picture is centered in the meme design, with example text at the top and bottom.
4. To select the text for editing, use the **Type Tool** or double-click on it.
5. Enter the wording you want for your meme. The Guided Workspace's Tool Options bar allows you to modify the font, size, color, and style of the text. When you're finished typing, press the green check mark () to save your changes.

Note: If you are changing the top text, clicking the green check mark selects the below text for editing as well.

6. (Optional) Resize your picture by doing one of the following:
- To zoom out, move the Zoom slider to the left, and to zoom in, drag it to the right.
- To flip your picture, click the horizontal or vertical flip button.
- Choose **Fit Photo to Canvas** to extend the photo to fill the full canvas. When you choose this option, the Zoom and border modification tools are disabled.
- Double-click the image to bring up the heads-up display (HUD). You can use the HUD to rotate your picture left or right, zoom in or out, or change the main image. Once you've made the necessary adjustments, click the green check mark to save your work.

Note: Resize the picture frame by dragging the bounding box around it. Drag a corner handle to scale the image accordingly.

7. (Optional) Change the border by doing one of the following:
- To enter the Border Presets dialog, click the **Border Preset button**. You have a choice of 12 pre-made borders.
- To choose a solid color, use the color picker. The border or color of your choice is added to the meme template.
8. (Optional) Click the Effects button to see five pre-configured effects for your picture. To add an effect to your picture, just click on it. By pressing the Reset option, you can return to your original picture.
9. **Once you have gotten the required result, select Next to choose how you want to proceed:**
- **Save / Save As**: Save the new image in any of the formats provided.
- **Continue editing - Quick / Expert:** Select if you would like to work on the picture in Quick mode or Advanced Mode.

Multi-Photo Text Guided Editing

Use the Multi-picture writing guided edit to create visual writing with a different picture within each word. To make a visually rich shot, use the Multi-shot Text guided edit to use any photo as a background, add text, and insert a photo within each word.

Here are the steps:

1. **Perform one of the following:**
   - Launch **Photoshop Elements** and open a picture.
   - From the Photo Bin, choose a photo.

Note: The first picture you choose is used as the background photo. Since you can't alter the background picture later, be sure you've chosen the right one.

2. Choose **Guided > Fun Edits > Multi-Photo Text** from the menu.
3. Click Input Tool, then click anywhere on the image to input your text. The Guided Workspace's Tool Options bar allows you to modify the font, size, and style of the text. When you're finished typing, press the green check mark to save your changes.
4. Select whether you want to use the Fit or Fill options to resize the text on your picture.
   - **Fit**: Extends the text to fill the width of the image. The font's aspect ratio is preserved.
   - **Fill**: Extends the text to cover the photo's height and breadth.

Note: You can also move the textbox by dragging it.

5. To make each character in the text into a picture frame, select **Create Frames**.

6. **To add a picture to the text, do one of the following:**
   - To explore and pick a picture, click on the instructive text inside a character frame. This option allows you greater choice over the picture you want to use on a character.
   - Select one or more photos from a single folder by clicking **Computer**.
   - Select **Photo Bin** to use photos from the photo bin. The Photo Bin's drop-down list enables you to pick a photo from Elements Organizer or an album.

If you pick additional photos from the computer or the Photo Bin contains more photos than the number of character frames, photos are inserted in an orderly fashion inside each frame. All excess photographs are discarded. However, if you choose fewer photographs, you will have some blank character frames.

7. (Optional) Change the background color by making it transparent, white, or black, or selecting a color from the Color Picker.
8. (Optional) Apply one of the three preset effects to your text. Choose from Small, Medium, and Large. The buttons change the text's Bevel, Drop Shadow, and Strokes.

9. **(Optional) Change or exchange photographs in text frames by doing one of the following:**
   - To activate the heads-up-display (HUD), double-click on a character frame. You can use the HUD to rotate your picture left or right, zoom in or out, and change the photo. Once you've made the necessary adjustments, click the green check mark to save your work.
   - Double-click a character frame and drag the picture onto the photo frame you want to exchange the photo with. Drop the picture when you see a double-arrow cursor. Images are exchanged between the source and target frames.

10. Once you have gotten the required result, select **Next** to choose how you want to proceed. You can either save it, continue editing, or share it to your preferred social media platform,

The Double Exposure Guided Edit

The Double Exposure guided edit allows you to merge two photographs to produce a strange double-exposure effect. You can either import a picture from your computer or choose from the available sample images.

Here are the steps:

1. **Perform one of the following:**
- Launch Photoshop Elements and open an image.
- From the Photo Bin, choose a photo.
2. Navigate to **Guided > Fun Edits > Double Exposure**.
3. (Optional) Using the crop tool, crop the shot to maintain your subject in the middle of the frame.
4. Using the Auto or Quick selection tools, choose the main subject of your shot.
5. **Perform one of the following:**
- Select Import a photo from your computer to add a background image.
- Choose one of the example photos provided. The Intensity slider may be used to change the intensity of the background.
6. (Optional) Use the **Move Tool** to reposition the topic or background picture.
7. (Optional) Select an effect from the list of available possibilities. The strength slider allows you to change the strength of the effect.
8. Once you have gotten the required result, select Next to choose how you want to proceed by saving the image, continuing editing, or sharing it on any of your favorite social media platforms.

The Painterly Guided Edit effect

Painterly is a method of producing creative output by painting your picture with a brush on various textured canvasses and adding various painting effects. This Guided Edit can be found under **Guided > Fun Edits > Painterly**.

The steps:

1. Launch Photoshop Elements and open an image.

2. Navigate to **Guided > Fun Edits > Painterly**.
3. Select **Paint Brush**. You are going to choose the area of the picture on which you will work for the remainder of the project
   - **Display / Hide:** Show can be used to paint over parts you wish to expose. Hide can be used to paint over sections you want to hide
   - **Presets**: Select the type of brush you want to use to get the desired impact for your painting.
   - **Size**: To change the size of the brush strokes on your picture, use the Size slider.
   - **Opacity:** To determine the strength of the original revealed after painting with the brush, use the opacity slider.
   - **Brush Angle**: To rotate the brush, use the Brush Angle setting.

4. Choose a color for the remainder of the photo's canvas. You have a choice of two colors: black or white. To change the color, click **Select Custom Color** and then click anywhere on the disclosed section of the image.

5. Choose a texture for the canvas (the background).
6. To emphasize the texture, choose **Effect** and apply an effect.

7. Once you have gotten the required result, click **Next** to choose how you want to proceed:
   - **Save - Save / Save As**: Save the new image in any of the formats provided.
   - **Continue editing - Quick / Expert**: Select if you would like to work on the picture in Quick mode or Advanced Mode.

The "Out of Bounds" Guided Edit effect

In Guided Edit, the **Out Of Bounds option** lets you create a frame for a picture and show a part of the image outside the frame.

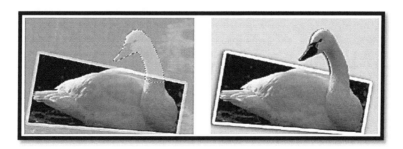

Here are the steps:

1. Click **Out Of Bounds** from the Guided Edits window.
2. To add a frame to the picture, select **Add Frame**.
3. Drag the frame's corners to leave a portion of the main subject outside the frame.
4. When you hit **Control + Alt + Shift (Command + Option + Shift on Mac OS)** and sliding the frame handles, you can add a viewpoint. Select the **Commit button**.
5. Drag the edges to change the width of the frame border. Select the **Commit button**.
6. Select the section of the picture that should extend beyond the frame using the Quick Selection tool.
7. Click to see the Out of Bounds Effect.
8. (Optional) Proceed to add a shadow.
9. (Optional) Click the **Add A Background Gradient button**.
10. To go to the Share window, select **Next**, or Cancel to exit Out of Bounds Guided Edit.

The Share window appears to the right of your image. You can save the image in the same place or as another picture in this panel. Take the image to the Quick Edit or Expert Edit rooms. You can also post the image to Flickr or Twitter.

Save as: Save/Save As

Put your adjusted image in a folder on your computer. If you haven't already saved your adjustments, you'll be prompted to choose a folder on your computer to save your image to. Use the **Save As option** to save the altered image to a different folder or with a different name. Select several advanced picture formatting settings in the JPEG settings dialog. If you don't want to make any changes, click OK to accept the settings that Photoshop Elements has applied.

Continue editing in Quick / Advanced Mode

Go to the Quick Edit or Expert Edit rooms with your photo. This signifies you've made changes in the Guided Edit mode and are currently making changes in the Quick or Advanced Modes.

Share on Flickr or Twitter

Share your newly adjusted photo on Twitter with your family and friends. Upload your photos to Flickr, where you can create and share photo albums.

Note: Photoshop Elements 2024 will prompt you to provide permission for it to upload your images to Flickr and Twitter. This is, however, a one-time event for each of them.

11. Click the **Done button**.

Create a Picture Stack

Picture Stack Guided Edit allows you to add frames to your photos, giving them the appearance of a creative collage.

Here are the steps to create a picture stack:

1. Launch **Photoshop Elements** and open an image.
2. Navigate to **Guided > Fun Edits > Picture Stack**.
3. Choose the quantity of photos you want in your photo collage from the drop-down menu.
4. Use one of the three presets to add a border to your images. You can select from Small, Medium, and Large.
5. To adjust the background, select one of the following buttons:
- Solid color
- Gradient

Set the color, blending mode, and opacity in the dialog box. Select OK.

6. Once you have gotten the required result, select **Next** to choose how you want to continue:
- **Save - Save / Save As:** Save the new image in any of the available formats.
- **Continue editing - Quick / Expert:** Select if you would like to work on the picture in Quick mode or Advanced Mode.

Create a Puzzle Effect

The Puzzle Effect Guided Edit gives the visual appearance of an image being generated by assembling a puzzle. You can use the Guided Edit to take a few puzzle pieces from their slots and move them about to create the sensation of an incomplete problem.

The steps:

1. Open Photoshop Elements 2024 and choose your image.
2. To choose the size of the tiles into which your picture will be cut, choose Small, Medium, or Large.
3. To make the problem seem more realistic, choose a few tiles that are not in their proper spot. Choose the **Select Puzzle Piece Button**, then select a tile from the puzzle. The tile has been chosen.
4. To remove the chosen tile, select **Extract Piece**. The Move Tool is chosen by default.
5. Drag the chosen tile to any spot on the canvas, or rotate or resize it using the handles.

Note: Steps 2, 3, and 4 should be repeated to remove and relocate several tiles.

6. (Optional) Use the **Eraser Tool** to erase any unwanted artifacts created as a consequence of using this Guided Edit.
7. To go to the Share window, select **Next**, or **Cancel** to exit Pop Art Guided Edit.

The Share window appears to the right of your image. You can save the image in the same place or as another picture in this panel. Take the image to the Quick Edit or Expert Edit rooms. You can also go on to post the image to Flickr or Twitter.

8. Select **Done** to complete the sharing or continuation process.

Special Edits

Depth of Field Guided Editing

The Depth of Field effect blurs out the rest of the picture to concentrate on certain sections of the image.

Simple Method

A duplicate of the background layer is made and a consistent blur is added to it in this method. Choose the areas you would like to focus on. The amount of blur added to the remainder of the picture may be adjusted.

Here are the steps:

1. Select **Depth of Field** under the Special Edits section of the Guided mode.
2. Select **Simple**.
3. Choose the **Add Blur button.** Across the picture, a uniform haze emerges.
4. To specify focus areas, click **Add Focus Area** and drag the pointer over the image's focus areas.
5. Drag the Blur slider until you reach the appropriate blur effect for the remainder of the picture to personalize the blur.
6. After you've obtained the required result, select **Next** to choose how you want to proceed:
- Save, continue editing, or share to X (Twitter) or Flickr**.**

Custom Method

Using the quick selection tool, you choose the things you want to focus on. The blur is applied to regions of the picture that have not been chosen. The amount of blur added to the remainder of the picture may be adjusted.

The steps:

1. Select **Depth of Field** under the Special Edits section of the Guided mode.
2. Select **Custom**.
3. Move the Quick Selection tool over the part of the picture that you wish to concentrate on.
4. Click the **Add Blur button**. The remainder of the picture is blurred uniformly.
5. Drag the Blur slider until you reach the appropriate blur effect for the remainder of the picture to personalize the blur.
6. After getting the required result, select **Next** to choose how you want to continue:
- **Save:** Save the new image in any of the available formats.
- **Continue editing - Quick / Expert**: Select if you would like to work on the picture in Quick mode or Advanced Mode.

The Text and Border Overlay Guided Edit

Add elegant borders to your photos that tell your narrative. Using the Text and Border Overlay guided edit, you can give your shot a wonderful new style with a mix of glossy borders and text.

Here are the steps:

1. Launch Photoshop Elements 2024 and open a picture.
2. From the Photo Bin, choose a photo.
3. Choose **Guided > Special Edits > Text and Border Overlay** from the menu.
4. Click **Select a Border** and select a border from the list.

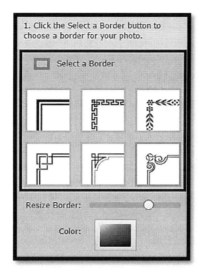

5. To change the size of the border, use the **Resize Border slider**.
6. Click the **Color Picker option**, and then choose the color for the border.

7. Choose **Add Text Overlay**. The Type Tool is activated when a text frame appears above the border.
8. Enter the new text. The Guided Workspace's Tool Options bar allows you to modify the font, size, color, and style of the text. When you're finished typing, press the green check mark to save your changes.
9. By clicking a dot on the border, you can move the text.

10. To see pre-configured text styles that you may apply to the text, click the **Text Style button.** To apply a text style to the text, click on it. Return to the original text style by pressing the **Reset button**.
11. Once you have gotten the required result, click Next to choose how you want to move on:
    - **Save:** Save the new image in any of the formats provided.
    - **Continue editing - Quick / Expert:** Select if you would like to work on the picture in Quick mode or Advanced Mode.

.The Perfect Portrait Guided Edit

Create a great portrait with Guided Edit by erasing flaws and improving different elements of the picture using simple tools.

Here are the steps

1. Select **Perfect Portrait** under the Special Edits section in the Guided mode.
2. Improve the skin's texture.
3. To smooth the skin, click the **Smooth Skin button**. You can change the smoothness effect by using the Strength slider.
4. To increase clarity, select **Increase Contrast**.
5. Using the available sliders, click **Features** to alter the Lips, Eyes, Nose, Face Shape, and Face Tilt for a chosen face.
6. Improve the appearance of your face.
   - To remove minor faults, select **Remove Blemishes**.
   - To brighten your smile, go to Whiten Teeth.
   - In the Open Closed Eyes dialog, the person's face is highlighted with a circle highlighter to signify that the face was recognized in the image.
   - (Optional) The Try Sample Eyes list displays a few examples. You can choose a face that closely resembles the main image. Photoshop Elements replaces the closed eyes in the main shot with the chosen face.
   - To brighten the eyes, select **Brighten Eyes.**
   - To darken the eyelashes and brows, select **Darken Eyebrows.**
7. Make any necessary adjustments.
   - Select **Add Glow.** Adjust the sliders until you get the results you want.
   - To make the chosen face look thinner, select **Slim Down.**

Note: Each click heightens the sensation.

8. Once you have gotten your outcome, select **Next** to choose how you want to continue:
   - **Save:** Save the new image in any of the formats accessible.
   - **Continue editing - Quick / Expert:** Select if you would like to work on the picture in Quick mode or Advanced Mode.

Photomerge Guided Edits

Use Photomerge Group Shot

To get the ideal group shot from various photographs, use Photomerge Group Shot. Ensure you select many photos from the same photo session for the best results.

Here are the steps:

1. Select the group photos you want to use as source images for the Photomerge Group Shot by doing one of the following:
- Select the photos in the Elements Organizer.
- Open the pictures in Photoshop Elements.
2. Select **Photomerge > Photomerge Group Shot** in the Guided Room.
3. Drag the greatest group shot from the shot Bin to the Final window.
4. Other photos in the Photo Bin are color-coded to help you keep track of them. Mark areas that you want to combine into the final image using the Pencil tool. Use the Pencil tool to add extra information or the Eraser tool to erase stuff to fine-tune the final picture.
5. **Set one or more of the following:**

Show Strokes

Select this option to display the Pencil strokes you highlighted in the original picture.

Show Regions

Select this option to make the specified areas visible in the final picture.

Advanced Options

For Advanced Options, expand or collapse this arrow.

Alignment Tool

To align several photographs, use the **Alignment Tool**, then add three markers in the source image and three marks in the end image before clicking **Align photos**. Photomerge Group Shot employs auto alignment. Only use the Alignment Tool if the automated alignment does not deliver the desired results.

Pixel Blending

Blend pixels by selecting this option.

6. After you've obtained the required result, click **Next** to choose how you want to proceed:
   - **Save :** Save the new image in any of the formats provided.
   - **Continue editing - Quick / Expert**: Choose if you would like to work on the picture in Quick mode or Advanced Mode.

Use Photomerge Scene Cleaner

To produce the ideal scenery shot from many photos, use Photomerge Scene Cleaner. You can, for example, remove undesired components such as visitors who have unwittingly strolled into the landscape.

Note: Use photos from the same scene shot from the same viewpoint for the best results.

The steps:

1. **Choose between 2 to 10 photos for the Photomerge Scene Cleaner by doing one of the following:**
- Select the photos in the Elements Organizer.
- Open the pictures in Photoshop Elements.
2. Click **Photomerge > Photomerge Scene Cleaner** from the Guided room.
3. Choose the finest image and drag it from the Photo Bin to the Final window.
4. Select a picture from the picture Bin (which is color-coded to help you keep track). It is shown in the Source window.
5. To add or delete areas from the Final window, perform any of the following:
- In the Final window, use the Pencil tool to outline the area to be removed.
- To add an area to the Final window, mark it in the Source window using the Pencil tool.
- Use the Pencil tool to add extra material or the Eraser tool to erase stuff to fine-tune the final picture.
6. (Optional) Choose one of the following options:

Show Strokes

Displays your Pencil strokes in the original picture.

Show Regions

The specified sections are revealed in the final picture.

7. (Optional) If the photos aren't aligned correctly, click the Advanced Options button to access the following:

Alignment Tool

The alignment of the several photos is corrected. Place three marks in the source picture and three markers in the final image using the Alignment Tool. Align Photos after dragging marks to comparable locations in each photo. Auto alignment is used by Photomerge Scene Cleaner. The Alignment Tool should be used only if the automated alignment does not deliver the desired result.

Pixel Blending

Blends pixels using various settings. Experiment to see whether this option enhances the picture.

8. (Optional) Repeat step 5 with additional photos from the Photo Bin for use in the Source window.
9. After you've obtained the required result, select **Next** to choose how you want to proceed:
   - **Save:** Save the new image in any of the formats provided.
   - **Continue editing - Quick / Expert**: Choose if you would like to work on the picture in Quick mode or Advanced Mode.

Photomerge Faces

To build a composite face, use Photomerge Faces to integrate several facial characteristics.

The steps:

1. Select the face photos you want to use as source images for Photomerge Faces by doing one of the following:
   - Select the facial image photos in the Elements Organizer.
   - Navigate to the facial image photos.
2. Select **Photomerge > Photomerge Faces** in the Guided Room.
3. As your basic picture, choose a face shot from the shot Bin and drag it to the Final window.
4. Click the **Alignment tool** on another picture in the Photo Bin. Align Photos after placing the three alignment marks on the eyes and mouth of the source and final images.
5. Other photos in the Photo Bin are color-coded to help you keep track of them. Mark the regions that you want to integrate into the final image using the Pencil tool. Use the Pencil tool to add extra information or the Eraser tool to erase stuff to fine-tune the final picture.
6. **Set the following settings:**

Show Strokes

Select this option to display the Pencil strokes you highlighted in the original picture.

Show Regions

Select this option to make the specified areas visible in the final picture.

7. **Once you have gotten the required result, select Next to choose how you want to continue:**
- **Save:** Save the new image in any of the formats provided.
- **Continue editing - Quick / Expert:** Choose if you would like to work on the picture in Quick mode or Advanced Mode.

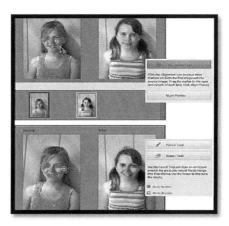

Photomerge Exposure

To properly manage scenarios in images with exposure issues, use Photomerge Exposure. You can merge two images to get a properly exposed image.

For instance, if you have a photograph with a window in the background and want an ideal photo with the following properties:

- A clear view of the countryside beyond the window.
- A decent exposure of the room's darker items.

In such cases, either the countryside outside the window or the contents within the room are often overexposed. **Do the following to obtain a flawless photo:**

- Take two or more shots with various exposures of the same scene. Take the shots at various exposure values with little shaking for the best results.

As an example:

- To appropriately expose the subject (the things within the room), shoot two or more photos with the flash switched on.

- Take one more snap without the flash to correctly illuminate the background (the view beyond the window).

Use Exposure Bracketing on your camera to capture the same subject with a variety of exposure settings.

- Combine the photos to generate a flawlessly exposed image.

Photomerge Exposure allows you to blend two photos to create a properly exposed image. **The following modes are available for photo merge exposure:**

- Manual Mode
- Automatic Mode

Note: Use images captured at multiple exposure settings, such as Exposure Bracketing, to get the best results while using the Automatic mode. Use images taken with the flash switched on and off to get the best results while using manual mode.

Automatic Photomerge Exposure

Elements Organizer can be used to choose the needed photographs and the Photo Bin can be used to select and deselect photos.

Follow the steps below:

1. Select **Photomerge > Photomerge Exposure** in the Guided room, and then perform one of the following:
- In Elements Organizer, pick a minimum of two and a maximum of ten photos, then click Photomerge > Photomerge Exposure in the Guided room.
- Select **File > Open** to open the necessary files.
  - To display all open files in the photo bin, choose **Show Open Files** In The Photo Bin.
  - Choose at least two and no more than 10 photos from the Photo Bin.
  - Select **Photomerge > Photomerge Exposure** in the Guided Room.
2. Select **Automatic** in the Photomerge Exposure.
3. **Choose one of the following alternatives:**

Simple Blending

You cannot adjust the Photomerge Exposure settings with this option. When you choose this option, the blended picture is shown.

Smart Blending

When you select the smart blending option, you can change the settings using the sliders. You may see the final image depending on the options you enter.

You can change the following options:

Highlight

Allows you to change the size of the information in the spotlight.

Shadows

Brighten or deepen the shadows.

Saturation

Allows you to adjust the color's intensity.

4. **Once you have gotten the required result, select Next to choose how you want to continue:**
- **Save**: Save the new image in any of the formats provided.
- **Continue editing - Quick / Expert**: Choose if you would like to work on the picture in Quick mode or Advanced Mode.

Manual Photomerge Exposure

Manual Photomerge Exposure is the default setting for Photomerge Exposure if you are using photos shot with your flash on.

Here are the steps:

1. Select **Photomerge > Photomerge Exposure** in the Guided room, and then perform one of the following:
 - In Elements Organizer, choose **Photomerge > Photomerge Exposure** with a minimum of two and a maximum of 10 photos.

- Select **File > Open** to open the necessary files.
  - To display all open files in the photo bin, choose **Show Open Files In The Photo Bin**.
  - Choose at least two and no more than 10 photos from the Photo Bin.
  - Select **Photomerge > Photomerge Exposure** in the Guided Room.
2. Click **Manual** in the Photomerge panel. The source picture is the first image in the picture Bin. As the final shot, you can choose an image from the shot Bin.
3. Choose the following exposed sections from the original image:
   - Select the **Pencil Tool** and paint exposed areas of the source picture with the mouse. Change the source picture and, if required, choose areas from it.
   - Select the **Eraser Tool** and use the mouse to paint over any locations you want to expose – this operation will deselect any areas selected by the Pencil Tool.

Above the first chosen final picture, you can now see a final image with various sections cloned from different source photographs.

4. Set the following settings:

Show Strokes

To see your Pencil strokes in the source picture, click.

Show Regions

To display the selected areas in the final picture.

5. More options:

- Using the Opacity Slider, adjust the transparency of these chosen sections to correctly blend them with the background.
- Click the **Edge Blending button** to smooth the blended edges.

Note: The Opacity Slider only affects the areas chosen from the presently displayed source picture. If you wish to adjust the transparency of the areas picked from the other photos, switch to a different source image. It remembers the value that was used for a certain picture.

6. Choose **Advanced Option** and then Alignment Tool to fix the alignment of numerous photos. Align Photos after placing three markers in the source picture and three marks in the final image. Select the **Done button**.
7. Choose **Next** to know how you want to continue:
- **Save:** Save the new image in any of the formats provided.
- **Continue editing - Quick / Expert:** Select if you would like to work on the picture in Quick mode or Advanced Mode.

Combine photos with Photomerge Panorama

To stitch/merge many images, use the Photomerge Panorama Guided Effect. For the stitching procedure to operate properly, the images must contain common, overlapping parts from the scene captured.

Here are the steps:

1. Choose **Guided Room> Photomerge > Photomerge Panorama** after selecting numerous photographs with overlapping material from the Photo Bin.

2. Choose the pan motion/layout settings for your photos in the Photomerge Panorama panel's Panorama settings box. To view the various options, click the triangle.

Auto Panorama

Analyze the source photos and choose between a Perspective and a cylindrical layout to provide the best photo merge.

Perspective

Creates a consistent composition by identifying one of the source photos as the reference image (by default, the center image). The remaining photos are subsequently modified (repositioned, stretched, or skewed as needed) to fit the overlying content layer.

Cylindrical

By presenting individual pictures as on an unfurled cylinder, this layout reduces the "**bow-tie**" distortion that may occur with the Perspective layout. Content that overlaps is still matched. The reference picture is in the middle. This is ideal for making large panoramas.

Spherical

Aligns and transforms the photos as if they were being used to map the interior of a spherical. If you have a collection of 360-degree pictures, use this to create 360-degree panoramas. Spherical may also be used to create excellent panoramic images from other file sets.

Collage

Aligns the layers, matches overlapping content, and changes any of the source layers (rotate or scale).

Reposition

The layers are aligned and overlapping material is matched, but no source pictures are transformed (stretched or skewn).

3. Select the **Settings checkboxes** to fine-tune the look of the resulting panorama.

Blend Images

Finds the best boundary between the photographs and produces seams based on them, as well as color-matching the images. A basic rectangular blend is done when Blend Images Together is turned off. If you want to retouch the blending masks by hand, this may be preferable.

Vignette Removal

Removes and compensates for darker edges produced by lens defects or incorrect lens shading in photos.

Correction of Geometric Distortion

Makes up for barrel, pincushion, and fisheye distortion.

Content-Aware Fill Transparent Areas

Seamlessly fill the transparent regions with comparable image content nearby.

4. Select the **Create Panorama button**. Photoshop Elements analyzes the photos and begins the panorama creation process.
5. When you create a panorama in Photoshop Elements, the new picture appears in the Expert view.

Note: A dialog appears asking whether you wish to fill the transparent panoramic boundaries. If you choose **Yes**, Photoshop Elements will cover the borders with content-aware fill swaths.

6. After you've obtained the required result, click **Next** to choose how you want to continue by saving the image in your preferred format, continue editing, or sharing to your favorite social media platform.

The Actions Panel

An action is a sequence of actions (tasks) that you may replay on a photo. These actions can take the form of menu commands, panel selections, tool actions, and so on. An action that generates a snapshot effect, for example, is a set of processes that alters the picture's size, applies an effect to the image, adds a border that extends below the image, and finally saves the file in the correct format. Photoshop Elements has a collection of actions in the Actions panel (**Window > Actions**). In a picture, you can use one or more of these actions. Photoshop Elements does not support the creation of action files. You can, however, load additional action files (.atn files) produced in Adobe Photoshop. Photoshop actions including steps that are not supported by Photoshop Elements will not play. Not all Photoshop actions are compatible with Photoshop Elements. **Here's how to play an action file on an image:**

The steps:

1. Open the picture you want to process with an action.
2. If the Actions panel isn't visible, go to **Window > Actions**.
3. Click an action or the triangle next to an Action Set in the Actions window.
4. To apply the action to the picture, either clicks the **Play button** or the **Actions panel menu** and then selects **Play**.

Manage action files

Add actions

Click the panel menu symbol in the Actions panel, and then select **Load Actions**. Select a.atn file and then access the new actions from the Actions panel.

Remove actions

Select an action or action set in the Actions window, and then click the **Delete button**. To confirm the deletion of the action, click OK.

Reset actions

Click the panel menu icon in the Actions panel, then select **Reset Actions**. All actions that were previously accessible in Photoshop Elements have been reinstated.

Frequently Asked Questions

1. How do you use Fun Edits?
2. How do you use black and white edits?
3. How do you use the move and scale object guided edit?
4. How do you combine photos with photomerge panorama?
5. How do you manually align your photos for photo merging?
6. How do you clean up faces with the perfect portrait guided edit?

PART III

THE ADVANCED PHOTO EDITING WORKSPACE

CHAPTER FIVE

GET TO KNOW THE PHOTOSHOP ELEMENTS TOOLBOX

Overview

Chapter five digs deep into the world of advanced photo editing workspace. Here, you will learn about the different Photoshop Elements toolboxes and how to use every one of them to make your image stand out.

The Tool Options

The Color Picker

Use the Adobe Color Picker to choose the foreground or background color by selecting from a color spectrum or by numerically specifying colors. Furthermore, you can pick colors based on the HSB or RGB color models, or you can choose solely web-safe colors.

Here are the steps:

1. To open the Color Picker, select the foreground or background color boxes in the toolbox.
2. Place your cursor within the color area. When you click in the color field, a circle marker appears in the field to show the color's location, and the numerical values alter to reflect the new color.
3. To change colors, drag the white triangles along the slider.
4. To specify a number graphically, try any of the following:
- In the text box below the RGB values, enter the hexadecimal value for your color. (Web designers often employ hexadecimal color values.)
- For RGB color, choose a radio button and enter component values ranging from 0 to 255 (0 being no light and 255 being the strongest light).
- For HSB color, pick a radio button and enter percentages for saturation and brightness; enter hue as an angle from 0° to 360° that corresponds to a point on the color wheel.
5. The new color is shown in the top portion of the color rectangle to the right of the color slider. The original color is visible at the rectangle's bottom.
6. To begin painting with the new color, select **OK**.

Note: Colors can be selected using either your system's built-in color picker or a plug-in color picker. Select **Color Picker** from **Preferences > General.**

The Eyedropper/Sampler Tool

The eyedropper tool in Adobe Photoshop Elements is one of the most user-friendly. It is often used by all digital artists, editors, and other Photoshop users. To choose a color from an image or any Photoshop project, use the Eyedropper tool. In other words, the eyedropper tool is used to sample a color from a given picture and then use that sample color in whatever manner you desire, such as the background, foreground, and so on. The eyedropper tool's symbol/icon is as follows:

If you have the Caps lock on, the eyedropper tool's symbol will change to a plus sign with a circle in the center.

How to use the eyedropper tool

As previously stated, the eyedropper tools only duty is to choose a color from any section of the picture.

Now, consider the following case in further depth:

1. In Photoshop Elements, open an image

2. From the tool palette, select the eyedropper tool. Now, with the eyedropper tool chosen, move your cursor over the picture (be sure to tick the "**Show sampling ring**" option in the settings box).
3. **After you've selected the eyedropper tool, move your cursor over the picture and click to choose the sample image. As demonstrated in the picture below, a ring will appear on the screen:**

The foreground color is visible, and the color of the sample ring corresponds to the color of the point of the eyedropper tool to which it points. The color changes as we move the pointer. As a result, the eyedropper tool is quite handy for selecting many colors from a photograph.

The Eyedropper tool's options

Now that we've learned how to use and operate the eyedropper tool, let's look at the options available on the options bar that shows when we choose the eyedropper tool.

Let's take a closer look at each of them:

1. **Sample Size**

It specifies the size of the sample area from which the eyedropper tool will choose the color.

There are seven sample size options:

- **Point Sample**: When this size is enabled, the tool will choose the color from the pointed pixel (i.e. where the cursor is).
- **3*3 average**: If this option is selected, the tool will choose a color from the 3*3 square average.
- **5*5 average**: If this size is enabled, the tool will choose the average color from a 5*5 pixel squares nearby.
- **11*11 average**: If this option is selected, the tool will choose the average color from a surrounding square of 11*11 pixels.

- **31*31 average**: If this option is selected, the tool will choose the average color from a nearby square of 31*31 pixels.
- **51*51 average**: If this size is enabled, the tool will choose the average color from a 51*51 pixel square nearby.
- **101*101 average:** If this option is selected, the tool will choose the average color from a surrounding square of 101*101 pixels.

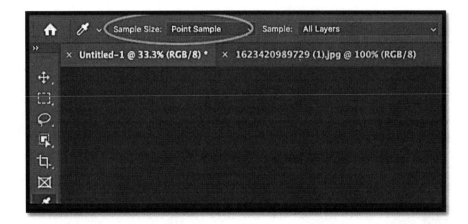

2. **Sample**

There are five options here including the following:

- **Current layer**: When this mode is chosen, the eyedropper tool will only choose colors from the currently selected layer.
- **Current layer and below**: When this option is activated, the eyedropper tool will choose a color from the current layer as well as the layers below the currently chosen layer.
- **All layers**: As the name implies, the eyedropper tool will choose a color from all levels in the document.
- **All layers no adjustment:** When this option is activated, the eyedropper tool will choose the color by combining all visible layers in the document, but the adjustment layers will be ignored.
- **Current and Below no adjustment:** When this option is activated, the eyedropper tool will choose the color from the current and layers below the current layer, but the adjustment layer will be disregarded if it exists below the current layer.

   3. **Sampling Ring**

This is a straightforward option. If you activate it, the ring with the selected color will appear on your screen. Most users normally keep it checked. Since it allows people to quickly choose the correct color by seeing the color change and then observing the changes from the background and foreground color sections.

The Color Swatch Panel

The Color Swatches panel (**Window > Color Swatches**) is a wonderful location to save the colors you often use in your photos. By clicking a color swatch in the Color Swatches tab, you can choose a foreground or background color. You can add and remove colors to build a custom swatch library, save a swatch library, and reload it for usage in another picture. By selecting an option from the More menu, you can modify how thumbnails are shown in the Color Swatches panel. Although you can add as many colors as you like to the Color Swatches panel, you should keep its size and structure under control to maximize efficiency. Creating libraries may help you organize and regulate panel size by grouping similar or specific swatches. The different swatch libraries are located in the Photoshop Elements installation folderPresetsColor Swatches (for Mac, Photoshop Elements installation folderSupport FilesPresetsColor Swatches). When you save custom libraries to the Color Swatches folder, they appear instantly in the panel libraries pop-up menu.

Select a color while using the Color Swatches window

Here are the steps:

   1. Choose **Window > Color Swatches** if the Color Swatches window is not already open.
   2. (Optional) Select a swatch library name from the Swatches menu in the Color Swatches window.

3. **Perform one of the following:**
   - To choose a foreground color, select one from the panel.
   - Ctrl-click (Command-click in Mac OS) a color in the panel to choose it as the background color.

Add a color to the Color Swatches panel

If you have a color that you often use, you can store it as a swatch in the Color Swatches window. Saved swatches are added to the panel's color library. You must save the complete library to permanently store your custom swatches.

The steps:

1. In the toolbox, change the foreground color to the color you want to add.
2. In the Color Swatches panel, try one of the following:
   - At the lower side of the panel, click the **New Swatch button**. The color swatch is added and designated Color Swatch 1 by default.
   - From the More menus, choose **New Swatch**.
   - Hover the cursor over an empty area in the Color Swatches panel's bottom row (the pointer transforms into the Paint Bucket tool) and click to add the color.

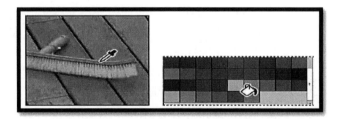

3. Select **OK** after giving the new color a name.
4. If asked to save the swatch library, enter a new name in the Save dialog box and press the **Save button**.

Save and use custom swatch libraries

The steps:

1. **In the Color Swatches panel, try any of the following:**
   - Select **Save Swatches** from the More menu to store a library of swatches. Save the file to the Photoshop ElementsPresetsColor Swatches (For Mac, Photoshop

ElementsSupport FilesPresetsColor Swatches) folder to have the set appear in the panel's swatch libraries pop-up menu.

Note: You must restart Photoshop Elements to view the new swatch set in the menu.

- Select **Load Swatches** from the More menu in the panel to pick and load a swatch library.
- To replace the existing swatch library with a different library, go to the More menu on the panel and select **Replace Swatches**.

Reset a swatch library to its default color swatches

The steps:

1. In the Color Swatches panel, choose a swatch library from the pop-up menu.
2. Select **Preset Manager** from the More option in the Color Swatches panel.
3. Select **Swatches** from the Preset Type option in the Preset Manager dialog box.
4. From the More menus, choose **Reset Swatches** and confirm the operation when requested.

Delete a color from the Color Swatches panel

1. **Perform one of the following:**

- Move the color swatch to the panel's Trash button, and then click **OK** to complete the deletion.
- Change the cursor to a scissors icon (Option key on Mac OS) and click a color in the Color Swatches window.

2. If asked to save the library, enter a name in the Save dialog box and press the **Save button**.

Note: You must resave the library that contains the swatches to permanently remove them.

3. The Color Swatches panel (accessed by choosing **Window > Color Swatches**) allows you to manage the swatches.
- Select Save Swatches from the More menu to store a library of swatches. To make the set displayed in the swatch library of the panel pop? Save the file to the Photoshop ElementsYour VersionPresetsColor Swatches folder (this is the default location that opens) from the pop-up menu. You must restart Photoshop Elements to view the new swatch set in the menu.

- Choose **Load Swatches** from the More menu in the panel to pick and load a swatch library.
- To replace the existing swatch library with a different library, go to the More menu on the panel and select **Replace Swatches**.

Additional Foreground/Background Color options

Select a color from the toolbox.

1. **Perform one of the following:**
- Choose the **Default Colors button** to make the foreground and background boxes black and white.
- Select the Switch Colors icon to change the colors in the two boxes.
- To change the foreground color, click the toolbar's uppermost color box and then choose a color from the Color Picker.
- To change the background color, click the toolbox's bottom color box and then choose a color from the Color Picker.

The Zoom Tool

You can enlarge an image and see the little details by using the zoom tool.

1. **Perform one of the following:**
- From the toolbar, choose the **Zoom tool** and then click the **Zoom In or Zoom Out button** in the Tool Options bar. Click on the area you want to enlarge. With each click, the picture is magnified or reduced to the next predetermined % and the display is centered on the spot you select. The magnifying glass looks empty when the picture has achieved its maximum magnification level of 3200% or the lowest reduction level of 1 pixel.

Note: Enlarge a part of a picture by dragging a Zoom tool over it. In the Tool Options bar, make sure the Zoom In button is chosen. Begin dragging a marquee and then hold down the spacebar while dragging the marquee to a new spot to move the zoom marquee around the picture.

- In the Tool Options bar, drag the **Zoom slider**.
- Go to **View > Zoom In or Zoom Out.**
- In the Tool Options bar, enter the appropriate magnification level in the Zoom text box.

Note: Hold down Alt to toggle between zooming in and zooming out while using a Zoom tool.

Display an image at 100%

The steps:

1. **Perform one of the following:**

   - In the toolbox, double-click the Zoom tool.
   - In the Tool Options menu, choose the **Hand or Zoom tool** and click the 1:1 button.
   - Select **View > Actual Pixels** from the menu, or right-click the picture and select Actual Pixels.
   - In the status bar, type 100% and hit Enter.

Fit an image to the screen

Here are the steps:

1. **Perform one the below:**

   - In the toolbox, proceed to click twice on the Hand tool.
   - From the opened Tool Options bar, ensure you select a Zoom tool or the Hand tool, and select Fit Screen button. Alternatively, right-click the picture and choose **Fit to Screen**.
   - Select **View > Fit On Screen**.

Both the zoom level and the window size are scaled to match the available screen area in these selections.

Resize the window while zooming

Here are the steps:

1. Click **Resize Windows To Fit in the Tool Options bar** when a Zoom tool is active. The size of the window varies as you enlarge or minimize the image's view.
2. When Resize Windows To Fit is off, the window remains the same size regardless of picture magnification. This is useful when dealing with tiled graphics or smaller displays.

Using the Navigator Panel

The Navigator panel allows you to change the magnification and region of view of the picture. The magnification is changed by typing a value into the text box, pressing the Zoom Out or Zoom In button, or sliding the zoom slider. To change the perspective of a picture, drag the view box in the image thumbnail. The image window's bounds are represented by the view box. You may also define the region of view by clicking on the image's thumbnail. Select **Panel Options** to adjust the view box color. Choose a color from the Color menu, or click the color swatch to launch the Color Picker and enter your own. Select OK.

Open multiple windows of the same image

Open numerous windows in Advanced Mode to present various perspectives of the same file. The Window menu displays a list of open windows, and thumbnails of each open picture appear in the Photo Bin. The number of windows per picture may be limited by available memory.

The steps:

1. Select **View > New Window For [image filename]** from the menu. You may need to adjust the second window to watch both concurrently, depending on the location of the first.

Note: When you're working with a zoomed picture, you can use the **New Window command** to view what the image will look like at 100% size in a different window.

View and arrange multiple windows

1. **Perform one of the following in Advanced Mode:**
- Select **Window > Images > Cascade** to show windows stacked and cascading from the top left to the bottom right of the screen.
- Select **Window > Images > Tile** to show windows edge-to-edge. The open windows are adjusted to fit the available area when you shut photos.
- Select **Window > Images > Match Zoom** to display all open pictures at the same magnification as the current image.
- Select **Window > Images > Match Location** to display all open photos in the same area (upper-left corner, middle, lower-right corner, and so on). All windows' views

change to reflect the current (frontmost) picture. The zoom level remains constant.
- To see other image-arranging possibilities, select **Layout** in the Taskbar and choose a new layout from the pop-up menu.

Note: Only when Allow Floating Documents In Advanced Mode is activated in preferences are the **Window > Images options** available.

Close the windows

1. **Perform one of the following in Advanced Mode to close the windows:**
- Select **File > Close** to close the current window.
- In the current window's title bar, click the **Close button**.
- In the Photo Bin, right-click a thumbnail and choose **Close**.
- Select **File > Close All** to shut all currently active windows.

The Move Tool

The Move tool allows you to cut and drag a pixel selection to a different spot in the image. The tool may also be used to transfer or copy selections between photographs in Photoshop Elements, as well as photos in other apps that handle selections.

Hold down Ctrl (Command on Mac OS) to activate the Move tool while another tool is chosen. (When the Hand tool is chosen, this strategy does not function.)

The steps:

1. Make a selection using a selection tool in the Edit workspace, then pick the **Move tool** from the toolbox.
2. Change the **Move tool settings** in the options bar (optional).
3. Drag the selection to a new location by moving the cursor within the selection boundary. If you have numerous places chosen, all pixel selections will move as you drag.

Move tool options

When you pick the Move tool, the options menu allows you to modify the following settings:

Auto Select Layer

Rather than the presently chosen layer, this command selects the topmost layer with pixels beneath the Move tool cursor.

Show Bounding Box

Displays the bounding box around the picture's selection or the currently chosen layer (if the image has no active selection). You can resize the selection or layer by using the boxes on the sides and corners.

Note: A Background layer's bounding box is not visible.

Display Highlights on Rollover

Individual layers are highlighted as the mouse moves over the picture. To pick and move a highlighted layer, click on it. Rollover does not highlight layers that are already chosen.

Arrange menu

The chosen layer is moved in front, between, or behind other levels. Bring To Front, Bring Forward, Send Backward, and Send To Back are all options. To organize a layer, choose it and then an item from the organize menu.

Align menu

Aligns the layers that have been chosen. Top edges, vertical centers, bottom edges, left edges, horizontal centers, and right edges are all options. Multiple layers can be aligned at the same time. To align layers, pick one, hold Shift, choose another, and then select an option from the Align menu.

Distribute menu

Layers are spaced evenly apart. Top edges, vertical centers, bottom edges, left edges, horizontal centers, and right edges are all options. Multiple layers might be spread apart at the same time. You must have at least three levels chosen for this option to be activated. To separate layers, pick one, hold Shift, choose another, and then select an item from the Distribute menu.

Copying selections or layers

You can copy and paste selections using the Move tool. Remember that when you copy and paste a selection or layer across pictures with various resolutions, the transferred data preserves its original pixel dimensions. As a result, the pasted section may seem out of proportion to the new picture. Before copying and pasting, use the **Image > Resize > Image Size command** to make the source and destination photographs the same resolution. Cut or copied selections are saved to the clipboard. At any one moment, just one selection is preserved in the clipboard.

Copy selections with the Move tool

Drag the selection from the current picture window into the other image window when copying between photographs. When you drag the selection into the image window, a border appears around it.

Here are the steps:

1. Choose the section of the picture you would like to copy.
2. Choose the **Move tool** from the toolbox in the Edit workspace.
3. While dragging the selection you wish to copy and relocate, hold down the Alt (Option) key.
4. **Do one of the following to create extra copies of the same selection:**

- While dragging the selection to each new place, hold down **Alt (Option in Mac OS)**.
- Hold down **Alt (Option in Mac OS)** and hit an arrow key to offset the clone by one pixel. (This moves and duplicates the pixels, resulting in a blur effect.)
- Press **Alt (Option in Mac OS) + Shift and** an arrow key to offset the duplicate by 10 pixels. (Rather than copying the pixels, this moves them.)

When you drag a selection (while holding down the Shift key) from one picture to another, the selection gets pasted in the middle.

Copy a selection using commands

1. Use a selection tool in the Edit workspace to choose the area you would like to copy.
2. **Perform one of the following:**
- To copy the selection to the clipboard, go to **Edit > Copy**.
- Select **Edit > Copy Merged** to copy all layers in the current selection to the clipboard.

Paste one selection into another

To paste a clipboard or copied material into a selection, use the Paste into Selection command. This command allows you to use items inside the specified region to avoid the pasted picture seeming flat and artificial.

To keep the reflection in a pair of sunglasses, for example, use a Hard Light blending mode at 85% opacity. When using blending modes in this manner, you must first create a new layer and then paste the selection onto it. Hold down **Ctrl (Command on Mac OS)** to activate the Move tool while another tool is chosen. (When the Hand tool is chosen, this strategy does not function.)

The steps:

1. Make a selection using a selection tool in the Edit workspace, then pick the **Move tool** from the toolbox.
2. Adjust the Move tool settings in the options bar (optional).
3. Drag the selection to a new location by moving the cursor within the selection boundary. If you have numerous places chosen, all pixel selections will move as you drag.

Move tool options

When you pick the Move tool, the options menu allows you to modify the following settings:

Auto Select Layer

Rather than the presently chosen layer, this command selects the topmost layer with pixels beneath the Move tool cursor.

Display Bounding Box

Displays the bounding box around the picture's selection or the currently chosen layer (if the image has no active selection). You can resize the selection or layer by using the boxes on the sides and corners.

Note: A Background layer's bounding box cannot be seen.

Display Highlights on Rollover

Individual layers are highlighted as the mouse moves over the picture. To pick and move a highlighted layer, click on it. Rollover does not highlight layers that are already chosen.

Arrange menus

The chosen layer is moved in front, between, or behind other levels. Bring To Front, Bring Forward, Send Backward, and Send To Back are all options. To organize a layer, choose it and then an item from the organize menu.

Menu alignment

Aligns the layers that have been chosen. Top edges, vertical centers, bottom edges, left edges, horizontal centers, and right edges are all options. Multiple layers may be aligned at the same time. To align layers, pick one, hold Shift, choose another, and then select an option from the Align menu.

Distribute the menu

Layers are spaced evenly apart. Top edges, vertical centers, bottom edges, left edges, horizontal centers, and right edges are all options. Multiple layers might be spread apart at the same time. You must have at least three levels chosen for this option to be activated. To separate layers, pick one, hold **Shift**, choose another, and then select an item from the Distribute menu.

Copying selections or layers

You can copy and paste selections using the Move tool or the Edit menu's Copy, Copy Merged, Cut, Paste, or Paste into Selection commands. Remember that when you copy and paste a selection or layer across pictures with various resolutions, the transferred data preserves its original pixel dimensions. As a result, the pasted section may seem out of proportion to the new picture. Before copying and pasting, use the **Image > Resize > Image Size command** to make the source and destination photographs the same resolution. Cut or copied selections are saved to the clipboard. At any one moment, just one selection is preserved in the clipboard.

Copy selections with the Move tool

Drag the selection from the current picture window into the other image window when copying between photos. When you drag the selection into the image window, a border appears around it.

Follow the steps below:

1. Choose the section of the picture you want to copy.
2. Select the Move tool from the toolbox in the Edit workspace.
3. While dragging the selection you want to copy and relocate, hold down the Alt (Option) key.
4. **Do one of the following to create extra copies of the same selection:**
- While dragging the selection to each new place, hold down Alt (Option in Mac OS).
- Hold down Alt (Option in Mac OS) and hit an arrow key to offset the clone by one pixel. (This moves and duplicates the pixels, resulting in a blur effect.)
- Press Alt (Option in Mac OS) + Shift and an arrow key to offset the duplicate by 10 pixels. (Rather than copying the pixels, this moves them.)

Note: When you drag a selection (while holding down the Shift key) from one picture to another, the selection gets pasted in the middle.

Copy a selection using commands

1. Use a selection tool in the Edit workspace to choose the area you would like to copy.

2. **Perform one of the following:**
   - To copy the selection to the clipboard, go to **Edit > Copy**.
   - Select **Edit > Copy Merged** to copy all layers in the current selection to the clipboard.

Paste one selection into another

To paste a clipboard or copied content into a selection, use the **Paste Into Selection command**. This command allows you to use items inside the specified area to avoid the pasted picture seeming flat and artificial. To keep the reflection in a pair of sunglasses, for example, use a Hard Light blending mode at 85% opacity. When using blending modes in this manner, you must first create a new layer and then paste the selection onto it.

The steps:

1. Use the **Copy command** in the Edit workspace to copy the part of the picture you wish to paste. (You can even copy images from other programs.)
2. Select the picture into which you want to place the copied image.
3. Select **Edit > Paste into Selection** from the menu. The copied image only displays inside the chosen boundary. You can move the copied picture inside the boundary, but it won't be visible if you move it fully outside of the border.
4. Drag the pasted picture to the right spot with your cursor inside the selection boundary.
5. When you're happy with the outcome, deselect the pasted picture to save your modifications.

Note: Hold down Ctrl (Command on Mac OS) to activate the Move tool while another tool is chosen. (The Hand tool is incompatible with this approach.)

Add to and subtract from a selection

The Select Subject command is used as follows:

1. **Click Select > Subject in either Expert or Quick mode**

In the Tool Options of the Quick Selection, Selection Brush, Magic Wand, Refine Selection, and Auto Selection Tools, you can additionally select the Select Subject button, as illustrated.

2. If your selection needs to be cleaned up after Step 1, use any of the selection tools to add to or remove from it.

The Lasso tool, which can be found under the Tool Options of the Auto Selection Tool, is our favorite for small cleanups.

- To add to your selection, hold down the **Shift key** while dragging over the picture portions you want to include.
- To erase from your selection, hold down the Alt (Option) key while dragging over your undesirable picture sections.

In the Tool options, you can also pick the Add to Selection and Subtract from Selection selections.

3. If you need to fine-tune your selections anymore, go to the Tool Options and alter the settings as needed.

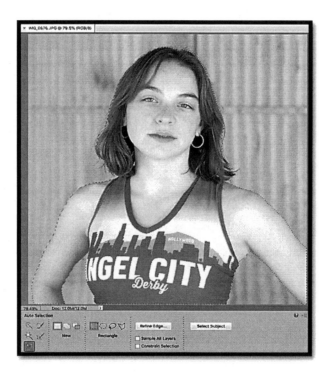

Refining the edges of a selection

You can refine the edges of your selection with the Refine Edge option. It doesn't matter how you obtained the choice; all that matters is that you have one. The command is found in the Tool Options menus of the Magic Wand, Lasso, and Quick Selection tools. And, of course, it's accessible via the Select menu.

Here's the lowdown on each of the settings for this option, as shown:

- **View Mode**: To preview your option, pick a mode from the pop-up menu. A tooltip will appear when you move your mouse over each setting. Marching Ants, for example, display the selection boundaries. Overlay allows you to see your selection while hiding the boundaries and adding a semi-opaque overlay of color to the unselected region. On Black and White display the selections against a black or white background, respectively. Show Original displays the picture without a preview of the selection. Show Radius indicates the size of the region where the edge refining is taking place.
- **Smart Radius**: Enabling this option allows Elements to automatically modify the radius for hard and soft edges near the chosen boundary. This option may not be appropriate if your border is consistently harsh or soft. This gives you greater flexibility over the radius setting.
- **Radius**: Determines the size of the selection boundary to be refined. To enhance the edge of sections with gentle transitions or a lot of detail, increase the radius. To find a decent setting, move the slider while looking at your selections.
- **Smooth**: Reduces jaggedness at the margins of your selection.
- **Feather**: Slide the slider to the right to produce a softer, blurrier edge.
- **Contrast**: Increasing the contrast removes artifacts while tightening soft edges. Before experimenting with contrast, try using the Smart Radius option.
- **Shift Edge**: Reduces or increases the size of your chosen region. Slightly reducing your selection border may assist in defringing (removing unwanted background pixels) your selection borders.
- **Decontaminate Colors**: Replace the background fringe with the colors of the element you've chosen. Because decontamination alters the colors of certain pixels, you will need to export to, or create, another layer or document to retain your present layer. Choose **Reveal Layer** as your View option to witness the decontamination in action.
- **Amount**: Modifies the degree of decontamination.
- **Output To**: Select whether you want to output your refined, decontaminated selection to a layer, layer mask, and layer, layer with a layer mask, new document, or new document with a layer mask.

- **Refine Radius tool:** On the left, choose the Paintbrush tool and brush around your border to change the region you're refining. Change your View mode to Marching Ants to see precisely what region is included or omitted. To change the brush size, use the right and left brackets.
- **Erase Refinements tool:** This tool (which resembles an Eraser) is likewise placed on the left and can be used to remove any undesirable refinements created using the Refine Radius tool.
- **Zoom tool:** Allows you to zoom in on your picture to observe how your settings affect it.
- **Hand tool**: Allows you to pan around your picture window to observe how your settings are affecting it.

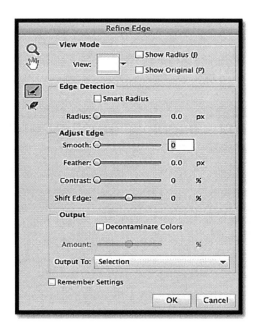

The Marquee Selection Tools

The Selection Brush is the simplest method to create a free hand selection in Adobe Photoshop Elements.

Selection Brush

To create a selection using the Selection Brush Tool, follow these steps:

1. From the Toolbar, choose the **Selection Brush tool**.

2. In the Options panel, you can change the shape and size of the brush.
3. From the fall-out Mode menu, choose **Selection or Mask**.
- The Selection mode is used to pick the pieces that must fall inside the contour of the selection.
- The Mask mode is used to select image fragments that must be removed from the selection contour.
4. Set the Hardness setting value.
5. If the Mask mode is enabled, you can change the Overlay Color and Overlay Opacity settings if the default values do not function.
6. If the Selection mode is enabled, paint over the areas of the picture that should fall inside the selection contour. If there is already a selection, a new selection will be added to it. When creating a new selection, keep the **Alt-key** held to deduct it from the previous one.
7. If the Mask mode is enabled, paint over the picture areas that should be omitted (these areas will be covered in semitransparent red). If there is already a selection, the painted pieces will be removed from it. You should maintain the Alt-key pressed when making the new pick to add it to the existing one.

In Adobe Photoshop Elements, you can also choose an image fragment using the following selection tools: Rectangular marquee, Elliptical marquee, Lasso, Polygonal Lasso, Magnetic Lasso, and Magic Wand. In the Toolbox, the Rectangular marquee and Elliptical marquee tools are concealed under the same icon. The Toolbox icon indicates the last tool that was chosen. Right-click on the arrow in the bottom right corner of the displayed icon to access the floating menu.

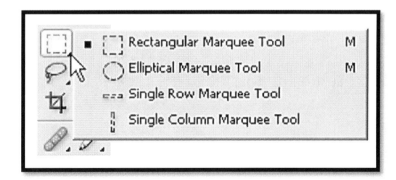

- **Rectangular Marquee**

This utility selects rectangular and square regions.

To choose a rectangle region, do the following:

1. Activate the Rectangular marquee tool by clicking on the icon or (if it was not the last tool used) selecting it from the floating window.
2. Place the mouse pointer in the picture where the corner of an imagined rectangle should be, and then hit the left mouse button.
3. While holding down the left button, move the pointer diagonally to the other corner and release the button.

Make a selection while holding down the **SHIFT key** to choose a square portion of the picture. Remember that if you already have a selected area, the new selection will be added to it. To prevent this, just hit the **SHIFT key** when you begin picking an area.

- **Elliptical Marquee**

This tool is for selecting ellipses and circles.

To choose an elliptical region, do the following:

1. Select the Elliptical marquee tool from the Toolbox by clicking on the icon, or pick it from the floating window if it was not the previous tool used.
2. Bring the mouse pointer to the corner of an imagined rectangle with an inscribed ellipse in the picture and push the left button.
3. While holding down the left button, move the pointer diagonally to the other corner and release the button.

When you hold down the Alt (Option) key when picking an elliptical or rectangular region, the selection is created from the center to the boundaries rather than from one corner to the other. The Lasso, Polygonal Lasso, and Magnetic Lasso tools are all concealed in the Toolbox under one icon. The Toolbox icon indicates the last tool that was chosen. Right-click on the arrow in the bottom right corner of the displayed icon to access the floating menu.

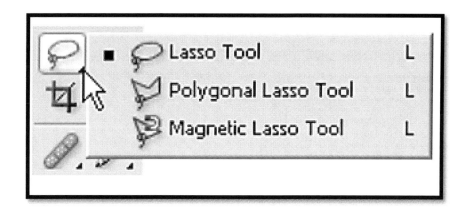

- **Lasso**

This tool is used to make freehand options.

To create a freehand selection, do the following:

1. Select the Lasso tool from the Toolbox by left-clicking on the icon, or from the floating window (assuming Lasso was not the previous tool used).
2. Bring the mouse cursor to the item to be picked and outline it while holding down the left mouse button.
- **Polygonal Lasso**

The contour of this tool is made up of straight segments and is used to produce freehand selections.

To make a choice, you should:

1. Click the **Polygonal Lasso tool**.
2. Place the cursor near the item to be delineated and hit the left mouse button - this will be the initial point of the contour.
3. Move the mouse to the next point of the contour, close to the first, and left-click it once more. The application will create a straight line between the two spots automatically.
4. Continue adding points in this manner until the whole object is delineated and the contour is closed.
- **Magnetic Lasso**

To create a freehand selection, use this tool.

When using Magnetic Lasso, you do not need to exactly follow the contour of the item. If the item shines out against the background, the chosen area's boundary will be automatically traced as you move the pointer along the object.

To choose an area using a magnetic lasso, do the following:

1. Select the **Magnetic Lasso tool** from the Toolbox.
2. Move the mouse cursor to the edge of the item to be chosen.
3. Start moving the pointer along the needed item by using the left button. Keep an eye out for fastening points that emerge as you outline the item and as you click. If a fastening point is no longer necessary, delete it using the **DELETE key** and return to the previous fastening point to continue outlining the item.
4. Close the contour, that is, connect the first and final fastening points, by moving the pointer to the first point or by double-clicking.

- **Magic Wand**

This tool is used to pick a color-coordinated area. Tolerance can be changed in the Options panel of the magic wand tool. The greater the value, the more colors will fall within the chosen region. The Tolerance value may be between 0 and 255. When Tolerance is set to 0, the specified region is represented by just one color; when Tolerance is set to 255, the whole picture is represented by all colors.

To choose a uniformly colored region, you should:

1. Click the icon to open the Toolbox and choose the magic wand tool.
2. Bring the pointer to the picture pixel that has to be included in the selection and left-click it. As a consequence, the pixel is surrounded by an outline. It comprises picture colors that are comparable to the color of the chosen pixel based on the Tolerance value. These selection tools are useful because of their versatility: you can add to, remove from, or intersect a selection.
3. To add an area to the previous selection, hold down the **SHIFT key** before using a selection tool and create a new selection while holding it down.
4. To remove a region from the previous selection, press the **Alt (Option in Mac) key** before using a selection tool and then create a new selection while holding it down.

5. When you press SHIFT and Alt at the same time (Shift and Option on a Mac), the previous and new selections intersect.

Quick Selection Tools

When you click and drag in a picture, the Quick Selection Tool in Photoshop Elements produces pixel selections based on neighboring pixel color and texture similarities. Depending on the boundaries of the picture and the difference in neighboring pixel color, this may make producing exact selections with this tool challenging. The Magic Wand Tool, Selection Brush Tool, Auto Selection, and Refine Selection Brush Tool all share a button in the Toolbox's "**Select**" button group. So, after selecting the button in the Toolbox is sure to choose the Quick Selection Tool from the Tool Options Bar. Set the Quick Selection Tool's selections in the Tool Selections Bar after selecting it in the Toolbox and, if necessary, the Tool Options Bar. Set the basic pixel selection options, such as brush size and selection mode, first. This tool has three modes: "**New selection**," "**Add to selection**," and "**Subtract from selection**."

Check the "**Sample All Layers**" option to sample the color from all layers beneath the tool's brush. Check the "**Auto-Enhance**" option to automatically improve pixel options made with the Quick Selection Tool. If you don't like the "**auto**" results, you can disable them by unchecking this option. Simply click or click and drag in the picture to make, add to, or remove from a selection after applying the chosen tool settings.

The Refine Selection Brush and Push Tool

In Photoshop Elements, the Refine Selection Brush Tool is a selection tool. It allows you to add or subtract pixels from an existing selection by automatically recognizing the image's edges. In Photoshop Elements, you can also use the Refine Selection Brush Tool to manually add or delete pixels from selections. In Photoshop Elements, you can now utilize the Refine Selection Brush Tool to smooth jagged edges inside existing pixel selections.

Using the Refine Selection Brush Tool

In Photoshop Elements, choose the Refine Selection Brush Tool from the Toolbox and, if required, the Tool Options bar to use it. Select the mode this tool uses to alter pixels in selections in the Tool Options Bar initially. You can manually add or subtract pixels from existing options by clicking the **"Add to selection" or "Subtract from selection"** buttons. These settings allow this tool to function similarly to the "**Selection Brush Tool**."

Alternatively, you can use the "**Push Selection**" button to move an existing selection line. The line is then forced to snap to the first adjacent picture edge it detects. The "Smooth selection" button, on the other hand, allows you to soften jagged edges inside existing selection lines. Set the pixel size of the tool using the "**Size**" slider after choosing the mode to use. Also, fill in the neighboring field with a pixel value. When using the "**Push Selection**" mode, set the picture edge snapping strength using the "**Snap Strength**" slider. When you drag this tool over a picture, the mouse pointer changes to two concentric circles. The inner circle represents the actual pixel selection brush size. The outer circle is the region around the brush that this tool searches for picture edges. The selection lines may then be snapped to the edges that it discovers.

How to Use the Add to or Subtract from Selection Mode

The setting you choose also influences how you use this tool. When in "**Add to selection**" mode either clicks and drags or clicks and hold the mouse button down. This adds the pixels under the inner circle to an existing selection or makes a new one. It quickly inserts pixels underneath the inner circle. Holding down the mouse button adds pixels to the selection inside the outside circle as well.

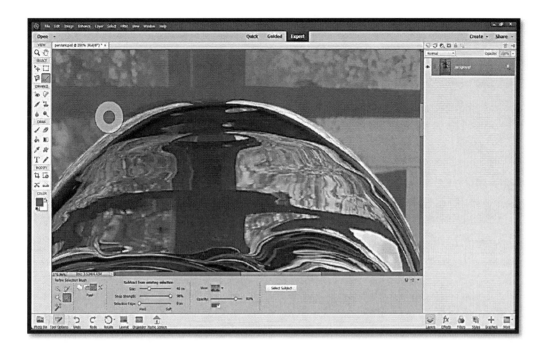

Similarly, if you're in "**Subtract from selection**" mode, click and drag or click and hold down the mouse button. This eliminates the pixels under the inner circle manually from an existing selection. It eliminates pixels directly under the inner circle. Clicking and holding the mouse button removes pixels from the outside circle selection as well. It does so depending on the edges of the picture.

How to Use the Push Selection Mode

If you choose the "**Push Selection**" option and want to extend an existing selection, position the cursor within it so that any selection line inside the outside circle snaps outward to expand that selection edge to the next picture edge discovered within the outer circle. Place the cursor outside the selection so that any selection line inside the outer circle snaps inward, contracting that selection edge to the next picture edge detected in the outside circle.

Smooth Selection Mode: How to Use It

If you are using "**Smooth selection**" mode, drag the cursor or click and hold the mouse pointer over the selection lines to which you want to apply smoothing in an existing selection.

Eye Tools: The Red Eye Removal Tool

Anyone who has ever taken a flash picture has seen red eyes—those burning, demonic eyes that make your tiny cherub appear like a character from an Anne Rice book. Red eye is a bigger issue with digital cameras than it is with film, but thankfully Elements includes a simple and effective solution for addressing it. All you have to do is use the Red Eye Removal tool to select the red spots and your issues will be cured.

This tool functions the same whether in Quick Fix or Full Edit mode. This is what you do:

1. Open an image.
2. Zoom in to see exactly where you're clicking. To enlarge the eyeballs, use the Zoom tool. You can also use the Hand tool to move the snapshot around so the eyes are in the middle.
3. Turn on the Red Eye Removal tool. In the toolbox, choose the red-eye symbol or hit Y.
4. Select the red portion of the pupil. The issue should be resolved with a single click. If it doesn't, undo it by using Ctrl+Z/-Z, and then try dragging the Red Eye Removal tool over the pupil. Sometimes one approach is superior to another. You can also change two options for this tool, as detailed later: Darken Amount and Pupil Size.
5. Click the red part of the opposite eye. Repeat on the other eye, and you're finished.

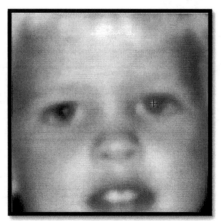

In Quick Fix and Full Edit, you can also use the Organizer's Auto Red Eye Fix. Simply hit **Ctrl+R/-R** in either window or go to **Enhance > Auto Red Eye Fix**. (In Full Edit, enable the Red Eye Removal tool, then click the Auto option in the Options bar.) The only disadvantage of using Auto Red Eye Fix in the Editor is that you don't receive a version set immediately, as you do when using the tool from the Organizer.

If you need to change how the Red Eye Removal tool works, the Options bar provides two settings, which you may disregard 99 percent of the time:

- Increase the amount of darkness. Increase the percentage in this box if the result is too light.
- The size of the pupil. Change this value to inform Elements how big an area to consider as part of the pupil.

Open Closed Eyes

Open closed eyes in your images with the Open Closed Eyes function. You can use the eyes from another picture on your computer or from the Elements Organizer catalog to open a person's eyes.

Here are the steps:

1. Launch Photoshop Elements and open a picture.
2. In Quick or Advanced Mode, do one of the following:
- Select the **Eye tool** and then, in the Tool Options box, select the **Open Closed Eyes button**.
- Go to **Enhance > Open Closed Eyes**.

In the Open Closed Eyes dialog, the person's face is highlighted with a circle highlighter to signify that the face was recognized in the image.

3. (Optional) The Try Sample Eyes list displays a few examples. You can choose a face that closely resembles the main image. Photoshop Elements replaces the closed eyes in the main shot with the chosen face.
4. **Perform one of the following:**
- Select a source picture from your computer by clicking Computer.
- Select a source picture from the Elements Organizer by clicking Organizer.
- Select a source picture from the presently open files by clicking the Photo Bin.

Note: If you like, you can use numerous source photographs. Photoshop Elements replaces the closed eyes in the main image with faces from these source photographs. Experiment with several eye replacements to obtain the best results.

5. Choose a face in the main picture whose eyes should be opened, and then click on any of the faces in the source photographs. To get the best results, experiment with various faces. If the skin tone in the source picture is different, Photoshop Elements matches the skin tone around the eyes to the main shot.
6. (Optional) Compare the results to the original picture by selecting the **Before/After button**
7. If you don't like the results, click Reset. You might experiment using a different source picture to see if you can achieve better results.
8. Select OK.
9. Save the picture after making the adjustments.

The Spot Healing Brush Tool

Photoshop Elements has various tools for removing minor faults from your photographs, such as spots or undesired objects.

Remove spots and small imperfections

The Spot Healing Brush effectively eliminates blemishes and other flaws from your images. To smooth out defects in an area, you can either click once on a blemish or drag.

The steps:

1. Choose the Spot Healing Brush tool.
2. Select a brush size. To cover the whole area with one click, use a brush that is somewhat bigger than the region you want to correct.
3. In the Tool selections box, choose one of the **Type options** listed below:

Proximity Match

The pixels surrounding the selection's boundary are used to locate an image area to use as a patch for the specified area. If this choice does not suffice, go to **Edit > Undo** and attempt the Create Texture option.

Create Texture

Makes a texture out of all the pixels in a selection to repair the region. If the texture isn't working, try dragging across the region again. To apply your adjustment to all layers of the picture, click Sample All Layers.

4. Click the picture area you want to change, or click and drag over a bigger region.

Remove unwanted objects with content-aware healing

Unwanted items or people may be removed from images without harming them. You can erase chosen items from a picture by using the Content-Aware option with the Spot Healing Brush tool. Photoshop Elements analyzes surrounding picture content to fill the selection smoothly while realistically preserving critical elements such as shadows and object boundaries.

Removing an unwanted object

1. Choose the Spot Healing Brush tool.
2. In the Tool Options bar, choose **Content-Aware**.
3. Remove the item from the photograph by painting over it.

Spot healing is most effective on tiny items. If the picture you're working on is enormous and contains a large undesired item, choose a high-end computer setup.

If you're having trouble viewing huge photos, consider the following solutions:

- Use a smaller brush stroke each time.
- Reduce the image size.
- Increase the amount of RAM allotted and restarts the program.

What is Anti-Aliasing?

Anti-aliasing is a digital image method used to smooth the jagged edges of visuals or text, particularly when scaling or distorting them. Anti-aliasing is used in Adobe Photoshop

Elements to enhance the look of selections and text by blending the edges with the background, resulting in a smoother and more visually attractive transition.

Anti-aliasing can be used in Adobe Photoshop Elements in the following ways:

1. On your computer, launch the Photoshop Elements program.
2. Either create a new document or open an existing one if anti-aliasing is desired.
3. Anti-aliasing is often used with selecting tools and text. Depending on what you're working on, choose the relevant tool:
- Marquee (rectangular or elliptical), Lasso, Magic Wand, and so forth.
- **Text Tool:** When dealing with text.
4. **Use Anti-Aliasing:**

For Selections:

- Use one of the selection tools to make your choice.
- Check the "**Anti-aliased**" option in the top settings bar. This is commonly indicated by a checkbox labeled "**Anti-alias**" or something like that.
- Once enabled, finish your selection or apply the transformation. The margins will seem smoother.

For Text:

- Choose the **Text tool**.
- Fill in the blanks with your text.
- Check the "**Anti-aliased**" option in the top settings bar. This is often found near the font and size settings.
- Finish your text input or make the modifications. Anti-aliasing will now be applied to the text edges.
5. **Adjust Anti-Aliasing Settings (Optional):** Extra anti-aliasing settings may be available. For example, you may be able to adjust the degree of anti-aliasing. Investigate the options accessible in the options bar and associated menus.
6. After you've applied anti-aliasing and made any necessary modifications, finish the operation you're working on, such as making the selection or completing the text.

Content-Aware Fill

Adobe Photoshop components' Content-Aware Fill function lets you eliminate undesired items or components from a picture while automatically filling in the background in a manner that fits in with the surrounding region. This function is very helpful for editing images and eliminating distracting elements.

Here's how to use the Content-Aware Fill in Adobe Photoshop Elements:

1. Open Adobe Photoshop Elements and choose the picture to be edited.
2. Select the object or area to be removed using your preferred selection tool (e.g., Lasso tool, Marquee tool).
3. Once you've decided, go to the "**Edit**" menu and pick **"Content Aware Fill" or "Fill Selection."**
4. The Content-Aware Fill dialog box will open, enabling you to fine-tune your settings. Options may include **"Color Adaptation," "Rotation Adaptation," and "Scale,"** among others. These options influence how the fill responds to its surroundings. To get the greatest results, play around with these settings.
5. To get a preview of the content-aware fill, click the "**Preview**" button. Check that the end outcome is acceptable.
6. If necessary, use the "**Adaptation**" sliders to fine-tune the fill. For example, you may modify the transparency of the fill by using the "**Opacity**" slider.
7. When you're happy with the preview, click the "OK" button to activate the Content-Aware Fill.
8. After applying the fill, zoom in and study the altered area carefully. Additional modifications may be required to produce a perfect mix.
9. Once you're happy with the outcome, save your changed picture.

The Healing Brush Tools

The Healing Brush tool in Adobe Photoshop Elements is a powerful tool for repairing defects in your photographs by sampling pixels from one region and perfectly blending them into another. In Photoshop Elements, there are two types of Healing Brush tools: Spot Healing Brush and Healing Brush. Here's how you can put them to use:

The steps:

1. Launch Photoshop Elements and open your image.
2. From the toolbar, select the **Spot Healing Brush tool**. It resembles a bandage.
3. Change the brush size with the bracket keys ([and]) or the Brush Size slider in the options bar.

4. In the options bar, you can select one of three healing modes:
   - **"Content-Aware":** Matches the texture, lighting, and shading of the sampled pixels automatically.
   - **"Create Texture":** Keeps the sampled area's texture.
   - **"Proximity Match":** The sampled pixels are matched, but the texture is not preserved.
5. Sample and Paint. Hold down the Alt key (Option key on Mac) and select an area of your image to use as a source for the correction.
6. Press and hold the Alt key while clicking or dragging over the area you want to repair.

Healing Brush Tool

The Healing Brush tool is similar to the Spot Healing Brush in functionality, but it gives you more control over the sampling process.

1. Select the Healing Brush tool from the toolbar (it resembles a bandage with a brush).
2. Determine the Source Point. Alt-click (Option-click on Mac) on an area you want to use as the healing source point.
3. Use the options bar to change the brush size and hardness.
4. Paint Over the Healed Area. Drag your mouse over the area you want to repair. The pixels from the source point that were sampled will be blended into the target region.

Tips:

- **Use a Soft Brush**: A soft-edged brush works best for most adjustments since it blends more smoothly.
- **Change Opacity**: In the settings box, you can change the opacity to alter the intensity of the repair.
- **Undo/Redo:** If you're unhappy with the outcome, use **Ctrl+Z (Command+Z** on Mac) to undo and try again.
- **Working on a Duplicate Layer**: Consider working on a duplicate layer so that you can simply compare the before and after and make non-destructive modifications.

The Smart Brush Tools

The Smart Brush Tool in Photoshop Elements is a flexible tool that enables you to carefully apply different modifications and effects to particular parts of your image. It's a non-destructive tool, which means it won't change your original picture forever. Instead, an adjustment layer is created to implement the modifications.

The steps:

1. Open Adobe Photoshop Elements and choose the picture to be edited.
2. Select the Smart Brush Tool from the toolbar on the left side of the screen. It resembles a paintbrush with a star symbol.
3. At the bottom of the screen, you'll see a menu from which you may choose the sort of change you wish to make. Adjust Exposure, Saturation, Hue, Sharpen, and so forth.
4. After choosing an adjustment type, you may be able to customize the effect with further settings. Make changes to these settings to suit your needs.
5. Drag the Smart Brush over the parts of the picture where you wish the correction to be applied. The chosen effect is applied to the areas you paint over with the brush.
6. Use the Selection Brush icon in the tool options bar to add or delete regions if you need to modify or change the selection.
7. After applying the adjustment, you can fine-tune it using the adjustment layer's attributes. In the Layers panel, find the adjustment layer and double-click it to see its properties.
8. Don't be afraid to try out various changes and settings. If you make a mistake, you may undo it by pressing Ctrl+Z or Command+Z.

The Clone Stamp Tool

Adobe Photoshop Elements' Clone Stamp Tool is a flexible tool that enables you to clone pixels from one part of a picture and paint them onto another. It may be used to remove undesired items, alter photos, and duplicate components.

Here's a quick overview of how to use the Clone Stamp Tool:

1. Begin by opening the photo you want to work on in Photoshop Elements.
2. Select the Clone Stamp Tool from the toolbar on the left side of the screen. It resembles a rubber stamp.

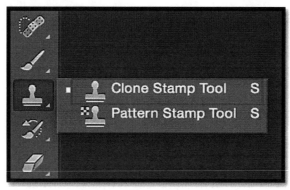

3. Before you begin cloning, you may decide to fine-tune the brush settings to your specific requirements. Using the options at the top of the screen, you can adjust the brush size, hardness, and opacity.
4. Set the sample point by holding down the Alt (Option) key and clicking on the region you wish to clone. This establishes a starting place for the Clone Stamp Tool to copy pixels from.
5. Start cloning by releasing the Alt key and moving the cursor to the region where you wish the cloned pixels to be painted. To begin cloning, click and drag. As you move the cursor, you'll get a preview of the region you're duplicating.
6. To continue copying, remove the mouse button and then click again. Hold down the Alt key and click on a new region to change the sampling point.
7. Options for blending modes and opacity can be found at the top of the screen. Experiment with these settings to get the desired outcome. Blending modes govern how copied pixels interact with existing pixels in the target region.
8. Use the zoom tool to zoom in for fine work and out for a larger picture.
9. If you make a mistake, hit **Ctrl + Z (Command + Z on Mac)** to undo your actions. You can also undo it by hitting **Shift + Ctrl + Z (on a Mac, Shift + Command + Z).**
10. Once you're pleased with the outcome, save your photo.

The Pattern Stamp Tool

The Pattern Stamp Tool in Adobe Photoshop Elements is a function that enables you to paint with a pattern rather than a plain color. It is a version of the Clone Stamp Tool, which duplicates pixels from one part of a picture and applies them to another area. The Pattern Stamp Tool, however, uses a pattern as the source rather than a particular portion of the picture.

The Pattern Stamp Tool can be used as follows:

1. Open the picture you wish to work on in Adobe Photoshop Elements.
2. Locate the Stamp Tool in the toolbar on the left side of the screen. To expose the hidden tools, click and hold the Clone Stamp Tool icon, then pick the Pattern Stamp Tool from the dropdown menu.
3. The Pattern Stamp Tool's options bar is located at the top of the screen. Click on the pattern swatch to bring up the Pattern Picker, where you can choose the pattern to use. Photoshop Elements has many preset patterns, but you may also create your own.
4. Before you begin painting, you should check the tool settings. You can change the brush size, opacity, and blending mode using the options bar. Experiment with these options to get the desired result.
5. Determine the Source Point. Hold down the Alt (Option) key while clicking on the region of the picture where you want to sample the pattern. This establishes the source point.
6. Let go of the Alt key and begin painting in the areas where you want the pattern to appear. The chosen pattern will be added to the picture as you paint, replacing the current pixels.
7. Create a new source point at any moment by releasing the mouse button and the Alt key. This enables you to keep adjusting the design as you paint.

8. Play around with various patterns, brush sizes, and opacities. If you make a mistake, you may undo it by pressing Ctrl+Z (or Command+Z on a Mac).

Blur, Smudge, and Sharpen

The Blur Tool

The Blur Tool is one of the retouching tools included with Adobe Photoshop Elements. Its major purpose is to blur parts of a picture, assisting in the creation of different creative effects or the correction of defects. This tool is particularly beneficial for photographers and digital artists who wish to highlight certain areas in a shot or create a more visually appealing arrangement.

Use the Blur Tool

1. Open the picture you want to work on in Adobe Photoshop Elements.
2. Locate the Blur Tool in the toolbar on the left side of the screen. It resembles a water droplet.

3. You can choose to change the brush settings before adding the blur. To access settings like size, hardness, and opacity, clicks on the brush symbol in the top options bar. These settings should be adjusted depending on the size and type of the region you wish to blur.
4. Select the Blur Strength. A "**Mode**" dropdown menu can be seen in the settings bar. Select the sort of blur you want to use. "**Normal**" for a basic blur and "**Gaussian**" for a more natural, gradient-like blur are the most prevalent selections. Using the "**Strength**" slider, you may change the blur's strength or intensity.

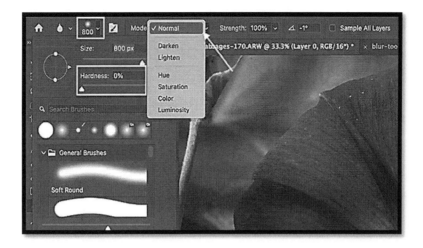

5. Select the Blur Tool and drag it over the area you wish to blur. Based on your brush settings and strength, the tool will soften the pixels in that location.
6. If the first blur is too strong or too faint, you may undo the operation (Ctrl+Z or Command+Z) and re-adjust the settings before applying it again. Experiment with various brush sizes and intensities until you get the look you want.
7. Zoom in on the picture to obtain a closer look for accurate work, particularly when working with minor details. This will allow you to apply the blur more precisely.
8. Once you're happy with the adjustments, save your picture to save the changes.

Blur Tool Tips

- **Use layers:**

Consider working on an image duplicate layer. In this manner, you can compare the changes and make modifications as required by adjusting the visibility of the original layer.

- **Play around with Blending Modes**

After you've applied the blur, experiment with adjusting the blending mode of the blurred layer to see if it improves the overall look.

- **Merge with Selections**

Before applying the blur, you can use selection tools to separate certain regions. This enables more precise and targeted blurring.

The Smudge Tool

Adobe Photoshop Elements' Smudge Tool is a powerful brush tool that lets you blur or smear colors in your picture, replicating the impression of running your finger over wet paint. It's especially great for making subtle color transitions, softening edges, and giving a painterly touch to your digital artwork or images. The Smudge Tool is represented by an icon that looks like a pointing hand with a droplet in the toolbar on the left side of the screen.

Using the Smudge Tool in Adobe Photoshop Elements:

1. Load the picture you want to work on into Adobe Photoshop Elements.
2. Look in the toolbar on the left side of the screen for the Smudge Tool. It's commonly found alongside the Blur and Sharpen tools. To use the Smudge Tool, click on its icon.

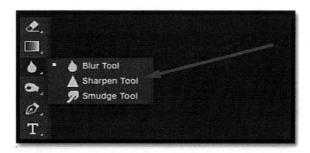

3. Before you begin smearing, you may fine-tune the Smudge Tool settings to create the appropriate effect. The following selections may usually be found in the selections Bar at the top of the screen:

- **Strength**: This determines the smudging effect's severity. A greater strength number indicates more smudging.
- **Brush**: Select the kind and size of the brush. Different brush shapes and sizes will provide different outcomes.
- **Smudging Mode**: The mode controls how the smudging interacts with the existing colors. The default option is typically Normal, however, you may experiment with various settings such as Darken, Lighten, and so on.

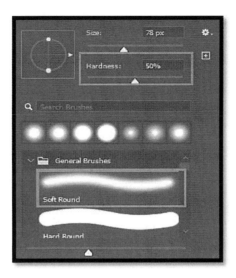

Smudge Your Image

- Place your mouse over the area you want to blur.
- To apply the smudge effect, click and hold the mouse button.
- Drag the cursor in the desired direction for the smudging to occur.

Experiment with Different Techniques

The Smudge Tool is flexible, and you can use it in a variety of ways:

- **Color Blending:** Use the Smudge Tool to mix neighboring colors to create a seamless transition.
- **Softening Edges:** Smudge around the edges of items to soften them and give them a more **natural appearance.**
- **Adding Texture**: To add texture to your picture, experiment with various brush shapes and sizes.
4. If you're unhappy with the outcome, you can undo (Ctrl+Z or Command+Z) and redo (Ctrl+Y or Command+Y) your changes.
5. When you're finished smudging, save your picture to save your adjustments.

The Sharpen Tool

The Sharpen Tool in Adobe Photoshop Elements is a useful tool for improving the clarity and sharpness of certain areas of a picture. It is classified as a retouching tool and is especially good for fine-tuning details in images.

Here's how to use the Sharpen Tool in Adobe Photoshop Elements:

Sharpening the Tool

1. Open Adobe Photoshop Elements 2024.
2. Select the picture you want to work on by selecting **"File" > "Open."**
3. In the toolbar, look for the Sharpen Tool. It resembles a triangle pointing to the right and is located among the Blur and Smudge tools.

4. If you don't see it, click and hold on the Blur or Smudge tool icon to see the other tools, which include Sharpen.
5. **Change the Brush Settings:**
- Adjust the brush settings to your liking before using the Sharpen Tool.
- Use the slider in the Options bar at the top of the screen to adjust the brush size. Choose a size that corresponds to the region you wish to sharpen.
- You can also change the brush's hardness. A softer brush has a more progressive impact, but a rougher brush has a more defined and intense sharpening effect.
6. **Determine the Strength:**
- A "**Strength**" slider can be found in the Options bar. This adjusts the sharpening effect's intensity.
- Begin with a lesser strength and progressively raise it until the desired degree of sharpness is achieved. Over-sharpening might result in unnatural-looking outcomes, so be careful.
7. For more accuracy, zoom in on the region you want to sharpen. This helps you to see the details more clearly and guarantees that the sharpening effect is applied precisely where it is required.

8. **Use the Sharpen Effect as follows:**
   - Drag the Sharpen Tool over the areas you want to improve. The tool works by raising the contrast between neighboring pixels, resulting in sharper edges.
   - Move the brush in the direction of the details you want to draw attention to. If you're sharpening someone's eyes, for example, follow the outlines of the eyes for a more natural effect.
9. If you are unhappy with the outcome, you can reverse the previous action by hitting **"Ctrl + Z" (Windows) or "Command + Z" (Mac).** Experiment with various brush sizes, strengths, and methods to get the desired effect.
10. When you're finished sharpening, save your picture by selecting **"File" > "Save" or "File" > "Save As"** to make a new version of the file.

Tips:

- Apply the Sharpen Tool selectively to certain regions of the picture rather than evenly to the whole image.
- Use the strength setting sparingly to prevent a harsh and unnatural look.
- Always work on a duplicate layer or retain a backup of your original picture to ensure the file's integrity.

The Sponge, Dodge, and Burn Tools

The Sponge Tool

The Sponge Tool in Adobe Photoshop Elements enables you to saturate or desaturate certain parts of a picture softly. It's an excellent tool for boosting or reducing the color intensity of certain regions, giving you greater control over the color balance in your images.

To use the Sponge Tool, follow these steps:

1. To begin, launch Photoshop Elements.
2. Select the picture you want to work on by navigating to **"File" > "Open"** and choosing it.
3. Locate the Sponge Tool in the toolbar on the left side of the screen. It has the appearance of a sponge. If you can't locate it, click and hold on to the Dodge Tool or Burn Tool to see a fly-out menu with the Sponge Tool.
4. **Tool Configuration**

The Options Bar is located at the top of the screen. You may change the brush size, mode, and strength here.

- **Brush Size:** Change the size of the brush to fit the area you're working on.
- **Mode**: Choose **"Saturate"** or **"Desaturate"** mode. "**Saturate**" boosts color intensity while "**Desaturate**" reduces it.
- **Strength**: This regulates how strong the impact is. A greater strength value will have a more noticeable impact.

Using the Sponge Tool

1. Select "**Saturate**" or "**Desaturate**" depending on whether you want to raise or reduce the color intensity.
2. Adjust the power based on how strong you want the color shift to be. Lower levels have a softer impact.
3. Change the brush size to suit the area you're working on. A wider brush is better for covering greater areas, while a smaller brush is better for tiny details.
4. Drag the Sponge Tool over the area you want to change. Based on the mode and intensity you choose, the tool will either add or remove color as you drag.
5. If you make a mistake, use Ctrl + Z (Windows) or Cmd + Z (Mac) to undo your previous action. Press Ctrl + Shift + Z (Windows) or Cmd + Shift + Z (Mac) to redo an activity.
6. Once you're happy with the adjustments, save your picture by selecting **"File"** > **"Save"** or **"File"** > **"Save As"** to preserve the original image.

Tips

Apply a Light Touch

The Sponge Tool is most effective when used lightly. Build up the impact gradually to get the desired outcome.

Experiment with Strength

As required, adjust the strength setting. Higher strength numbers cause more obvious alterations, whilst lower strength values provide a more subtle impact.

Zoom in for more detail

When working with little or detailed sections, zoom in on your picture to work on finer details.

The Dodge Tool

Adobe Photoshop Elements' Dodge Tool is a strong tool for selectively lightening or brightening certain sections of a picture. It is one of three tone correction tools, along with the Burn and Sponge tools. The Dodge Tool is modeled after the old darkroom method of dodging, in which photographers deliberately expose areas of an image to light during the printing process.

Understanding the Dodge Tool

Location

- The Dodge Tool is often accessible in the Tools panel, alongside the Burn Tool and Sponge Tool. Its icon is a little magnifying glass with a hand on it.

Function

- The Dodge Tool's principal purpose is to lighten or brighten certain sections of a picture. It operates by raising the pixel exposure in the targeted region.

Tonal Range

- The Dodge Tool can be used for highlights, midtones, or shadows, giving you flexibility over which tonal ranges are impacted. The tonal range can be selected from the options bar at the top of the screen.

Exposure Settings

- The Exposure setting controls how much the tool influences the picture. A higher exposure setting has a greater impact, whilst a lower setting has a more subtle effect. In the settings bar, you can change the Exposure setting.

How to Use the Dodge Tool

1. Open Photoshop Elements and choose the picture to be edited.
2. In the Tools panel, click or press 'O' to choose the Dodge Tool icon.

3. In the settings bar, adjust the brush size to fit the area you're working on. Adjust the Range (highlights, midtones, or shadows) and Exposure settings to get the desired look.
4. Gently brush the area you want to brighten. A soft-edged brush may be used for smoother transitions and a hard-edged brush for more defined modifications.
5. Zoom out and evaluate the adjustments you're making regularly. To fine-tune the effect, you can undo (Ctrl + Z) or change the tool settings.
6. Save your adjusted picture after you're pleased with the modifications.

Tips

Experiment on a Duplicate Layer

Always work on a duplicate layer before making modifications to the main picture. This enables you to compare the changed and original versions and offers a non-destructive editing method.

Merge with Selections

Confine the impact on certain areas by using selection tools (e.g., Marquee, Lasso) in conjunction with the Dodge Tool.

Experiment with Blend Modes

Changing the mix mode of the Dodge Tool layer sometimes provides unexpected effects. For tonal modifications, the blend modes Overlay and Soft Light are often used.

The Burn Tool

The Burn Tool is generally used to carefully add darkness or shadows to a shot. It's part of the Dodge/Burn/Sponge tool set, which also includes the Dodge Tool for lighting and the Sponge Tool for adjusting color saturation.

Use the Burn Tool

1. Open Adobe Photoshop Elements and choose the picture to be adjusted.
2. In the toolbar on the left side of the screen, choose the Burn Tool. It resembles a hand with a pointing index finger.
3. **Adjust Tool Settings:**

The Options Bar is located at the top of the screen. You can change the settings for the Burn Tool here:

- **Range**: Use this setting to specify whether you want to affect shadows, midtones, or highlights.
- **Exposure**: This determines the strength of the darkening effect. A lesser exposure has a more subtle impact, but a larger exposure has a more obvious effect.
4. Change the brush size to suit the area you wish to darken. You may accomplish this by using the bracket keys ([and]) on your keyboard or by clicking on the brush size drop-down in the Options Bar.
5. Drag your mouse over the areas you wish to darken. As you drag, you'll see that the picture darkens. Use caution and a little touch, since you may always go over an area many times for a more dramatic impact.
6. If the effect is too powerful, you can reverse it (Ctrl + Z on Windows, Command + Z on Mac) and lower the Exposure in the Options Bar. Increase the Exposure if it isn't powerful enough.
7. Experiment with various tonal ranges of burning. Burn shadows to enhance depth, or highlights to highlight certain areas.
8. For more exact editing, use the Zoom Tool (magnifying glass icon) to zoom into the picture and change the brush size appropriately.
9. Save your adjusted picture after you're pleased with the modifications. Use **"File"** > **"Save As"** to save the original while creating a new version with your changes.

Tips

- **Feathered Edges:** For a more natural transition between burnt and non-burned regions, use a soft-edged brush.
- **Multiple Passes**: Applying the effect gradually with numerous passes is generally preferable to attempting to get the desired outcome in a single stroke.
- **Experiment**: Don't be scared to try various exposure settings and brush sizes to determine what works best for your particular photo.

The Brush Tools

The Impressionist Brush

The Impressionist Brush is a tool in Adobe Photoshop Elements that belongs to the creative brush group. It is intended to mimic the appearance and feel of classic art methods, notably the painting style of the Impressionist movement. The Impressionist style is distinguished by loose, emotive brushstrokes that capture the spirit of a subject rather than exact details.

How to Use Adobe Photoshop Elements' Impressionist Brush

1. Open the picture you want to work on in Adobe Photoshop Elements.
2. Locate the Brush tool in the toolbar on the left side of the screen. Click and hold the Brush tool to bring up a dropdown menu with several brush selections.
3. From the menu, choose the Impressionist Brush. It can be used in conjunction with other creative or textured brushes.
4. Before you begin painting, you should modify the brush settings. Brush size, opacity, and flow are among the options available. These options can be found in the tool options bar at the top of the screen.
5. To create the desired effect, experiment with various brush sizes and opacities. A bigger brush size generates wider strokes, whilst a lower opacity might give a more delicate application.
6. Change the foreground and background colors to your liking. Select the color swatches at the bottom of the toolbar to do so. The Impressionist Brush will add color depending on the current color of the foreground.
7. Begin painting your picture with the Impressionist Brush chosen and your settings changed. To obtain the desired artistic impression, experiment with various strokes and brush sizes.
8. The brush strokes will give the artwork a rich and emotive appearance reminiscent of Impressionist paintings.
9. Use the Undo (Ctrl+Z or Command+Z) and Redo (Ctrl+Y or Command+Y) commands if you make a mistake or want to compare various brushstrokes.

Once you're happy with the outcome, save your photo. You can save it in a variety of formats, including JPEG and PNG.

The Color Replacement Brush

The Color Replacement Brush in Adobe Photoshop Elements is a tool for replacing one color in a picture with another. It is very handy for activities such as adjusting the color of an item or correcting color inconsistencies.

In Adobe Photoshop Elements, use the Color Replacement Brush as follows:

1. Open the picture you want to work on in Adobe Photoshop Elements.

2. In the left-hand toolbar, select the "**Color Replacement Brush**," which looks like a brush with a little color swatch.
3. Before you begin painting, you should modify the brush settings. The Options Bar, located at the top of the screen, allows you to change the brush size, hardness, and other settings. Set the brush size to fit the area you're working on.
4. A color swatch is available in the Options Bar. Click it to launch the Color Picker, and then choose the color to replace the current one.
5. **Sampling Method:**

Select a sample technique. Continuous, Once, and Background Swatch are the three possibilities.

- **Continuous**: As you paint, sample the color continuously.
- **Once**: Only sample the color when you begin painting.
- **Background Swatch**: Replace the background color with the color of your choice.

6. Set boundaries. The "**Limits**" option in the Options Bar specifies the color range that will be substituted. There are three options: **"Discontiguous," "Contiguous," and "Find Edges."** Select the one that best meets your requirements.
7. Drag the Color Replacement Brush over the area you want to change the color of. The utility will replace the original color with the color you choose.
8. If you discover that the tool is influencing more colors than you intended, change the "**Tolerance**" option in the Options Bar. A smaller tolerance restricts the range of impacted colors, while a larger tolerance includes a wider range.
9. You may need to make extra tweaks after the first pass. To fine-tune the results, you may switch between the Color Replacement Brush and other tools such as the normal Brush and the Eraser.
10. Once you're happy with the edits, save your picture to save the changes.

Brush settings and options

Eraser Tools

The Eraser

The Eraser tool in Adobe Photoshop Elements is a key tool that enables you to selectively delete areas of an image or layer. It functions effectively as a digital eraser, allowing you to eliminate pixels and expose the layers underlying.

The steps:

1. Launch Photoshop Elements.
2. Select the picture or layer to be edited.
3. Select the Eraser tool from the toolbar. It resembles a pink eraser symbol and is located with other brush tools.
4. To pick the Eraser tool, click on it or hit the 'E' key.
5. Before you begin erasing, you may want to change the tool settings. The Options Bar is located at the top of the screen. You may adjust the brush size, hardness, and opacity here. You can change the size and softness of the eraser by using these settings.
6. Select the Eraser tool and drag it over the area you want to delete. The pixels just under the brush cursor will be deleted, showing the layers beneath.
7. The Eraser tool, like the Brush tool, has several modes. The modes can be found in the Options Bar

Mode Options

- **Brush Mode:** This mode erases pixels depending on the brush form specified.
- **Pencil Mode:** Regardless of brush form, erases with a harsh edge.
- **Block Mode:** Erases in a square form using Block Mode.

Play around with these modes to see what effects you can get.

8. The transparency of the eraser is controlled by the opacity. With a lesser opacity, the erasing action is slower.
9. In the Options Bar, change the opacity to adjust how much of the underlying picture is seen.
10. If you make a mistake, use the **'Undo'** command (Ctrl + Z on Windows, Command + Z on Mac) to undo your previous action. You can also undo activities (Ctrl + Shift + Z or Command + Shift + Z) if necessary.
11. Once you're happy with the adjustments, save the picture in the right format.

Tips:

- For smoother transitions between erased and unerased regions, use a soft-edged brush.
- To obtain the desired effect, experiment with various brush sizes, opacities, and modes.

- For non-destructive editing, consider working on a duplicate layer or utilizing layer masks.

The Background Eraser Tool

The Background Eraser Tool in Adobe Photoshop Elements is a useful tool for quickly removing the background from a picture. This technique is very handy when you wish to isolate a topic in the front from its background. The Background Eraser Tool may help you obtain clean and exact options while working on graphic design, picture editing, or collages.

The steps:

1. Load the picture you want to work on into Adobe Photoshop Elements.
2. Use the Background Eraser Tool. The Background Eraser Tool can be found in the toolbar on the left side of the screen. It seems to be an eraser with a miniature pair of scissors attached. If you can't locate it, it's probably grouped with the standard Eraser Tool, so click and hold on the eraser icon to see the other eraser options, then choose the Background Eraser Tool.
3. Adjust Tool Settings

Before you begin wiping the background, you must first configure the tool. The Background Eraser Tool's options bar is located at the top of the screen.

Here are some important settings:

- **Color Sampling**: This controls how the tool samples colors. Select "**Continuous**" for a continuous color transition or "**Once**" for a one-time sample.
- **Limits**: Select "**Contiguous**" to delete just pixels with identical colors next to each other, or "**Discontiguous**" to erase similar pixels anywhere in the picture.
- **Tolerance**: This setting governs the tool's sensitivity to color fluctuations. With a larger tolerance, you can remove a wider variety of colors.
- **Brush Size:** Change the size of the brush to suit the specifics of your picture. For wider regions, use a larger brush, and for finer details, use a smaller brush.
4. Place the pointer on the background to be removed and click. Within the tolerance range, the tool will sample the color at the cursor and remove comparable hues. Drag the pointer over the background to watch it deleted as you go.

5. You may need to fine-tune your options as you work. Adjust the Tolerance setting if the tool is removing too much or too little. You can also change the brush size or switch different Sampling modes for more accuracy.
6. Zoom in on your picture for more thorough work. This helps you to observe and alter tiny regions more precisely.
7. After you've removed the background, you should polish the borders for a more professional appearance. You can accomplish this by selecting Refine Edge from the options menu. This lets you smooth off the edges, feather the selection, and alter the contrast.
8. When you're happy with the background removal, you can either keep it translucent or replace it with a new one. Save your picture in a transparency-supporting format, such as PNG.

Advanced brush tool settings

Tablet Settings

1. To begin, launch Adobe Photoshop Elements.
2. Check that your graphic tablet or pen is correctly connected to your computer.
3. Click the "**Edit**" button at the top of the screen.
4. From the drop-down menu, choose "**Preferences**".
5. In the Preferences menu, look for a "**Tablet**" or "**Stylus**" option. To access tablet settings, click on it.

Tablet Configuration Options

Tablet Input

Turn on or off tablet input. To use the tablet with Photoshop Elements, make sure the option is switched on.

Pressure Sensitivity

Change the tablet pen's sensitivity to adjust how much pressure impacts brush size, opacity, and other factors. Higher sensitivity gives for more control.

Tilt Sensitivity

If your tablet supports tilt, you can vary the angle at which the pen is held about the tablet surface by adjusting the sensitivity. This may have an impact on brush behavior.

Customizable Buttons

Many graphic tablets have customizable buttons. You can designate certain functionality (such as undo, redo, or brush size) to these buttons in Photoshop Elements for easier access.

Eraser Settings

You can change the behavior of your stylus if it has an eraser end. You may, for example, configure it to function as a typical eraser or switch to a different tool.

Using Tablet Settings

Brush Control

Tablet settings make sketching and painting seem more natural. Pressure sensitivity can be used to alter brush size and opacity, resulting in a more dynamic and expressive painting experience.

Precision Editing

Tablets provide more exact control than mice, making thorough retouching and tiny tweaks simpler.

Tilt for Realism

If your tablet has tilt sensitivity, you can use it to simulate the angle of conventional drawing tools, giving your digital work a more realistic feel.

Workflow Customization

Tailor the tablet buttons to your workflow to speed up the editing process. This may save you time and improve the efficiency of your experience.

The Magic Eraser Tool

The Magic Eraser Tool in Adobe Photoshop Elements is a strong tool for removing similar colored regions in a picture fast and effortlessly. It works by choosing a base color and removing any pixels in the picture that are close to that color. This tool is very good for eliminating backgrounds that have a continuous and distinct color.

The steps:

1. Open the picture you want to work on in Adobe Photoshop Elements.
2. Select the Magic Eraser Tool from the toolbar on the left. It resembles a wand with a star emblem.
3. You must first set the Tolerance level before using the Magic Eraser Tool. Tolerance defines how similar a pixel's color must be to the specified color for it to be erased. A smaller tolerance erases just colors that are quite similar, while a larger tolerance erases a wider spectrum of hues. The Tolerance option is located at the top of the screen. Set it to the suitable value for your picture. To get the proper balance, you may need to experiment.
4. **Select Anti-aliasing and Contiguous Options:**
- Anti-aliasing smoothes the erased area's edges, resulting in a more natural transition. This option should be kept ticked in general.
- Contiguous restricts erasing to regions that are related to the clicked point. If this option is not chosen, the tool will remove any pixels in the picture that match the specified color, regardless of their closeness.
5. Move the mouse over the background area you wish to erase and click once. The Magic Eraser Tool will assess the color and begin deleting pixels within the tolerance range that closely matches the specified color.
6. You might fine-tune the selection depending on your picture and the Tolerance level. Adjust the Tolerance and click again if the tool is deleting too much or too little.
7. Continue clicking on background regions until you have eliminated the whole undesirable piece. If you're eliminating a complicated background, you may need to click many times to cover all color variants.
8. When you're happy with the outcome, save your picture. This may be accomplished by going to "**File**" and choosing **"Save" or "Save As."**

The Paint Bucket (Fill) Tool

The Paint Bucket Tool, also known as the Fill Tool in Adobe Photoshop Elements, is a useful function that enables you to fill a specified area or layer with a color or pattern. This tool is very helpful for quickly applying color to a small area of your picture.

Here are the steps:

1. Open the picture you want to work on in Adobe Photoshop Elements.

2. Locate and pick the Paint Bucket Tool from the toolbar on the left side of the screen. It is symbolized with an icon that resembles a bucket of paint being poured.

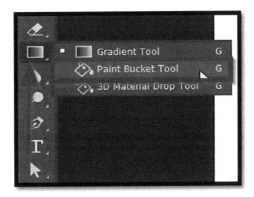

3. Select Your Fill Options. You must first configure the fill selections before using the Paint Bucket Tool:

- **Foreground Color**: The color you want to use for the foreground. By clicking on the foreground color swatch at the bottom of the toolbar and picking a color from the Color Picker, you may change the color of the foreground.
- **Pattern**: If you want to fill the selection with a pattern rather than a solid color, use the Pattern Picker.
- **Tolerance**: This setting affects the range of colors that the Fill Tool will influence. A larger tolerance setting will allow for a wider spectrum of colors.

4. The Contiguous option in the options bars controls whether the tool fills just neighboring pixels with comparable colors. Only neighboring pixels with identical colors will be impacted if Contiguous is selected. If this option is left unchecked, all pixels within the tolerance range, regardless of position, will be filled.

5. Place the Paint Bucket pointer over the area to be filled and click. Based on your preferences, the tool will fill the specified area with the desired color or pattern.

6. If necessary, you can fine-tune the fill by modifying the tolerance, altering the hue, or changing the pattern. Simply continue the procedure until the desired outcome is obtained.

Tips:

- **Undo**: To undo a previous operation, use the Undo command (Ctrl+Z on Windows, Command+Z on Mac).
- **Layer Selection**: Before using the Paint Bucket Tool, be sure that the relevant layer or region is chosen. For this, you can use selecting tools such as the Marquee or Lasso Tool.

The Gradient Tool

The Gradient Tool in Adobe Photoshop Elements is a strong function that enables you to create seamless transitions between colors or tones in your photographs. Gradients are progressive color mixes that may be applied to backgrounds, text, or any specified section of an image.

Here are the steps:

1. To begin, launch Adobe Photoshop Elements.
2. Select an existing picture or create a new document in which to apply the gradient.
3. Locate the Gradient Tool on the left side of the screen in the toolbar. It frequently coexists with the Paint Bucket Tool.
4. The Options Bar is located at the top of the screen. You can change the gradient settings here before applying it. To access the Gradient Editor, click on the gradient preview.
5. In the Gradient Editor, you can select a pre-made gradient or make your own by adjusting the color stops. Color stops are markers that specify the gradient's colors. To get the desired color effect, you can add, remove, or relocate these stops
6. In the Options Bar, you can choose between gradient kinds. Linear, radial, and angle are the most prevalent. Each kind generates its gradient style.
7. Change the gradient mode to influence how the new gradient merges with the current material. Normal, Dissolve, Behind, Clear, and more options are available. You can also modify the gradient's transparency by adjusting its opacity.
8. To design the gradient, click and drag on your canvas. The gradient's direction and extent are determined by the direction and length of your drag.
9. If you're not happy with the original outcome, you may still make changes. After sketching the gradient, use the Move Tool or the Gradient Tool to further adjust it.

10. Experiment with different blending settings in the Layers panel to generate different blending effects between the gradient and the underlying layers.
11. Once you're satisfied with the gradient effect, save your work to save the changes.

The Shape Tools

The Rectangle Tool, Ellipse Tool, and sss Tool

The Rectangle Tool, Ellipse Tool, and Rounded Rectangle Tool are fundamental form tools in Adobe Photoshop Elements that enable you to construct geometric shapes in your projects. These tools are useful for a wide range of design tasks, such as creating backgrounds, buttons, and graphical elements. Let's look at each tool and how to use it:

Rectangle Tool

Functions:

- Depending on how you use it, the Rectangle Tool produces rectangular or square shapes.
- You can draw both filled and unfilled rectangles.

How to Use It

- From the toolbar on the left side of the screen, select the Rectangle Tool. It appears to be a rectangle or a square.
- Create a rectangle on your canvas by clicking and dragging.
- Hold down the Shift key while dragging to limit the dimensions and make a perfect square.
- Click and hold the mouse button to complete the shape.

Ellipse Tool

Functions:
- Use the Ellipse Tool to make circular or elliptical shapes.
- Enables you to draw both full and empty ellipses, like the Rectangle Tool.

How to use it

- From the toolbar, choose the **Ellipse Tool**. It resembles a circle or an ellipse.
- Create an ellipse on your canvas by clicking and dragging.

- While dragging, hold down the Shift key to limit the dimensions and make a perfect circle.
- Click and hold the mouse button to complete the shape.

Rounded Rectangles Tool

Functions:

- The Rounded Rectangle Tool is a Rectangle Tool variant that produces rectangles with rounded edges.
- It enables you to modify the amount of rounding by adjusting the radius of the corners.

How to Use It

- From the toolbar, choose the **Rounded Rectangle Tool.** It has the appearance of a rectangle with rounded sides.
- Create a rounded rectangle on your canvas by clicking and dragging.
- You can limit the dimensions by holding down the Shift key while dragging.
- After releasing the mouse button, you can change the roundness of the corners by entering a radius number in the top-right options bar.

Tips

Fill and Stroke Variations

Using the settings in the toolbar at the top, you can change the fill and stroke (outline) colors of the shapes.

Editing Shapes

After you've created a form, you can use the Move Tool (V) and the selections in the options bar to change its size, location, and other features.

The Polygon Tool

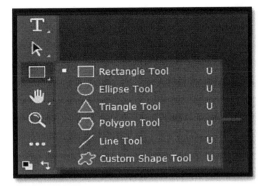

Adobe Photoshop Elements contains a Polygon Tool for making polygons with numerous sides. This tool is excellent for drawing triangles, rectangles, pentagons, hexagons, and other forms.

How to Use the Polygon Tool

1. To begin, launch Adobe Photoshop Elements.
2. Begin by creating a new document or opening an existing picture to which you want to add a polygon.
3. Choose the Polygon Tool. The "**Shape Tool**" icon can be found on the left toolbar. Hold your mouse over this symbol to show a menu of shape tools. Choose the "**Polygon Tool**" option from the menu.
4. **Options Bar Settings:**

After selecting the Polygon Tool, the Options Bar at the top of the screen will provide several tool options. Here are some examples of frequent configurations:

- **Sides**: Define the number of polygon sides.
- **Radius**: The distance between the center and a vertex. If you leave this field empty, the polygon will be generated by clicking and dragging to determine its size.

5. Click on the canvas where you want the polygon's center to go, and then drag to determine the size without releasing the mouse button. When you're happy with the form, let go of the mouse button.
6. Change the polygon after you've created it. To pick and move the complete form, use the Direct Selection Tool or the Move Tool. Use the Pen Tool to make changes to specific points.

7. The fill and stroke selections for the polygon may be set in the selections Bar. By choosing the relevant options, you can choose a fill color, a stroke color, or a stroke.
8. A polygon is typically formed on a new shape layer when it is drawn. This enables you to modify and change the form apart from the other parts in your picture.
9. Once the polygon has been formed, you can edit its size, location, color, and other features using different adjustment and transformation tools.
10. Enhance the look of the polygon by using layer styles such as drop shadows, gradients, or patterns.
11. Save your work regularly to prevent losing any changes.

Tips

Hold the Shift Key

Hold down the **Shift key** while dragging the mouse to build a regular polygon (with equal sides).

Adjust After Creation

You can always return to the polygon and change it by choosing the Shape Layer in the Layers Panel and using the Direct Selection or Move Tool.

Combine Shapes

Combine the form tools to create more complicated shapes. For example, you can build a star by connecting a polygon with a line.

The Line Tool

The Line Tool enables you to create a two-point line on the canvas. Lines may be drawn as vector forms, pathways, or pixels. Choose Shape mode if you want to draw a non-destructive, scalable line that you may tweak at a later date. Choose Pixels mode when dealing with rasterized material such as pixel graphics.

Draw a line

Follow these short steps to create a line:

1. **Select the Line tool**

From the toolbar, click and hold the Shape tool group icon to bring up the different shape tool possibilities. Select the Line tool.

Set the width of your line

Shape mode

Set the width of a form line using the Weight settings in the options bar. For optimal results, ensure the Align setting in the Stroke selections is set to Center or outside. If Inside alignment is selected, the stroke weight will be hidden. In the settings bar, you can change the color and thickness of the stroke. You may also specify the width of your line without including a stroke.

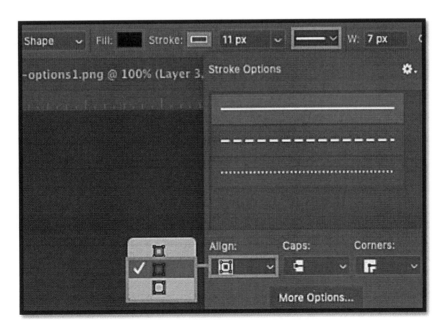

Path or Pixels Mode:

Set the Weight in the settings bar to determine the width of your pixel line.

Note: The Line tool does not support Pixels mode or Weight in Photoshop versions 22.0-22.2.

2. Proceed to click and drag.

To draw a line, click on the canvas, drag, and release. Hold down shift while dragging and drawing the line to limit the line angle to a multiple of 45 degrees.

Shape mode options

Line Mode

- Select **Shape** to make a vector line.

Fill Color

- Choose a color from the list or click the color picker to do so. Alternatively, you may choose a color by clicking the color swatch in the Appearance section of the Properties window. This will be utilized to fill the arrowhead's center.

Stroke Color

- Choose a color from the list or click the color picker to do so. Alternatively, you can choose a color by clicking the color swatch in the Appearance section of the Properties window. This will color the line as well as the arrowheads outside.

Stroke Width

- Enter the width of the stroke in pixels.

Weight

- Fill in the line **Weight** in pixels.

Additional Options

- **Preset**: Select a solid line, dashed line, or dotted line from the drop-down menu, or select **More Options** to build a custom line preset.
- **Align**: Choose **Center or Outside**. If Inside alignment is chosen, the stroke weight will not be shown.
- **Caps**: There are three line cap forms to pick from: Butt, Round, and Square. The forms of the beginning and end of the line are determined by the line cap shapes.
- **Dashed Line**: Change the appearance of your dashed line by putting numbers in the repeating pattern for the number of dashes and spaces.

Pixel mode options

Line Mode

- Select Pixels to build a pixel-based line.

Mode

- Choose the desired mix mode. **Normal** is the default setting.

Opacity

- Change the Opacity value from 1 to 100%.

Weight

- Enter the line width in pixels.

Additional options

To activate canvas morph controls, click the **gear symbol** on the Line tool options bar and choose **Live Shapes Controls**. This enables you to rotate and resize canvas lines. The arrowheads will be scaled as well.

The Properties section also allows you to change the Transform and Appearance settings. This can be activated from the main menu by selecting **Window > Properties**.

Draw an arrow

Simply add arrowheads to a line to make an arrow. Click the **gear icon** on the Line tool settings bar after drawing a line and adjusting the stroke color and width. Check **Start** to add an arrow at the beginning of your line; check End to add an arrow at the end of your line. Check both **Start** and **End** to add arrows to both ends.

- Define the arrowhead's width and length in pixels. Arrowheads in version 22.0 and beyond are specified in absolute pixels rather than percent weight.
- Adjust the **Concavity**, which is the degree of curvature on the broadest section of the arrowhead where it meets the line. Enter a value for Concavity between -50% and +50%.

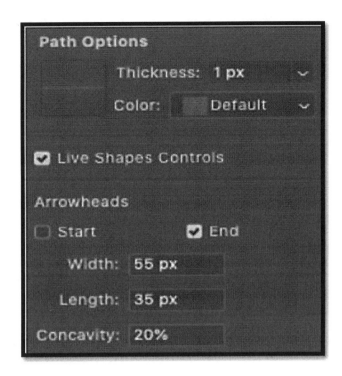

Making a Curved Line in Photoshop Elements

1. **In your Photoshop Space, create a new layer**

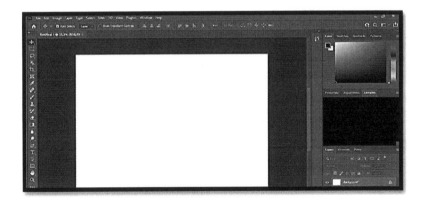

If you want to create a new layer in Photoshop, you can do it by clicking on the **Create a New Layer button** in the left corner. This feature is available in any version of Adobe Photoshop and will undoubtedly be helpful in the long term. In most situations, the icon is a folded corner on a piece of paper. Do not forget that the majority of your work in Adobe Photoshop will begin with either importing the picture or establishing a new layer and then working on that layer. When you click the "**Create a New Layer**" button, a new layer will appear above the Background Layer, which you can work on and construct to progress. Making a new layer above the background layer ensures that the work you perform on the top layer will not alter your original picture, allowing you to work with peace of mind. By default, the name of this layer will be Layer 1. On it, we must draw the Curved Line.

2. **Make a round selection using the Elliptical Marquee tool**

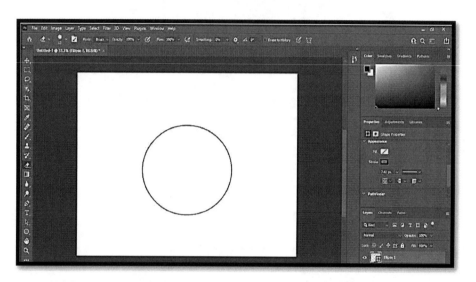

The Elliptical Marquee tool is used in the second phase of learning how to produce a curved line in Photoshop Elements. This tool can be found in your Toolbox, which is located on the left side of your screen. When you hover your cursor over the tools, you will see an Elliptical Marquee tool, which is formed like a flat rounded circle. You must then click on the tool and drag it diagonally across your canvas, ensuring that you have a shape Selection where the top or bottom side of the Selection can be used as the Curved Line. If the curve is too tight and you want to make it less curving, just slide your mouse farther laterally toward the left or right side of the screen. Following that, you can modify the shape of the Selection by going to the Select **Menu** and then selecting "**Transform Selection**." By clicking and dragging on any of the 8 handles, you can simply resize the picture. When you are satisfied with the adjustment, click the **green Mark** and you are finished.

3. **Using or Applying Strokes on the Selections Tools**

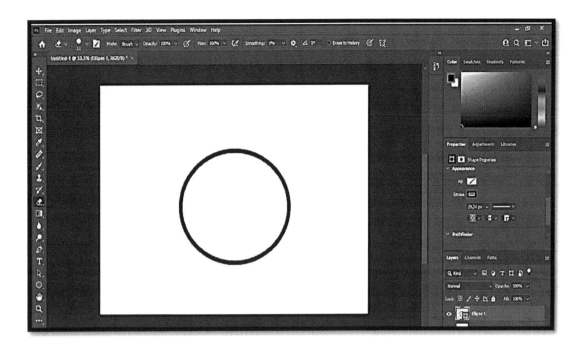

To achieve this, go to the **Edit Menu box** and choose "**Stroke (Outline) Selection...**" from the drop-down menu. After selecting this menu, you will be presented with a "**Stroke**" Dialogue Box with a few selections. There will be a box with a number in it named "**Width**" there. When you put a number into the box, the larger the number becomes, the broader our Stroke becomes. When you're pleased with the width, click "**OK**" to exit the dialogue window. Undo and deselect are available by hitting the Control-D (Windows) or Command-D (Mac) keys.

4. **Remove any unwanted sections of your line**

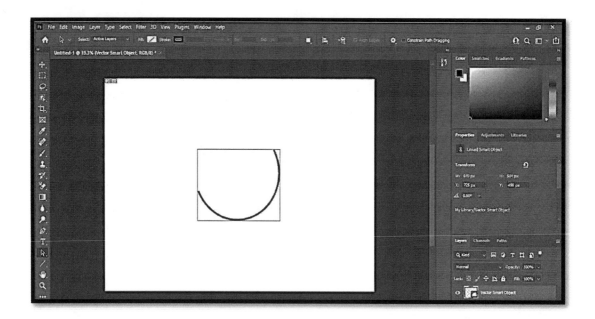

You can delete undesired items by hitting the **Eraser button** in the Toolbox. You must make the cursor for the Eraser Tool bigger than the Stroke that you have produced. You can also adjust the size by pressing the left and right Bracket Keys on your keyboard. Then, by dragging, you may remove the unwanted portion of the Stroke. After that, a last touch and you will now have the lovely and smooth Curved Line that you want.

Typing Tools

The Pencil Tool

The Pencil Tool in Adobe Photoshop Elements is a basic drawing and painting tool that enables you to make freehand drawings and lines. It's a handy tool that's often used for drawing, outlining, and adding tiny details to images

How to Find the Pencil Tool

1. Launch Adobe Photoshop Elements and go to the "**Expert**" workspace to access more sophisticated tools.
2. Locate the toolbar on the left side of your screen. The Pencil Tool is represented by a pencil-shaped symbol.
3. In the toolbar, click the **Pencil Tool icon** to activate it.

4. Change the Pencil Tool Settings. The Options Bar is located at the top of the screen. You can change the Pencil Tool's brush size, opacity, and blending mode using this menu.
5. Select the appropriate brush size depending on the thickness of the lines you wish to draw.

Using the Pencil Tool

Freehand Drawing

- Using the Pencil Tool, create freehand lines on the canvas by clicking and dragging.
- The lines you create will have a firm edge and will move with the cursor.

Brush Size Adjustment

- To change the brush size, use the settings in the settings Bar. A smaller brush is good for tiny details, while a bigger brush is good for wide strokes.

Adjusting Opacity

- In the Options Bar, choose the opacity level to decide how transparent or opaque the drawn lines are. Lowering the opacity might result in a more delicate and blended look.

Changing Blending Modes

- Use the Options Bar's blending modes to adjust how the pencil strokes interact with the underlying picture or layers. Blending modes that are often used include Normal, Multiply, Overlay, and so on.

Erasing with a Pencil

- To erase a part of your drawing, use the Pencil Eraser mode by holding down the 'E' key while using the Pencil Tool. You can erase using the same settings as the Pencil Tool.

Undo and Redo

- If you make a mistake, you can fix or redo your actions by using the "**Undo**" (Ctrl + Z or Command + Z on Mac) and "**Redo**" (Ctrl + Shift + Z or Command + Shift + Z on Mac) commands.

Save your Work

- Always remember to save your work frequently to prevent losing any modifications. To save your project, go to the "**File**" menu.

The Crop Tool

The Crop tool deletes the area of a picture that surrounds the selection. Crop the picture to eliminate distracting background components and concentrate on your target item. By default, when you crop a picture, the resolution stays the same as the original image.

The steps:

1. Choose the Crop tool.
2. Select one of the following crop ratios from the drop-down list on the left of the Tool Options panel, or enter new custom values in the Width and Height fields in the options bar, to change the crop ratio from that of the original photo:

No Restriction

Allows you to resize the picture to any size.

Use the Photo Ratio

When you crop a picture, the original aspect ratio is shown. The Width and Height fields display the cropped image's dimensions. You can change the picture resolution using the Resolution box.

Note: When you enter numbers for the crop tool's Width and Height, the drop-down list shows Custom as the preferred option.

3. Drag over the picture portion area you want to save or keep. The crop marquee appears as a bounding box with handles at the corners and sides when you release the mouse button.
4. (Optional) Make any of the following changes to the crop marquee:
- In the Tool Options panel, change the aspect ratio by selecting values from the drop-down list on the left.
- To move the marquee, set the cursor within the bounding box and drag, or use the arrow keys to move the marquee.
- Drag a handle to resize the marquee. When **No Restriction** is selected from the drop-down list, you can constrain the proportions while scaling by holding **Shift** while dragging a corner handle.
- In the options bar, click the **Swap icon** to swap the Width and Height values.
- To rotate the marquee, move the pointer outside the bounding box (it will turn into a curved arrow) and drag. (In Bitmap mode, you cannot rotate the crop marquee for a picture.)

Change the Crop tool preferences to change the color and opacity of the crop shield (the cropped area surrounding the image). Select **Edit > Preferences > Display & Cursors** and enter a new Color and Opacity value in the Preferences dialog box's Crop Tool area. Deselect **Use Shield** if you don't want to see a colored shield during cropping.

5. To complete cropping, select the **green Commit button** in the lower-right corner of the marquee, or double-click the bounding box. To stop the cropping process, hit Esc or click the red stop icon.

Crop to a selection boundary

The Crop tool eliminates the regions that lie outside the current selection. When you crop to a selection boundary, Photoshop Elements reduces the picture to the bounding box that includes the selection. (Irregularly shaped selections, such as those generated by using the Lasso tool, are cropped to a rectangular bounding box that includes the selection.) When you use the Crop command without creating a selection, Photoshop Elements trims the picture by 50 pixels from each visible edge.

The steps:

1. Use any selection tool, such as the Rectangular Marquee tool, to choose the section of the picture you want to keep.
2. Select **Image > Crop**.

Automatic cropping recommendations

The Crop tool and method are an integral aspect of the picture editing process. From the latest Photoshop Elements versions, the Crop tool automatically provides four ready-to-use recommendations. You can select the greatest crop for your requirements from one of them. You may even continue to crop as much as you want to, after accepting one of the four options or rejecting all four suggestions.

To use the automated cropping suggestions:

1. Launch Photoshop Elements and open an image.
2. Click the **Crop tool.** Four thumbnails depicting the automated recommendations are available in the Tool Options window.
3. Select the thumbnail that you believe is the greatest match. When you pick a different aspect ratio from the drop-down list in the Tool Options panel, you will get additional possibilities.

Note: Hover your mouse over the Crop Suggestions button in the Tool Options panel to get a preview of the crop recommendation.

Use grids to improve cropping results

Grid Overlay

In the picture, a grid guide is created. Before cropping the picture, use the grid to arrange items.

The Cookie Cutter Tool

The Cookie Cutter tool cuts a picture into the form you want. Drag a shape onto your picture to crop the shot into that form. You can also drag and resize the bounding box to crop the appropriate area.

The steps:

1. Select the Crop tool in Advanced Mode.
2. In the Tool Options window, click the **Cookie Cutter icon** and then choose a shape. Select a different library from the Shapes drop-down to browse additional libraries.
3. To choose a shape, double-click it.
4. Drag the form border inside the picture and move it to the appropriate place in the image.

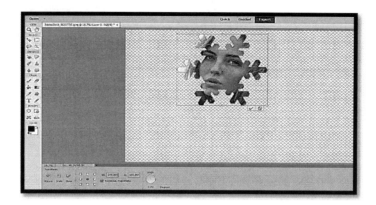

5. To complete the cropping, click the **Commit button** or hit **Enter**. To stop the cropping process, hit **Esc** or click the stop button.

The Perspective Crop Tool

The viewpoint Crop tool allows you to crop a picture while changing its viewpoint. This is handy if your picture has some distortion. When an item is shot from a non-straight angle or when wide-angle lenses are employed to picture a huge span of an object, distortion develops. For example, while photographing a tall structure from the ground level, the building's borders look closer to each other at the top than at the bottom.

Here are the steps:

1. In Photoshop Elements, open a picture.
2. Click the **Perspective Crop tool** from the Modify section of the toolbar in Advanced Mode.
3. Draw a marquee or border around the item whose perspective you want to fix, and then crop the picture to that area.

4. To change the form of the marquee, drag the corners of the selection. Hover over any corner, then click and drag the corner when the cursor becomes white. For optimum results, match the marquee's vertical edge with a pattern or item in the picture to seem vertical.

5. In the Tools Options panel, you can also enter settings for the width (W), height (H), and Resolution fields. The finished picture is scaled to the desired height, breadth, and resolution.

6. Click ✔ to change the viewpoint and crop the picture to the marquee area.

The Recompose Tool

In Adobe Photoshop Elements, the Recompose Tool enables you to change the composition of a picture without damaging its primary parts. It's especially handy for enlarging photos without losing crucial details or changing the composition's overall balance.

Use the Recompose Tool as follows:

1. Open Adobe Photoshop Elements.
2. Navigate to **"File" > "Open"** and choose the picture file you want to work on.
3. In the toolbar, look for the Recompose Tool. It often appears as an icon with two overlapping rectangles or boxes.
4. After activating the Recompose Tool, create a selection around the area you want to maintain in your picture. Typically, this is accomplished by clicking and dragging your mouse to form a bounding box.
5. After you've made your selection, you may relocate or enlarge it by moving the bounding box's borders or corners.
6. Use the "**Protect**" brush to identify certain items inside the chosen area that you want to protect against deformation. This assures that certain regions do not alter throughout the recomposition process.
7. Once you're happy with the changes, click the "**Go**" or "**Apply**" button to finish the recomposition.
8. Examine the recomposed picture. If you need to make any extra changes, you may undo and restart the procedure, or you can use other tools to do so.
9. Once you've achieved the desired outcome, save your adjusted picture. To save it as a new file, choose **"File" > "Save As" or "File" > "Save"** to overwrite the old file.

The Content-Aware Move Tool

Photoshop Elements' Content-Aware Move function lets you pick and move things inside a picture while automatically filling in the background where the object was originally placed. This is very handy for rearranging parts in a shot or making minor changes without leaving visible seams.

How to Use Photoshop Elements' Content-Aware Move

1. Open the picture you want to work on in Adobe Photoshop Elements.

2. Locate the "**Move**" tool in the toolbar on the left. If it isn't visible, click and hold the "**Spot Healing Brush**" tool to bring up a fly-out menu. From this menu, choose the "**Content Aware Move" tool.**

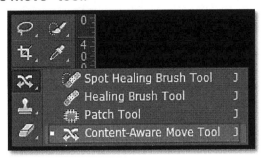

3. The tool options bar is located at the top of the screen. Change the brush size to match the size of the item you want to move. In the options box, you can alternatively choose "**Move**" as the mode.
4. Click and drag the item you wish to move around. This makes a selection around the selected region.
5. After selecting the object, click and drag it to the new place inside the picture. As you move the item, you'll see a preview of it.
6. Let go of the mouse button to drop the item into its new location. Using Content Aware technology, Photoshop Elements will automatically fill in the area where the item was previously positioned with content from the surrounding area.
7. After repositioning the item, you may need to use other tools like the Spot Healing Brush or Clone Stamp to further enhance the picture and make the adjustments seamless.
8. Once you're happy with the changes, save your changed picture.

The Straighten Tool

An image might be misaligned due to camera shaking. For example, the horizon in a sunset photograph may not be completely horizontal. You may realign the shot in Photoshop Elements to make the horizon completely horizontal. To realign a picture vertically or horizontally, use the Straighten tool (P). You can also select to automatically resize or crop the canvas to allow for picture straightening.

- In Quick mode, with the Straighten tool (P) selected, draw a line parallel to the horizon (when visible). When not visible, draw a line that you believe must represent the photo's horizontal axis.

- The picture is straightened, and any empty borders that result from the choice you selected are immediately filled.

Straighten a picture manually in Advanced Mode

The steps:

1. Choose the **Straighten tool**.
2. Choose from the following options buttons:

Grow or Shrink Canvas to Fit

The canvas is resized to suit the rotating picture. Straightening causes the image's corners to extend beyond the current canvas. There are patches of vacant background in the straightened picture, but no pixels are cut.

Crop to Remove Background

Crops the picture to eliminate any apparent blank background region after straightening. Some pixels have been cropped.

Crop to Original Size

The canvas remains the same size as the original picture. Other pixels in the straightened picture are cut, while others are blank. **Do one of the following to straighten the image:**

- Draw a horizontal line along an edge to align horizontally. For example, consider the view of a train with an incorrectly oriented horizon. Draw a horizontal line parallel to the track of the train.

- Draw a vertical line along an edge to align it vertically. For example, you may have a picture of an incorrectly oriented tower. Draw a vertical line perpendicular to the tower.

Automatically Fill Empty Edges

Instead of filling in background color or transparent pixels, the Straighten tool now provides an improved option to intelligently fill the borders with appropriate picture data. Only the Grow or Shrink and Original Size modes include the Autofill edges option. Select Autofill edges before drawing a line to facilitate picture straightening. When you draw the line, any gaps around the photo's boundaries are instantly and intelligently filled.

Straighten a picture manually in Quick mode

The steps:

1. Choose the **Straighten tool.**
2. Choose from the following options buttons:

Keep the Canvas Size

The canvas is resized to suit the rotating picture. Straightening causes the image's corners to extend beyond the current canvas. There are patches of vacant background in the straightened picture, but no pixels are cut.

Maintain the Image Size

Resize the picture to eliminate any apparent blank background space after straightening. Some pixels have been cropped.

3. **Do one of the following to straighten the image:**
   - Draw a horizontal line along an edge to align horizontally. For example, consider the view of a train with an incorrectly oriented horizon. Draw a horizontal line parallel to the track of the train.
   - Draw a vertical line along an edge to align it vertically. For example, you may have a picture of an incorrectly oriented tower. Draw a vertical line perpendicular to the tower.

Automatically Fill Empty Edges

Instead of filling in background color or transparent pixels, the Straighten tool now provides an improved option to intelligently fill the borders with appropriate picture data. Choose **Autofill edges** before drawing a line to facilitate image straightening. When you draw the line, any gaps around the photo's boundaries are instantly and intelligently filled.

Straighten a picture automatically

- Select **Image > Rotate > Straighten Image** to automatically straighten the picture while leaving the canvas surrounding it. There are patches of vacant background in the straightened picture, but no pixels are cut.
- Select **Image > Rotate > Straighten and Crop Image** to automatically straighten and crop the picture. Although there are no sections of blank background in the straightened picture, some pixels are clipped.

Frequently Asked Questions

1. How do you use the color swatch panel in Photoshop Elements 2024?
2. How do you use the color picker option?
3. How do you use the zoom and hand tool?
4. How do you use the marquee selection tools?
5. How do you use the red eye removal tool?
6. How do you use the smart brush tools?
7. How do you use the background eraser tool?
8. How do you use the shape tools?
9. How do you use the cropping tools?
10. How do you use the sponge, dodge and burn tools?

CHAPTER SIX

SELECT AND ISOLATE AREAS IN YOUR PHOTOS

Overview

Chapter six delves into the world of selecting and isolating areas in your image in Photoshop Elements 2024. Here, you will learn about selection, the select menu, edge detection, how to use selection to protect an area and so much more.

Working with Selections

A selection is a defined section of a photograph. When you make a selection, the region around it becomes editable (for example, you may brighten one section of a photo without changing the rest). A selection may be made using either a selection tool or a selection command. The selection is surrounded by a selection border that you may conceal. You can change, copy, or remove pixels inside the selection boundary, but you can't touch anything beyond the selection border until you deselect it. Adobe Photoshop Elements has selection tools for several types of selections. The Elliptical Marquee tool, for example, picks circular and elliptical regions, while the Magic Wand tool may choose an area of similar hues with a single click. With one of the Lasso tools, you may make more complicated selections. You may even use feathering and anti-aliasing to soften the edges of a selection.

Why Do You Need to Use "Select" and "Isolate" in Adobe Photoshop Elements:

Selecting Editing

- **Function**: The major purpose for using these tools is to undertake selective picture manipulation. When you choose and isolate particular parts, you can make changes to just those areas while leaving the rest of the picture alone.
- For example, you could want to improve the color of a certain item, eliminate a bothersome feature, or add a filter to a specific area of the shot.

Complex Image Manipulation

- **Function**: Isolating components or objects enables individual handling in more complicated compositions with many elements or objects. When dealing with

layered photos or integrating many images into a single composition, this is extremely beneficial.
- As an example, you may need to take a person from one shot and position them in another.

Masking and Layering

- **Function**: Selecting and isolating items is critical when dealing with masks and layers. Masks allow you to control the visibility of certain areas of a picture, while layers allow you to stack and organize various components.
- For example, you can use masks to flawlessly merge two photos, resulting in a composite that seems natural and well-integrated.

Detailed Corrections

- **Function**: When conducting complex repairs, such as retouching particular areas or altering exposure in limited parts, choosing and isolating provides more precision and accuracy.
- For instance, you could want to brighten the eyes, smooth the skin, or fix the exposure of a certain portion of the shot.

How to Use Adobe Photoshop Elements' "Select" and "Isolate" Functions:

1. Make a selection around the area you want to isolate using tools like the Marquee Tool, Lasso Tool, or Magic Wand Tool.
2. Use tool options like feathering to improve the selection edges.
3. When working with complicated shapes and intricate edges, use selection refinement tools such as the Refine Edge dialog to fine-tune the selection.
4. After selecting the appropriate region, use the **"Layer via Copy" or "Layer via Cut"** options to create a new layer containing just the specified information. This isolated layer can now be modified separately from the remainder of the picture.
5. Use layer masks to regulate the visibility of the chosen area. Transparency is controlled by white, black, and gray hues. Use a brush to refine the transition between the isolated region and the background
6. For non-destructive editing, apply adjustment layers to the separated pieces. Changes can be made without affecting the original pixels.
7. Use the "**Save Selection**" option to save selections for later use. You may then recall and apply the same option later in your process.

Feathering

Smooth the edges of a selection by anti-aliasing

Anti-aliasing and feathering may be used to soften a selection's rough edges. Anti-aliasing softens the color transition between edge pixels and background pixels, smoothing the jagged edges of a selection. No detail is lost since only the edge pixels change. When cutting, copying, and pasting selections to build composite pictures, anti-aliasing comes in handy. The Lasso, Polygonal Lasso, Magnetic Lasso, Elliptical Marquee, and Magic Wand tools all include anti-aliasing options. To anti-alias, select the **Anti-Alias option** before making the selection; anti-aliasing cannot be added to an existing selection.

The steps:

1. Select the Lasso, Polygonal Lasso, Magnetic Lasso, Elliptical Marquee, or Magic Wand tool from the Edit workspace.
2. In the settings bar, choose **Anti-aliased.**
3. Choose in the image window. Feathering softens the edges of a selection.
4. When you use feathering, you can soften the rough edges of a selection. Feathering blurs edges by creating a transition between the selection and the pixels around it. This blurring may result in some detail loss near the selection's edge.

The Elliptical Marquee, Rectangular Marquee, Lasso, Polygonal Lasso, or Magnetic Lasso tools may be used to make a feathered selection. Using the Select menu, you can also apply feathering to an existing selection. When you move, cut, copy, or fill the selection, feathering effects appear.

Define a feathered edge for a selection tool

1. Do one of the following in the Edit workspace:
- From the toolbox, choose any of the lasso or marquee tools and enter a Feather value in the options bar to set the breadth of the feathering. The feathering process starts at the chosen boundary.
- In the options bar, choose the Selection Brush tool and a soft-edged brush from the brushes pop-up panel.
2. Make a choice or selection in the image window.

Define a feathered edge for an existing selection

Here are the steps:

1. To create a selection in the Edit workspace, use a selection tool from the toolbox.
2. Select **Feather** from the drop-down menu.
3. In the Feather Radius text box, enter a number between 2 and 250, then click OK. The breadth of the feathered edge is defined by the feather radius.

The Select menu

The Select menu is quite useful for editing and refining options within your photos. Selections are an important part of image editing because they enable you to isolate select regions for manipulation while leaving the rest of the picture alone.

Here's a list of the most common options in the Select menu:

1. **All**: Select the whole canvas, highlighting the entire picture. It comes in handy when you want to execute actions on the full picture or clear an existing selection.
2. **Deselect**: If you have a selection already, this option eliminates it, leaving the whole picture unselected. It's useful when you want to start a fresh selection or work on the complete picture.
3. **Reselect**: This option enables you to reapply your previous selections. If you mistakenly deselected or lost your selection, you can quickly restore it with this option.
4. **Invert**: Flips the current selection. If you have a choice, this option chooses everything that was not chosen, and vice versa. It comes in handy when you wish to change the background or other non-selected sections.
5. **Feather**: This option softens a selection's edges. Feathering produces a seamless transition between chosen and unselected regions, which reduces the illusion of a harsh border. The feather radius may be specified in pixels.
6. **Modify:**
- **Border**: This command adds a boundary to an existing selection. The border's width may be specified in pixels.
- **Smooth**: Softens a selection's edges by averaging the pixel values at the border.
- **Expand**: Enlarges a selection by a given number of pixels.
- **Contract**: Shrinks a selection by a given number of pixels.

7. **Similar**: Select regions with pixel values that are comparable to the current selection. This might help you quickly choose places with similar colors or tones.
8. **Grow**: Expand the selection to include neighboring pixels that are comparable to the ones you've chosen. It's very effective for picking adjacent sections with comparable hues.
9. **Transform Selection**: You can enlarge, rotate, or skew an existing selection, giving you additional control over the shape and orientation of the chosen region.
10. **Save Selection:** This option allows you to store your current selection as a named channel. This is important if you want to reuse the selection or apply various effects to the selected area in the future.

One-Click Select Subject, Background, or Sky

With a single click, you can automatically select the Subject, Sky, or Background in your shot. Photoshop Elements recognizes the Subject, Sky, or Background in your shot using Adobe Sensei AI technology*.

To get the one-click selection options, follow these steps:

1. To open the specified picture, choose **File > Open or Open in the Quick or Advanced workspace**.

Use one of the following procedures to access the one-click selection options:

- From the Select menu, choose **Subject, Background, or Sky**.

- Proceed to open any of the Selection tools from the **Tools panel > Select any of the Subject, Sky, or Background options** from the action bar.

Allow Photoshop Elements a few seconds to automatically choose your photo's Subject, Sky, or Background. The selection will be apparent as marching ants, or a moving, dotted line.

Refine the automatic selection

To change the selection, choose one of the Selection Brushes under Tool Options and click Add to Selection or Subtract from Selection. You may also refine the selection by selecting **Select > Refine Edge**.

Note: Using the new Quick Actions menu, you can quickly pick the Subject, Sky, or Background in your images.

Refine the edge of your selection

Refining the borders of a selection in Adobe Photoshop Elements may substantially enhance the quality and appearance of your adjustments.

Here are the steps:

1. Load the picture you want to work on into Adobe Photoshop Elements.
2. Make a preliminary selection around the item or region you want to improve using any selection tool from the toolbar (e.g., Marquee, Lasso, and Magic Wand).
3. Once you've made your first choice, go to the top menu and click "**Select**," then "**Refine Edge**" from the drop-down menu.
4. Modify the Edge Settings

You can fine-tune your pick using the sliders and settings in the Refine Edge dialog box. Here are some important settings to pay attention to:

- **View Mode:** Use the dropdown menu to choose various view modes, such as **"On White" or "On Black,"** to improve the visibility of the edges you're working on.
- **Edge Detection:** This determines how the program detects the edges of your selection. To enhance edge recognition, play around with the Radius and Smart Radius settings.
- **Smooth**: This slider aids in the smoothing of jagged or rough edges. Be careful not to over-smooth, since this might make your choice seem odd.
- **Feather**: Feathering provides a gentle transition between the chosen and unchosen sections. To adjust the amount of feathering, move the slider.
- **Contrast**: Increasing contrast helps to refine your selection's edges. This is beneficial for low-contrast selections.

5. Output Settings

The Output settings are located at the bottom of the Refine Edge dialog box:

- **Output To**: Depending on your preferences, you can output the selection to a new layer, a new layer with a layer mask, or another selection.
- **Decontaminate Colors**: Enabling this option might assist in eliminating color fringing around the margins if your selection requires removing a background.

6. Once you're happy with the changes, click the "OK" button to apply the new edge settings.
7. If you export to a new layer with a layer mask, you can adjust the mask using the Layer Mask settings. Paint on the mask using the Brush tool in black and white, exposing or concealing areas of the selection as desired.
8. Finish your adjustments and save your photo with the refined selection.

Refine Edge Adjustments

Edge refinement in Adobe Photoshop Elements is essential for making accurate selections and masks in your photographs. Refining edges offers a smooth and seamless outcome whether cutting out a subject, generating a composite picture, or making specific edits.

Here are the steps:

1. Launch the image you want to work on in Adobe Photoshop Elements.
2. Proceed to make a preliminary selection of the region you wish to improve using any selection tool (e.g., Lasso, Magic Wand, and Quick Selection).
3. To open the Refine Edge Dialog Box while your selection is active, go to the top menu and click **Select > Refine Edge.**
4. View Options

Several view options are available in the Refine Edge dialog box to help you see your decision more clearly. Typical alternatives include:

- **On White/On Black**: Displays your selections against a white or black background, respectively.
- **Overlay**: Place your selections on top of the original picture.
- **On Layers:** Displays your selections against a background that you may change.

5. Change the detection of edges:

To fine-tune your selections, use the sliders in the Edge Detection section. These are some examples:

- **Radius**: This setting controls the size of the edge-detecting region.
- **Smart Radius**: Adjusts the radius automatically for various parts of the selection.
- **Adjust Edge**: This option moves the selection border in or out.

6. The "**Smooth**" slider softens the edges of your choice. Be careful not to overdo it, since this might cause the corners to seem fuzzy.
7. Use the "**Feather**" slider to create a smooth transition between chosen and unselected sections. This is beneficial for preventing sharp edges.
8. Use the "**Contrast**" slider to improve the separation of the chosen and unselected sections.
9. Use the "**Shift Edge**" slider to adjust the selection border inside or outward as desired. This might be beneficial for repositioning the selection.

10. Select the output for your refined selection at the bottom of the dialog box. A new layer, a new layer with a layer mask, or a selection without generating a new layer are all options.
11. Select the "**Preview**" option to see how your revised selection appears in the context of your picture. Make any other changes that are required.
12. When you're finished refining the edge, click "**OK**" to save your changes and close the Refine Edge dialog box.
13. After you've refined the edge, zoom in on your picture to look for any spots that require further work. If more refining is desired, use the brush tool on the layer mask.

Use a selection to protect an area

Making selections is a key ability that enables you to isolate and edit certain areas of a picture. Protecting an area with a selection often entails ensuring that any changes you make affect just the chosen area and leave the rest of the picture alone.

Follow the steps below to use a selection to protect an area:

1. Open the picture you want to work on in Adobe Photoshop Elements.
2. Select the proper selection tool for your requirements from the toolbar on the left side of the screen. The "**Rectangular Marquee Tool**" (for rectangular selections) and the "**Lasso Tool**" (for freehand selections) are the most regularly utilized tools. The "**Magic Wand Tool**" can also be used to select areas depending on color.
3. Draw a boundary around the area you wish to protect using the chosen tool. For example, if you're using the Rectangular Marquee Tool, you can draw a rectangle by clicking and dragging. Trace around the area you wish to protect using the Lasso Tool.
4. Use the selecting tools' selections to narrow your selection. For example, using the Rectangular Marquee Tool, you can add to an existing selection by holding down the Shift key, or remove from it by holding down the **Alt/Option key.** You can modify your selection using the Lasso Tool by altering the location of the anchor points.
5. Feathering makes the transition between the chosen and unselected sections seamless. Go to the top menu and click "**Select**" > "**Feather**." Enter a pixel value for the feathering effect.

6. After you've made your selection, any modifications you make (such as tweaks, filters, or painting) will only affect the area included in the selection.
7. After making the adjustments, it's critical to deselect the area to avoid mistakenly changing the protected zone. Select **"Select" > "Deselect"** from the top menu, or use the keyboard shortcut Ctrl+D (Windows) or Command+D (Mac).
8. After you've protected the required area, save your work to save the modifications. To save a new version, go to **"File" > "Save" or "File" > "Save As"**.

Cut and paste a selection into another photo

Follow the steps below:

1. Adobe Photoshop Elements should now be open on your PC.
2. Select "**Open**" from the "**File**" menu to open the picture from which you want to make a selection.
3. Repeat the procedure for the second picture where you wish to paste the selection.
4. In the picture from which you want to make a selection, highlight the region you wish to cut using the selection tool of your choice (e.g., Rectangular Marquee Tool, Lasso Tool).
5. Once the area has been chosen, use Ctrl + X (Windows) or Cmd + X (Mac) to cut it. Alternatively, go to the "**Edit**" menu and choose "**Cut**."
6. Switch to the second picture by clicking on its tab.
7. To paste the selection onto the second picture, use Ctrl + V (Windows) or Cmd + V (Mac). Alternatively, go to the "**Edit**" menu and choose "**Paste**."
8. Position and adjust the pasted selection on the second picture as desired using the move tool (typically the arrow symbol).
9. If the edges of your pasted selection are too sharp, use tools like the Eraser or Layer Mask to soften them.
10. If required, adjust the opacity of the pasted layer to merge it flawlessly with the background.
11. Once you're happy with the outcome, save your altered picture. Go to "**File**" and choose **"Save" or "Save As"** to save a duplicate of your work.

Tips

Use layers

Using layers enables you to perform non-destructive changes. Each picture should be placed on its layer to make it easy to change and modify.

Redo and Undo

To reverse a mistake, use Ctrl + Z (Windows) or Cmd + Z (Mac). To undo, use Ctrl + Shift + Z on Windows or Cmd + Shift + Z on Mac.

Try something new

Experiment with different selection tools and blending selections to reach the desired outcome.

Fill or stroke a selection

Filling a Selection

The steps:

1. Open the picture you want to work on in Adobe Photoshop Elements.
2. Make the required selection using the selection tools (e.g., Marquee, Lasso, or Magic Wand). To choose an area, click and drag.
3. • Select the "**Paint Bucket**" tool from the Toolbar. This tool is used to color-fill regions. The Options Bar is located at the top of the screen. To choose the fill color, click on the foreground color swatch. A color picker will open, from which you may choose the required color.
4. Return the Paint Bucket tool to your picture once you've selected the fill color.
5. Click within the selected area to fill it with the color of your choice.

Stroking a Selection

1. In your picture, use the selection tools to make the required selection.
2. Select the "**Type**" tool (T) or any other tool that supports the Stroke option from the Toolbar.
3. In the Options Bar at the top of the screen, click on the color swatch to choose the stroke color. Using the color picker, choose the required color.

4. After selecting the stroke color, go to the Options Bar and choose the "**Stroke**" option. Enter a number in pixels to change the stroke width.
5. Return to your picture once you've selected the stroke settings.
6. To apply the stroke to the chosen region, use the "**Enter**" key or click on another tool.

Additional Suggestions

Redo and Undo

To reverse a mistake, use **"Ctrl + Z" (Windows) or "Cmd + Z" (Mac).** Changes may also be undone by pressing **"Ctrl + Shift + Z" (Windows) or "Cmd + Shift + Z" (Mac).**

Adjusting Selections

Fine-tune your selections with tools such as the Marquee, Lasso, and Magic Wand. The "**Select**" menu also includes options for changing and refining selections.

Layers

Using layers enables non-destructive editing. Consider establishing a new layer and applying the adjustments there before filling or brushing.

Frequently Asked Questions

1. How do you use the one-click select subject, background or sky in Photoshop Elements?
2. How do you refine edge adjustments in Photoshop Elements?
3. How do you use selection to protect an area?
4. How do you use the feathering option in Photoshop Elements?
5. How do you cut and paste a selection into another photo?

CHAPTER SEVEN

RESIZE YOUR IMAGES

Overview

Chapter Seven talks about resizing images in Adobe Photoshop Elements with a particular discussion on image and canvas size.

Image Size vs. Canvas Size

Understanding the concepts of image size and canvas size is critical for working successfully with digital photographs. Image size and canvas size both play important roles in the editing process and understanding these principles will allow you to manage your photographs with more accuracy. Let's take a closer look at each of these points:

Image Size

The dimensions of the actual picture or graphic you're dealing with are referred to as image size. It is often measured in pixels, inches, or other measurements according to the needs of your project.

Accessing Image Size

- To examine or adjust the picture size in Photoshop Elements, go to the "**Image**" menu bar, then "**Resize**," and finally "**Image Size**."

Resampling

- Resampling happens when the pixel dimensions of a picture are changed. Increased picture size may result in a loss of quality, while decreased size may result in a loss of detail. When resizing, keep the "**Resample Image**" option in mind.

Measurement Units

- Adjust the image size in various units such as pixels, inches, centimeters, and so on. The unit you choose is determined by the needs of your project.

Constraining Proportions

- The "**Constrain Proportions**" option is normally activated by default. When you change the width or height, the other dimension adapts correspondingly, preserving the original aspect ratio.

Resolution

- The number of pixels per inch (PPI) of a picture is referred to as its resolution. Higher resolution is often preferable for printing, whereas lesser resolution is sufficient for digital display. Adjust the resolution to meet your output requirements.

Canvas Size

Canvas size refers to the whole working area's dimensions, which include the picture and any extra space (or border) surrounding it. This is very handy when you want to expand the background of your picture or add a border to it.

Accessing Canvas Size

To change the canvas size, go to "**Image**" in the menu bar, then "**Resize**," and finally "**Canvas Size.**"

Anchor Points

When resizing the canvas, indicate which parts of the current canvas will remain fixed. This is accomplished by choosing an anchor point. For example, increasing the canvas size from the bottom causes the picture to rise upward.

Absolute vs. Relative

Specify an absolute size in inches or pixels or alter the canvas size relative to the existing dimensions (in percentage).

Adding a Border

A typical approach to creating a border around a picture is to increase the canvas size. If you wish to select a fixed size for the border, uncheck the "**Relative**" option.

Image Resizing

Here are the steps to resize an image in Photoshop Elements 2024:

1. On your PC, launch Adobe Photoshop Elements.
2. Click "**File**" on the top menu, then "**Open**" to pick the picture to be resized. You can also drag and drop the picture straight into the Photoshop Elements workspace.
3. Select your picture by clicking on the "**Move**" tool in the toolbar on the left side of the screen.
4. Go to the top menu and select "**Image**," then "**Resize**," and finally "**Image Size**."
5. Set the Dimensions

There are various selections for altering the picture size in the "Image Size" dialog box.

- **Width and Height**: Enter the image's desired width and height. To keep the original aspect ratio, make sure the "**Constrain Proportions**" option is selected. This prevents the picture from being distorted.
- **Set the resolution of your picture here**. This is often expressed as pixels per inch (PPI) or dots per inch (DPI). Web pictures typically have a resolution of 72 PPI, however, print photos may need a greater resolution, such as 300 PPI.
- **Resample Image**: Select or deselect this option depending on your requirements. Leave it checked if you want to keep the same picture quality but vary the proportions. Uncheck it if you wish to eliminate certain picture data to minimize file size.

6. After you've entered the required settings, use the "OK" button to save the changes.
7. Select "**File**" and then "**Save As**" to save the enlarged picture with a new filename, or "**Save**" to overwrite the original file.

Recommendations

- **Always work on a copy**: Before making any substantial modifications, duplicate your original picture. You can save the original file this way in case you need it later.

- **Save in another format**: Depending on your requirements, choose to save the scaled picture in a different format. JPEG is frequently an excellent option for online usage, although PNG is preferable for pictures with transparency.

Canvas Resizing

In Adobe Photoshop Elements, resizing the canvas enables you to adjust the proportions of your workspace without changing the size of your picture.

Here are the steps:

1. Launch Adobe Photoshop Elements and get to the location of the image file you want to work on by choosing **"File" > "Open"** and navigating to it.
2. Locate and select the "**Crop Tool**" in the toolbar on the left side of the screen, which looks like a square with diagonal lines.
3. The aspect ratio selections can be found in the options bar at the top of the screen. If you want to freely resize the canvas without regard for aspect ratio, select "**No Restriction**" from the dropdown option. If you wish to keep a specified width-to-height ratio, you can choose a specific aspect ratio.
4. To bring up the cropping handles, click on the picture using the Crop Tool. A bounding box will appear around your picture.
5. Hover your mouse over the bounding box's border or corner until you see a double-headed arrow. Resize the canvas by clicking and dragging. If you have precise size needs, you can also manually input the settings in the settings box.
6. If scaling the canvas leaves some space, you can relocate the picture inside the canvas by clicking and dragging it. This is optional and entirely up to you.
7. When you're happy with the new canvas size, hit **Enter** or click the checkmark symbol in the options box to save your changes.
8. Save your edited picture by going to **"File" > "Save"** or **"File" > "Save As"** and saving it as a new file. Make sure to save your photo in the correct file format and location.

Frequently Asked Questions

1. How do you resize images in Photoshop Elements?
2. How do you resize canvas?
3. How does image and canvas size compare in Photoshop Elements?

CHAPTER EIGHT

FIX AND ENHANCE YOUR PHOTOS

Overview

Chapter eight is all about fixing and improving the photos you have in Photoshop Elements. With the help of some tools and functions, you can fix and drastically improve your photos.

Auto Smart Tone

The Auto Smart Tone tool modifies the tonal value of your picture using an advanced algorithm. Your shot is corrected using the Auto Smart Tone function. You also have a joystick control that you can move around the picture to fine-tune the results. Photoshop Elements examines the tonal quality of the area being sampled as you move the joystick over various sections of your shot. The whole photo is then tone-corrected. Moving the joystick to various parts of the image will provide varied effects. Moving the joystick to the brighter areas of the picture (bright sky or grass) causes the whole image to brighten.

The Auto Smart Tone tool is available in two modes: Quick and Expert.

Apply Auto Smart Tone to a photograph

The steps:

1. When you have a picture open, go to **Enhance > Auto Smart Tone**. A preset tone adjustment is automatically done.
2. To fine-tune the generated picture, move the joystick control that appears on the image.
3. View the thumbnail pictures that are displayed in the four corners of the shot to see how the image will look when you move the joystick control in a given way.

Auto Smart Tone Learning

Choose **Learn** from this Correction when using the Auto Smart Tone function. When you choose this option, Photoshop Elements continues to learn from your editing activities. The system learns from picture tonal ranges before and after you use the Auto Smart Tone tool. This assists the Auto Smart Tone function in making more accurate automated tonal selections for a new picture. As a result, each time you use the feature on a picture, the algorithm offers tone treatment (joystick control positioning) based on past image adjustments. The more photos you adjust tonally using this tool, the smarter it grows at anticipating the kinds of changes you want on a new image. This learning is used by the feature to present you with comparable adjustments on photographs of the same kind.

Reset Auto Smart Tone Learning

Click **General > Reset Auto Smart Tone Learning** in the Preferences menu to reset the learning that the Auto Smart Tone feature has learned from your use and activities.

Adjust Color

The steps:

1. First of all, open Adobe Photoshop Elements.
2. Open the picture you want to adjust by going to **"File" > "Open"** and navigating to the image's location.
3. There are two settings in Photoshop Elements: Quick and Expert. Switch to Advanced Mode for more complex color tweaks by clicking on the **"Expert"** option in the top right corner.
4. In Advanced Mode, go to the **"Enhance"** option in the top menu bar.

5. Change the color

Color adjustment selections may be found under the "Enhance" menu. Here are some useful resources:

Adjust Color

Choose "**Adjust Color**" to see selections such as Adjust Hue/Saturation, Adjust Brightness/Contrast, and Adjust Levels. - Changing the Hue/Saturation value enables you to alter the overall color balance of the picture. - Brightness/Contrast controls the overall brightness and contrast of the image. - Levels provide more control over the tone range.

Color Variations

"**Color Variations**" is another option under the "**Enhance**" menu. It allows you to modify color balance and saturation visually. When you choose the option, a dialog box will display.

6. Use the Color Variations Dialog as follows:

The Color Variations dialog box shows your picture as well as color wheels depicting Shadows, midtones, and Highlights. These wheels may be used to make adjustments.

Choose a Tone Range

Click on the respective radio buttons to choose Shadows, Midtones, and Highlights.

Adjust Color Balance

Drag the sliders for "**More Cyan/Red,**" "**More Magenta/Green,**" and "**More Yellow/Blue**" to modify the color balance.

Adjust Saturation

To modify the strength of colors, use the "Saturation" slider.

7. Adjust using the Adjustments Panel:

• In Advanced Mode, use the modifications panel to fine-tune color modifications. If it isn't already open, select "**Adjustments**" from the "**Window**" menu.

Hue/Saturation Adjustment Layer

At the bottom of the modifications panel, click the "**Create Adjustment Layer**" button and choose "**Hue/Saturation**." This enables you to make non-destructive color modifications.

8. Once you're happy with the color changes, save the picture by going to "**File**" > "**Save**" or "**Save As.**"

Tips:

- **Undo/Redo**: To compare changes and rollback if required, use the "**Undo**" (Ctrl+Z/Command+Z) and "**Redo**" (Ctrl+Y/Command+Y) shortcuts.
- **Experiment**: Don't be scared to try out various settings to get the appearance you want.
- **Adjustment Layers:** Use Adjustment Layers wherever feasible for non-destructive editing, enabling you to adjust settings later without altering the original picture.

Preview Changes

Previewing changes is an important stage in the editing process to verify that changes have the intended impact.

Follow the steps below to preview changes:

1. Firstly, open Adobe Photoshop Elements.
2. Open the picture you want to change by going to "**File**" > "**Open**" and browse to the image's location.
3. Get acquainted with your workplace. The Tools panel on the left, the Options bar at the top, and the Layers panel on the right are the three primary panels in Adobe Photoshop Elements.
4. To make simple modifications, use the tools in the Tools panel. To make adjustments to your picture, for example, you can use the Crop tool, the Adjustments panel, or the Quick Selection tool.
5. You'll be working with the Layers panel whenever you're making changes that include layers, such as adding text or graphics. Before making any changes, make sure you have the relevant layer selected.
6. Adobe Photoshop Elements shows a real-time preview of the majority of changes. Keep an eye on your picture as you make modifications to observe the changes as they happen.

7. In the Tools panel, use the Zoom tool (magnifying glass symbol) to zoom in and out of your picture. This is useful for checking details and the overall composition.
8. To see your picture in a bigger size, hit the "F" key to activate Full Screen mode. By hitting the "F" key again, you can switch between Standard and Full Screen modes.
9. Use the "**Undo**" and "**Redo**" commands to compare the original picture to your altered version. To undo your previous operation, use Ctrl + Z (Windows) or Command + Z (Mac). To undo, use Ctrl + Y (Windows) or Command + Y (Mac).
10. The History panel records all of the actions you've taken. You may view the picture at that stage by clicking on "**Window**" > "**History.**" Click on a particular state in the history to return to that point.
11. If you wish to retain many copies of your picture, use the "Save As" option from the "File" menu. You can save numerous copies of your work with various modifications this way.
12. Select from the "**View**" menu to examine your picture in several settings, such as Standard, Before & After, or Side by Side.
13. If you want to print your picture, access print preview options by selecting "**Print**" from the "**File**" menu. This lets you preview how the picture will look on paper.
14. When you're finished making changes, save your file by going to "**File**" > "**Save**" or "**File**" > "**Save As**" if you want to make a new version.

Adjust Hue/Saturation

Here are the steps:

1. Open the picture you wish to work on in Adobe Photoshop Elements.
2. It's a good idea to duplicate the background layer before making any changes. This guarantees that you can always restore the original picture if necessary.
   - In the Layers panel, right-click on the background layer.
   - Select "**Duplicate Layer**" and press "OK."
3. Select "**Enhance**" from the top menu bar.
4. Choose "**Adjust Color**" and then "**Adjust Hue/Saturation**." Alternatively, you can enter the Hue/Saturation panel by pressing Ctrl + U (Windows) or Command + U (Mac).
5. **Change Hue**

There are three sliders in the Hue/Saturation panel: Hue, Saturation, and Lightness. To change the full-color spectrum, move the Hue slider left or right. This will alter the image's overall color tone. Moving it to the right, for example, warms the colors (more towards red and yellow), while moving it to the left cools them (more towards blue and green).

6. **Adjust the Saturation**

Adjust the strength or vividness of the colors with the Saturation slider. Moving the slider to the right increases saturation, making colors brighter, while moving it to the left desaturates the picture, making it look more grayscale.

7. **Adjust the Lightness**

The Lightness slider affects the color brightness. If you move it to the right, the colors will brighten, and if you move it to the left, they will darken.

8. As you make changes, click the "**Preview**" option at the bottom of the panel to see the results in real-time.
9. When you're finished adjusting, click the "OK" button to save your changes and dismiss the Hue/Saturation window.
10. To keep the original file, save your picture with a new name or version.

Remove Color and Replace Color

Color removal and replacement in Adobe Photoshop Elements requires a range of tools and strategies.

Here's a step-by-step approach to doing this:

Color Removal

Method 1: Using the "Magic Wand" Tool

The steps:

1. Open Adobe Photoshop Elements and select the picture to work on.
2. Locate the "**Magic Wand**" tool on the left side of the screen in the toolbar.
3. In the top selection bar, change the "**Tolerance**" level. Colors with a greater tolerance will be chosen from a wider range.
4. Check the "**Contiguous**" box if you want to choose just neighboring pixels.
5. Click on the image area with the color you want to delete. Based on your tolerance level, the "**Magic Wand**" will choose comparable colors.
6. To delete the chosen color, use the "**Delete**" key, or click the "**Layer Mask**" button at the bottom of the Layers panel.

Using the "Color Range" Tool

The steps:

1. Launch Photoshop Elements and open the picture.
2. In the menu, select **"Enhance," then "Adjust Color," and lastly "Remove Color."**
3. A dialog box will be shown. To adjust the range of colors to be eliminated, use the "**Fuzziness**" slider.
4. When you press the "OK" button, Photoshop Elements will erase the chosen color.

Replacing Color

1. Launch Photoshop Elements and open the picture.
2. From the toolbar, choose the "**Brush**" tool.
3. Select the new color by clicking on the foreground color square at the bottom of the toolbar.
4. In the top options bar, change the brush size, hardness, and opacity settings.
5. Drag the brush over the area where you want the color replaced
6. Use adjustment layers such as "**Hue/Saturation**" or "**Color Balance**" for more exact color alterations. These layers enable you to fine-tune the color substitution without altering the source picture directly
7. To obtain various color effects, change the blending mode of the adjustment layer.
8. Once you're happy with the color substitution, save your work.

Adjust Color Curves

Here are the steps:

1. Locate and launch Adobe Photoshop Elements.
2. Open the picture you want to work on by going to **"File" > "Open"** and searching for it.
3. Navigate to the "**Enhance**" menu.
4. Select "**Adjust Color**" from the drop-down list.
5. Select "**Adjust Color Curves."**
6. The Curves panel will be shown. A grid will appear, with a diagonal line going from bottom-left to top-right. This line displays your image's current tonal and color values.

7. Initially, the RGB curve is chosen to reflect the image's overall brightness and contrast. To make changes, click and drag the curve. Moving the curve upward illuminates the picture while moving it downward darkens it.
8. Select specific color channels (Red, Green, and Blue) from the drop-down menu above the grid. By adjusting these channels, you can fine-tune individual color tones in your picture.
   - **Red Channel:** Moving the curve upward enhances red tones while moving it below diminishes them.
   - **Green Channel:** Changing this curve affects green tones.
   - **Blue Channel**: This curve is in charge of blue tones.
9. Click on the curve to add control points. To fine-tune certain sections of the picture, you can add additional points.
10. Explore the Curves panel's preset selections to make predetermined modifications for typical upgrades.
11. Sliders for Highlights, Midtones, and Shadows are located underneath the grid. To further tweak the tone range of your picture, use these sliders.
12. Toggle between the original and altered versions of your picture; check the "**Preview**" box.
13. Once you're happy with your changes, click "OK" to save them.
14. Save your adjusted picture by going to **"File" > "Save As"** and selecting the format and location you want.

Adjust Color for Skin Tone

Adjusting Skin Tone in Photoshop Elements

1. To adjust skin tone in Photoshop Elements, use a selection tool to choose the parts of the skin to be adjusted.
2. Alternatively, choose the layer to modify.
3. From the Menu Bar, choose "**Enhance > Adjust Color > Adjust Color for Skin Tone.**"
4. Click on the skin region you want to adjust.
5. Click around until you get the results you want.
6. Use the "**Skin**" and "**Ambient Light**" sliders to make more changes.
7. The "**Tan**" slider adds and subtracts brown, while the "**Blush**" slider adds and subtracts red.

8. Sliding the "**Temperature**" slider to the right (warmer/red) or left (cooler/blue) affects the overall hue.
9. When done, click the "**OK**" button.

Defringe Layer

When you move or paste a selection, part of the pixels around the selection boundary are copied along with it. These additional pixels might create a fringe or halo around the selection's borders. The Defringe Layer command replaces the color of any fringe pixels with the color of surrounding pure-color pixels (pixels with no background color). For instance, if you choose a yellow item on a blue background and then move the selection, part of the blue background moves with it. The Defringe Layer swaps off blue pixels for yellow ones.

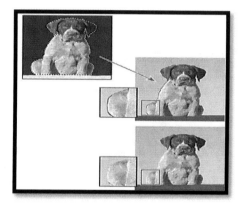

The steps:

1. Copy and paste a selection onto an existing or new layer.
2. Select **Enhance > Color Adjustment > Defringe Layer**.
3. Enter the number of pixels you want to replace around the item in the Defringe dialog box. A value of one or two should suffice.
4. Select **OK**.

Brightness/Contrast

The Brightness/Contrast command allows you to make adjustments to a picture that does not use its complete tonal range. Excessively dark images may be brightened up. This often throws off the image's contrast, which may also be modified in this window.

The steps:

1. Select **Enhance > Adjust Lighting > Brightness/Contrast** from the menu. There are currently no changes.
2. To brighten the picture, drag the Brightness slider to the right to 65 or input 65 into the Brightness text area.
3. Increase the contrast to 30 by sliding the Contrast slider to the right or putting 30 into the Contrast text box to restore some shadows. To compare before and after versions, check and then uncheck the Preview option to receive a quick look at your changes. Click OK.

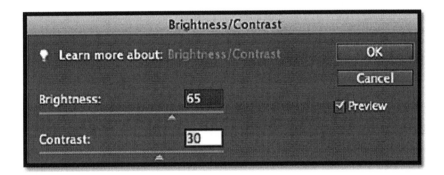

4. Select **File > Save** to save your changes. Deselect the Save in Version Set with Original checkbox and hit Save if the Save As dialog box appears. If Photoshop Elements prompts you to replace the file, choose Yes and then OK when the JPEG Options dialog box opens.

Shadows/Highlights

Brighten shadows, darken highlights, and change the mid tone contrast using Shadows and Highlights. You will work on a different rendition of the same picture in this assignment.

The steps:

1. Select the Shadow Highlight.jpg file in the Organizer, then click the arrow to the right of the Fix tab and select Full Photo Edit, or press Ctrl+I (Windows) or Command+I (Mac OS) to open the picture in the Editor.
2. Select **Enhance > Adjust Lighting > Shadows/Highlights** from the menu. By default, shadows are softened by 25%.

3. Notice how the picture has become dull and bluish-gray. Increase the midtone contrast to +30 by dragging the slider to the right or putting 30 into the Midtone Contrast text box to reclaim some contrast within the picture. Click OK.

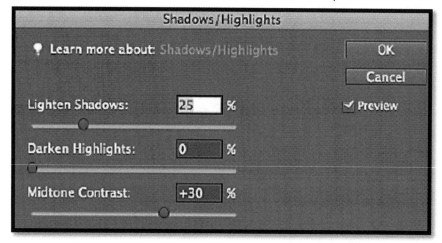

4. Select File > Save to save your changes. Uncheck the Save in Version Set with the original checkbox in the Save As dialog box, then click Save. If Photoshop Elements prompts you to replace the file, choose **Yes** and then OK when the JPEG Options dialog box opens.

Levels

Here's how to use Auto-Level in Organizer:

1. Open the Photoshop Elements Welcome screen.
2. To open the Organizer, select the **Organize Button**.
3. Choose the photo that needs level correction.
4. On the right-hand side, select the **Fix Panel button**.
5. Select the **'Auto Level'** option.

Let's look at how to perform custom settings in a photograph's Levels in Adobe Photoshop Elements... There are two ways to get into the Level Adjustment process:

1. Click **Levels > New Adjustment Layer > Layer Menu**.
2. Click on **Adjustment Layers** and then Levels in the Layer Palette.

Making tonal adjustments using Levels in Photoshop Elements

The Levels command displays a histogram that shows where the majority of the tones in a picture are situated. You have complete control over the image's darkest and lightest areas, as well as all of the midtones in between. You improved the shadows, highlights, brightness, and contrast in the previous two challenges, but you never completely eradicated the blue color cast. You'll now use Levels to improve the contrast of this shot and eliminate the blue color cast.

Histogram

The Histogram panel displays your image's tonal balance. It can determine if the picture has adequate information in the shadows (dark regions), mid-tones (middle tones), and highlights (bright areas). To open the Histogram panel, go to **Window > Histogram**. If you don't see the Histogram option, it's because the Histogram panel is only visible in Full Edit mode. To access the panel, click the Full button directly below the Edit tab, then choose Window > Histogram.

1. To access the Organizer, click the **Organizer icon**. Locate and pick the file Lighting Levels.jpg. To open the file in the Editor, click the triangle to the right of the Fix tab and choose Full Photo Edit. Within the Histogram panel, you'll see that the image's tonal information is visually represented as peaks and troughs. Shadow regions are shown on the left side of the Histogram panel, while highlight areas are shown on the right. The higher the peaks, the more of a certain pixel value appears in the picture. The majority of the "peaks" in this picture are on the left side of the histogram. This indicates that the picture lacks light tones, which would appear on the right side of the histogram and increase the image's contrast. You can disable the histogram for the time being by selecting **Window > Histogram** and unchecking it; you'll see it again when you learn about Levels.
2. Select **Enhance > Adjust Lighting > Levels** from the menu. There are three sliders at the bottom of your histogram in the Input Levels area of the Levels dialog box; the two end sliders control white and black, and the center slider controls the colors in between. Drag the white slider to the left, to 178, to bring it to the bottom of the histogram's initial peak. You have now turned all of the tones from 178 to 255 white, lightening the image.

3. To brighten the image even more, move the center slider to the left to 1.19. The picture would darken if you dragged the center slider to the right.

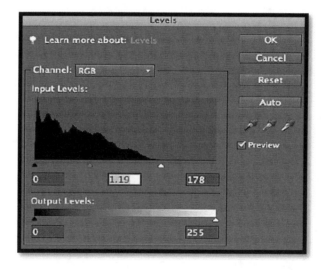

4. The picture is improving, but you still need to compensate for the blue color cast. Select the Blue channel from the Channel drop-down option at the top of the dialog box. To reduce the blue in the picture, move the center slider to the right to 75.

5. Click OK to save the changes. To save your changes, go to **File > Save**. Deselect the Save in Version Set with Original checkbox and hit **Save** if the Save As dialog box appears. If Photoshop Elements prompts you to replace the file, choose **Yes** and then OK when the JPEG Options dialog box opens.

Quick Fixes and Guided Fixes

Convert to Black and White

The steps:

1. Begin by launching Adobe Photoshop Elements on your PC.
2. Navigate to **"File" > "Open"** and choose the picture you want to convert to black and white.
3. Right-click on the Background layer in the Layers panel and choose "**Duplicate Layer**." This step assures that you're working on a duplicate of the original picture, with the original remaining intact.
4. With the copied layer selected, click "**Enhance**" from the top menu, then "**Convert to Black and White**." The picture will be desaturated and converted to grayscale as a result of this.
5. Adjust the brightness and contrast of your black-and-white picture as desired. Go to **"Enhance" > "Adjust Lighting" > "Brightness/Contrast."** Play around with the sliders until you get the desired effect.

6. Using filters, you can improve the black-and-white image even further. Navigate to the top menu and choose "**Filter,**" then "**Artistic,**" "**Stylize,**" or "**Filter Gallery**." Experiment with several filters to discover the one that best matches your picture.
7. To fine-tune the black-and-white conversion, choose **"Enhance" > "Adjust Color" > "Adjust Hue/Saturation."** You can fine-tune the grayscale conversion by adjusting the sliders for each color channel.
8. Once you're happy with the black-and-white conversion, save your work. Navigate to **"File" > "Save As"** and choose the format and location for your picture. To prevent overwriting the old file, give it a new name.
9. To save a copy of the original color picture, keep the original file and save the black and white version separately.

Colorize Photo

The steps:

1. Launch Photoshop Elements and open a picture.

2. Select **Enhance > Colorize Photo** from the menu. Option+Command+R (macOS)/Alt+Ctrl+R (Windows) can also be used.
3. In the Colorize Photo workspace, a preview is created. The panel on the right will show four color possibilities. Choose the one that is most convenient for you.

4. Click OK, or **Reset** if you want to go back to the original picture.

Change colors in specific areas of a photo

The steps:

1. Launch Photoshop Elements and open a picture.
2. Select **Enhance > Colorize Photo** from the menu. Also, use Option+Command+R (macOS)/Alt+Ctrl+R (Windows).
3. Change the toggle on the right panel to **Manual**.
4. In the right panel, choose the areas where you want to change the color using the Quick Selection Tool or Magic Wand Tool.
5. Select the Droplet tool and place the droplet in the region you wish to recolor. You may add as many droplets as you need.

Note: Control+D (Windows)/Cmd+D (MacOS) to concentrate on one option at a time. Select > Deselect can also be used to delete an existing selection before establishing a new one.

6. The Color Palette displays a selection of unique colors for each droplet. Simply click the chosen color from the hue Palette after selecting a droplet (selected droplets have a blue edge). To pick a color, you can either use the vertical slider in the **All-Applicable Colors box** or the icon. The most recently used color is shown next to the Color Palette swatches. You can use this to return to the previous color.

7. To display the result without droplets, turn off the **Show Droplets option**. Using the Before-After toggle, you can also see the original and altered picture. Click **Reset** to undo any changes and return to the original picture.
8. When you're satisfied with the outcome, click **OK**.

Haze Removal

How to Apply Haze Removal in Photoshop Elements

Here are the steps:

1. To manually remove haze or fog in Photoshop Elements, first choose the picture to be adjusted.
2. From the Menu Bar, select "**Enhance> Haze Removal**" to launch the "**Haze Removal**" dialog box.

3. In this dialog box, change the "**Haze Reduction**" slider to eliminate the desired amount of haze.
4. Use the "**Sensitivity**" slider to control how sensitive the software is to haze removal.
5. The "**Before/After**" toggle button allows you to flip between your image's before and after views.

6. After you've removed the haze, click the "**OK**" button to save your changes.
7. Save your picture before exiting Photoshop Elements to guarantee that your modifications are saved.

In the Remove Haze dialog, use the following controls:

- **Haze Reduction slider**: Adjusts the amount of haze eliminated.
- **Tolerance slider**: Sets the haze removal threshold value (Suggestions for a better name for this control/setting are appreciated).
- Before / After view toggle button
- Reset and OK buttons

Adjust Sharpness

Remove imperfections

The first step is to use the Spot Healing Brush Tool to eliminate any blemishes or defects on the skin since they will appear more accentuated when sharpened.

Duplicate your layer

Go to the Layers panel by navigating to **Window > Layers** - it'll be on the right side of the interface. Now, press Ctrl + J on a PC or Cmd + J on a Mac to duplicate the Background Layer.

Create a high-pass layer

Choose **Filter > Other > High Pass** and reduce the Radius amount in the High Pass dialogue box to a low number, generally about 3-5px. Select OK to apply the sharpening effect.

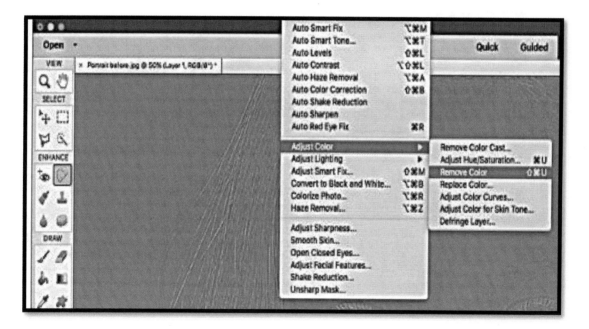

Remove the color

Your high pass layer now has a little amount of color, which when blended will distort the colors in your image. To avoid this, go to **Enhance > Adjust Color > Remove Color**.

Blend it in

It's now time to blend in the high pass layer to sharpen your photo, so go to the Layers panel and set the Blending Mode to Overlay by clicking on the drop-down box that reads Normal.

Mask it off

To completely mask off the layer, click the **Add Layer Mask button** and then press Ctrl / Cmd + I. Then, using a soft-edged white Brush Tool, paint over the elements of your images that you wish to sharpen, such as the facial characteristics.

Unsharp Mask

Here are the steps:

1. Open Adobe Photoshop Elements and choose the picture to be sharpened.
2. It's a good idea to duplicate the background layer before adding any sharpening filters. This allows you to subsequently compare the sharpened version to the original.
   - Right-click on the Background layer in the Layers window.
   - Select "**Duplicate Layer**" from the contextual menu.
   - In the Duplicate Layer dialog, press the "OK" button.
3. In the Layers panel, make sure the duplicated layer is selected.
4. Choose **Enhance > Unsharp Mask** from the menu bar.
5. Adjust the Settings

The dialog box Unsharp Mask will display. Here are the important settings:

- **Amount**: This affects the sharpening effect's intensity. Sharpness rises as the quantity value increases. Begin with a low value and progressively raise it until the desired outcome is obtained.
- **Radius**: This defines the size of the sharpened region surrounding each pixel. Smaller values concentrate on finer details, but bigger values have a wider impact. Experiment with various radius numbers to find the ideal balance.
- **Threshold**: This setting specifies how different the brightness of a pixel must be from the brightness of surrounding pixels before it is deemed an edge and sharpened. A higher threshold prevents delicate details from being sharpened and decreases noise. This should be adjusted depending on the features of your picture.

6. Check the "**Preview**" option in the Unsharp Mask dialog before making the adjustments. You can witness the impact on your photo in real-time.
7. When you're happy with the settings, click the "OK" button to activate the Unsharp Mask filter.

8. To compare the sharpened version with the original, toggle the visibility of the copied layer on and off. This will assist you in determining the influence of the Unsharp Mask filter.
9. If you're happy with the results, save the picture. You should save it as a new file to protect the original.

Smooth Skin

Make individuals appear their best in pictures by using automated skin smoothing.

Here's how it's done:

1. Launch **Photoshop Elements** and open a picture.
2. Select **Enhance > Smooth Skin**.
3. The face in your picture is automatically picked in the Smooth Skin dialog box. If the image contains many faces, all identified faces are highlighted. Click the face you want to change.

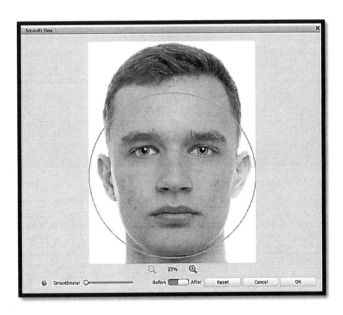

4. Use the Smoothness slider to create the desired effect.
5. (Optional) Review the modifications by using the Before/After toggle button.
6. To return to the original picture, select **Reset**.
7. When you're satisfied with the outcome, click OK.

Adjust Facial Features

The Adjust Facial Features command is a simplified, automated version of the iconic Liquify function, which is used to enhance numerous magazine photos. Although Adjust Facial Features does not allow for much manual manipulation, the result is rather spectacular, not to mention seamless and simple to use. Prepare to get retouching requests from friends and relatives.

Here's how to take advantage of this feature:

1. Select Expert or Quick mode for a picture.
2. Select **Enhance > Adjust Facial Features**. The dialog box Adjust Facial Features appears. A circle surrounds the region that will be impacted by the changes in the dialog box. It's worth noting that Elements first determines whether or not it's a face. We tested it with a cat picture. No such luck.
3. Use the sliders to change the appearance of facial characteristics such as the eyes, nose, lips, chin, and face.

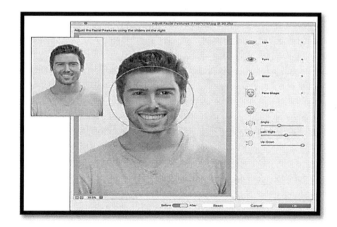

4. To examine your findings, toggle your Before and After buttons.
5. Are you satisfied? Select OK. Not pleased? Restart by clicking Reset.

Select **Preferences > Performance** and ensure that the Use Graphic Processor option is set to guarantee better and smoother performance when utilizing features such as the Adjust Facial Features, Lens Blur, and Liquify filters.

Shake Reduction

How to Use the Shake Reduction Tool

1. First, open the fuzzy picture you wish to sharpen in Photoshop.
2. Once you've opened the picture in Adobe Photoshop Elements, choose **'Enhance'** from the menu bar at the top of your screen. You'll see an option named Auto Shake Reduction in the drop-down menu.

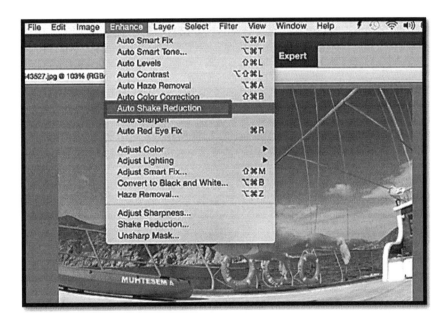

3. Select **'Auto Shake Reduction'** and let Adobe Photoshop Elements handle the rest.
4. If the auto results don't suit you, go back up to the **'Enhance'** option and this time select **Shake Reduction** from the drop-down menu at the bottom.
5. You can focus on the section of the image you wish to sharpen by adjusting the box in the middle of the image. Remember to experiment with the sensitivity slider to fine-tune the sharpness of your image. Finally, to compare outcomes, flick the Before/After switch back and forth.

Frequently Asked Questions

1. How do you use Auto Smart Tone in Photoshop Elements?
2. How do you remove and replace color?
3. How do you adjust lighting?
4. How do you convert photos from black to white?
5. How do you use haze removal?
6. How do you use an unsharp mask in Photoshop Elements?

CHAPTER NINE
WORK WITH PHOTOSHOP ELEMENTS LAYERS

Overview

Layers are overly important in Photoshop Elements, hence, the reason for talking about them. Chapter Nine talks about everything you need to know about layers in Photoshop Elements including selecting a layer to edit, copying layers from one image to another and so much more.

How layers work

Layers are helpful because they allow you to add components to a picture and work on them individually without permanently altering the primary image. You can change the color and brightness of each layer, add special effects, relocate layer content, set opacity and blending values, and so on. You may also modify the stacking order, connect layers to work on them concurrently, and use layers to build web animations. Layers are similar to layered, translucent sheets of glass on which pictures may be painted. The translucent regions of a layer allow you to see through to the levels below. You may work on each layer separately, trying to get the desired result. Until you integrate (merge) the layers, each layer stays separate. The Background layer is always locked (protected) in the Layers panel, which means you can't modify its stacking order, blending mode, or opacity (until you convert it to a normal layer).

The Layers panel organizes layers. Keep this panel open when working in Adobe Photoshop Elements. The active layer (the chosen layer that you are modifying) is visible at a glance. Layers may be linked so that they move as a unit, making layer management easier. Because numerous layers in a picture increase file size, you can minimize file size by combining finished layers. As you edit images, the Layers panel is a valuable resource. To operate with layers, you may also utilize the Layer menu. Ordinary layers are picture (pixel) layers. Other layer types you can use to generate unique effects include:

Fill layers

Include a color gradient, a plain color, or a pattern.

Adjustment layers

Allow you to fine-tune color, brightness, and saturation without affecting your picture permanently (unless you flatten, or collapse, the adjustment layer).

Type layers and shape layers

Allows you to create vector-based text and objects. You can't paint directly on an adjustment layer, but you may paint on its mask. You must first transform fill or text layers into standard picture layers before you can paint on them.

About the Layers panel

The Layers panel (**Window > Layers**) displays all layers of a picture, from the top layer to the lowest Background layer. If you are working in the Custom Workspace in Advanced Mode, you may drag the Layers panel out and tab it with other panels. For easier identification, the active layer, or the one you are working on, is highlighted.

Check which layer is active while you work on a picture to ensure that the changes and edits you make impact the proper layer. For example, if you choose a command and nothing happens, ensure you're looking at the current layer. Many actions can be completed by using the panel's icons, such as creating, concealing, and connecting, locking, and removing layers. With a few exceptions, your changes only impact the highlighted chosen or active layer.

Adding layers

In the Layers panel, newly added layers are displayed above the chosen layer. Layers may be added to a picture using any of the following methods:

- Add new, blank layers or convert selections to layers.
- Change a background layer to a regular layer, or vice versa.
- Copy and paste selections into the picture.
- Use the Type tool or a shape tool.
- Make a copy of an existing layer.

A picture may have up to 8000 layers, each with its blending mode and opacity. Memory restrictions, on the other hand, may reduce this limit.

Create and name a new blank layer

The steps:

1. In Photoshop Elements, do one of the following:
- In the Layers panel, click the **New Layer button** to create a layer with the default name and settings. The resultant layer is named after its creation order and is in Normal mode with 100% opacity. (To rename the new layer, double-click it and input a new name into the text box.).
- Select **Layer > New > Layer or New Layer** from the Layers panel menu to create a layer with a name and settings. Enter a name and other details, then click OK.

The new layer is automatically chosen and displayed in the panel above the previously selected layer.

Create a new layer from part of another layer

You can copy a part of a picture from one layer to another while keeping the original intact.

1. Make a selection on an existing layer.
2. **Select one of the following:**
- **Layer > New > Layer Via Copy** to create a new layer from the selected.
- **Layer > New > Layer Via Cut** to cut and paste the selection onto a new layer.

The chosen area is duplicated in a new layer at the same location relative to the image borders.

Convert the Background layer into a regular layer

The Background layer is the image's bottom layer. Other layers are stacked on top of the Background layer, which typically (but not always) includes the photo's actual picture data. The Background layer is always locked to safeguard the picture. You must first convert it to a normal layer if you wish to modify its stacking order, blending mode, or opacity.

1. **Perform one of the following:**
- In the Layers panel, double-click the **Background layer**.
- Navigate to **Layer > New > Layer from Background**.
- Choose the Background layer and then select **Duplicate Layer** from the Layers panel flyout menu to duplicate it as a new layer while keeping the Background layer intact.

Note: No matter how you convert the layer, you can make a duplicate layer of it; just click the converted Background layer and select **Duplicate Layer** from the Layer menu.

2. Give the new layer a name.

When you drag the Background Eraser tool onto the Background layer, it is changed to a standard layer and the erased portions become translucent.

Make a layer the Background layer

If the picture already has a Background layer, you cannot convert it to the Background layer. You must first transform the current Background layer into a standard layer in this situation.

The steps:

1. In the Layers panel, choose a layer.
2. Select **Layer > New > Background from Layer** from the menu. The background color is filled into any transparent portions in the original layer.

Create a new layer group

To avoid clutter and order the layers, establish a new group. Perform one of the following:

1. In Advanced Mode, select the **A New Group button** in the Layers panel to create a new group with default settings.
2. To establish a new group with customizable options, do the following:
- Go to **Layer > New > Group**.
- In the dialog box, provide a name and other selections before clicking OK.

Assign a color to a layer or a group

Color coding layers and groups aid in the identification of related layers in the Layers panel. Simply choose a color by right-clicking the layer or group.

Select a layer to edit

Here are the steps:

1. Open the project you're working on in Adobe Photoshop Elements.
2. If the Layers panel isn't already visible, go to the "**Window**" menu at the top and pick "Layers" to open it.
3. The Layers panel lists all of the layers in your project. A thumbnail picture and a name are assigned to each layer.
4. Choose **Layers**. There are numerous methods for selecting a layer:

Select the Layer

To choose a layer, just click on its thumbnail or name in the Layers panel.

Use the Move Tool

Select the Move tool by using the "V" key on your keyboard. In your document window, click on the element. If there is more than one layer at that moment, clicking will cycle between them.

Use the Tab Key

With the Move tool selected, you can cycle between the levels in your document by using the "**Tab**" key. Continue to press "**Tab**" until the required layer is chosen.

Right-click on the document and select

Right-click on a document window element. You may pick the layer you wish to select from the context menu.

5. To make it simpler to recognize and choose layers, alter layer visibility in the Layers panel by clicking on the eye symbol next to each layer. This toggles the visibility of the chosen layer.
6. Keyboard Shortcuts: Shortcut keys can be used to speed up layer selection. Select the layer below the current one by using the "[" key. Select the layer above the current one by pressing the "]" key.
7. Hold down the "Shift" key while clicking on the layers in the Layers panel to choose several layers. This is handy when you wish to make modifications to numerous levels at the same time.
8. If your project has a complicated structure, try grouping your levels. This facilitates the management and selection of associated layers.
9. By locking a layer, you can prevent unintentional alterations. In the Layers panel, right-click on the layer and choose "**Lock Layer**."
10. After selecting a layer, you may make changes like applying filters, altering opacity, scaling, or adding effects.

The Layer Panel

Adobe Photoshop Elements "**Layers**" panel is a critical component that enables users to work with several levels inside a project. Layers are effectively separate sheets piled on top of one another, each with its own set of components or modifications. Understanding the Layers panel is critical for non-destructive editing. The Layers panel is located in the bottom right corner of the screen by default. If the Layers panel does not display on your screen, you can access it (as well as any of Photoshop's other panels) by navigating to the Window menu in the Menu Bar at the top of the screen and selecting Layers. **A checkmark to the left of a panel's name indicates that the panel is now open on the screen:**

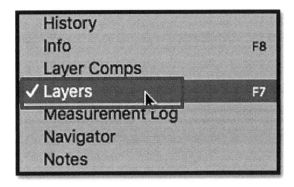

The Name Tab

First and first, how do we know we're looking at the Layers panel? We know since the name tab at the top of the panel says so:

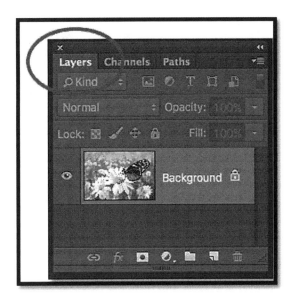

You may have noticed that there are two more tabs to the right of the Layers tab: Channels and Paths, which are both somewhat darker than the Layers panel tab. These are two more panels that are grouped along with the Layers panel. Since Photoshop has so many panels, placing them all on the screen while still allowing room to work might be difficult, therefore Adobe opted to arrange certain panels together into panel groups to conserve space. Simply click on the panel's tab to go to another panel in the group. The panel tab that is presently open in the group is highlighted. Don't be confused by the fact that the Layers panel is bundled with these two other panels. The Channels and Paths panels have nothing to do with the Layers panel except that they are both extensively used in Photoshop, so we can safely ignore them while we focus on the Layers panel.

The Layer Row

When we open a new picture in Photoshop, it opens a new document and is put on a layer. Layers in the document are represented in Photoshop as rows in the Layers panel, with each layer having its row. Each row contains different details about the layer.

However, when we add more layers, more rows will appear:

The Layer Name

Photoshop sets the new picture on the Background layer. The background is the term given to it since it acts as the background for our content. The name of each layer is printed in its row.

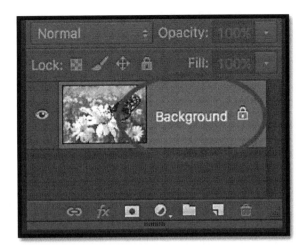

The Preview Thumbnail

A thumbnail picture to the left of a player's name is known as the layer's preview thumbnail since it provides us a little glimpse of what's on that particular layer.

The Active Layer

When a layer is highlighted, it indicates that it is the active layer at the time. Everything we do in the document affects the active layer's contents. When we create a new layer, Photoshop automatically makes it the active layer, but we may alter it manually by simply clicking on the layer we need.

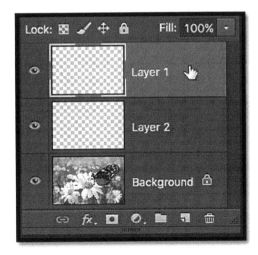

The Layer Visibility Icon

If you want to see the actual picture in the document again, simply switch off the blurred layer by clicking the layer visibility symbol to the left of the preview thumbnail. When the small eyeball appears, it indicates that the layer is visible on the page. By clicking the symbol, you can hide the eyeball as well as the layer:

The actual picture returns in the paper when the blurred layer is removed. The fuzzy layer is still there; we simply can't see it right now.

To reactivate the blurred layer, just click on the empty area where the eyeball used to be.

This restores the blurred layer of the document, obscuring the real picture once again.

Changing a Layer's Blend Mode

In the Layers panel, we can also modify a layer's blend mode, which affects how the layer blends in with the layer(s) underneath it. Blend Mode is located in the top left corner of the Layers panel, immediately below the name tab. It doesn't state "**Blend Mode**" anywhere, but it's the box with "**Normal**" in it by default. To change the blend mode, click on the term "**Normal**" (or whatever other blend mode is currently chosen), then choose a new blend mode from the list that displays.

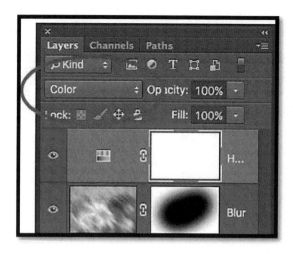

By changing the blend mode of the Hue/Saturation adjustment layer from Normal to Color, the adjustment layer now affects just the colors in the picture. The brightness levels (lights, darks, and all hues in between) remain unaffected.

Locking Layers

The Layers panel also provides many options for locking certain features of a layer. For instance, if a portion of a layer is transparent, we may lock the transparent pixels so that we only modify the layer's real contents and not the transparent portions. Alternatively, we may lock all pixels, whether transparent or not, to prohibit us from making any modifications to the layer. We may also lock the layer's location so that we don't mistakenly move it around within the page. There are four lock selections available, each represented by a little icon and positioned directly below the Blend Mode option. Lock Transparent Pixels, Lock Image Pixels (which locks all pixels on the layer, including the transparent ones), Lock Position, and Lock All are the options from left to right. To activate any of the lock options, click its symbol. When you click the same lock option again, it will be disabled. To access all of the lock settings, you must first choose an actual pixel layer (such as our Blur layer):

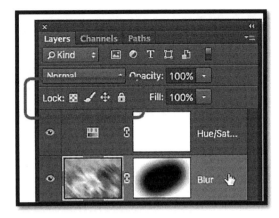

If you pick any or all of these settings, a little lock icon will appear on the far right of the locked layer, as seen on the Background layer, which is locked by default.

The Layer Search Bar

The Search Bar, which you'll find at the very top (just below the name tab), is a new feature that was initially introduced to Photoshop's Layers panel.

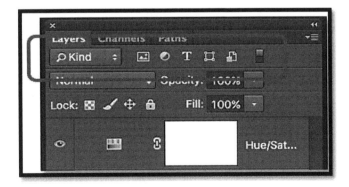

The Search Bar enables us to swiftly filter among the layers of a multi-layered document to discover a particular layer, see just certain kinds of layers, or view only the layers that meet specified criteria. To use the Search Bar, choose a filter type from the left-hand drop-down box. The filter type is set to Kind by default, which means we'll be asking Photoshop to show us just a certain sort of layer. You'll notice various selections to the right of the filter type box depending on whatever filters type you've selected. When you choose **Kind**, you'll see a row of icons, each representing a distinct kind of layer. Pixel layers, adjustment layers, type layers, form layers, and smart objects are shown from left to right. By selecting one of these symbols, you may narrow down the layers in your document to just those of that kind. By clicking several icons, you may examine two or more types of layers at the same time. Deselect an icon by clicking it again to remove it from the search.

In our document, for example, we presently have two-pixel layers and one adjustment layer. If we simply wanted to see the pixel layers, we could click the pixel layers symbol. In the Layers panel, this would hide our adjustment layer and leave just the two-pixel layers visible:

However, remember that filtering layers in the Layers panel does not turn off the other layers in the document. It just removes them from display in the Layers panel. Even though the Hue/Saturation adjustment layer is not now visible in the Layers panel, we may see its impact if we glance at our picture.

To display just the adjustment layer in my Layers panel, click on the pixel layers symbol again to deselect it, and then click on the adjustment layers icon beside it.

When you click on the Filter Type box, you'll get a list of all the ways we may filter our layers, such as by name, layer effect, blend mode, and more. To disable the filtering options, return the filter type to Kind and choose none of the icons. Alternatively, you can turn the filter selections on and off by clicking the light switches to the right of the Search Bar.

Changing the Thumbnail Image Size

Another useful feature of the Layers panel is the option to modify the size of the preview thumbnails. Larger thumbnails allow us to see the contents of each layer more easily, but they also take up more space, limiting the number of levels we can see at once in the levels panel without scrolling. Since large thumbnails cannot fit totally inside the layer row, your layer names may seem truncated.

To accommodate more layers into the Layers panel at once, we may make the preview thumbnails smaller by clicking on the Layers panel menu button again and selecting Panel Options.

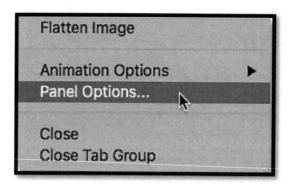

The Layers Panel Options dialog box appears. The Thumbnail Size option is at the top of the dialog box, with three sizes to pick from, as well as the option to turn off the preview thumbnails altogether (None).

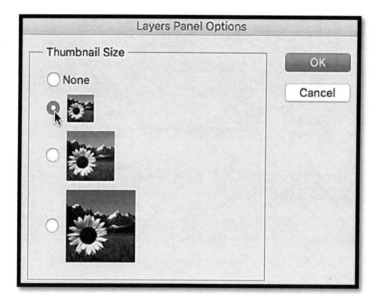

Once you've decided on a size, click OK to exit the dialog box. Everything fits much better on my Layers panel now that the preview thumbnails are much smaller. You can always go back and modify the thumbnail size.

Simplify or Flatten a Layer

When you need to apply filters or modify using painting tools, you must simplify a layer. It is critical to understand how to accomplish it correctly. Fortunately, it is not too difficult. Depending on the strategy you choose, you can complete the task in one or two phases. It's worth noting that "**Simplify**" and "**Rasterize**" are practically synonymous.

How to Simplify a Photoshop Layer

To simplify a layer in Photoshop, go to the "**Layers**" (F7) panel on the right side toolbar, right-click on the layer you want to simplify, and select "**Rasterize Layer**." Alternatively, you can go to "**Layer > Rasterize > Layer**" on the top-of-the-screen menu. As you can see, there are two alternatives. Let's start with the first option, which takes advantage of Photoshop's "Layers" panel.

Using Photoshop's Layers (F7) Panel to Simplify a Layer

Follow these methods to simplify a layer in Photoshop's layers panel:

1. On the right-side toolbar, open the "**Layers**" (F7) panel.
2. Right-click on the layer you want to simplify and choose **Simplify Layer**.
3. Choose "**Rasterize Layer**."

Simplifying a Layer in Photoshop Using the "Layer" Option in the Top Menu

Follow these methods to simplify a layer in Photoshop using the Layer option:

1. To simplify the layer you're working on, choose **"Layer > Rasterize > Layer"** from the menu at the top of the screen.
2. If you need to simplify all layers, go to **"Layer > Rasterize > All Layers"**.

Copy layers from one image file to another

Adobe Photoshop Elements enables you to design graphics and edit pictures for use in professional documents, websites, and online apps. Each graphic might have many distinct layers. Levels are picture parts that may be edited independently without affecting the content of other levels. To generate numerous overlapping pictures inside a photo, copy and paste the content of a layer. You may also copy and paste the layer into another graphic to move a portion of one image to another.

Here are the steps:

1. Open Photoshop Elements and the picture containing the layers you want to replicate. If you want to duplicate the layer in another picture, open that one as well.
2. In the Layers panel, click the thumbnail of the layer you want to duplicate.
3. To select the whole layer, use the "**Ctrl-A**" keyboard shortcut. You can also use the "**Select**" option to select "**All**."
4. To copy the chosen layer, use the "**Ctrl-C**" shortcut. You can also go to the "**Edit**" menu and choose "**Copy**."
5. Choose the picture where you want the cloned layer to be placed. This might be the same or a different picture.
6. "**Ctrl-V**" will paste a copy of the layer. You can also go to the "**Edit**" menu and choose "**Paste**."
7. Repeat for each layer you want to copy, and then save the changes to your image.

Layering Images in Photoshop Elements

Photo layering in Photoshop Elements is a two-step procedure. After opening two (or more) photographs in the Elements Editor, drag the image you want to add to another from the Photo Bin into the real image.

To begin layering pictures in Photoshop Elements Editor, open two or more photographs. Multiple photos can be selected in the Elements Organizer or opened directly in the Elements Editor. When you open many photos, the Photo Bin panel at the bottom of the window will automatically appear. If the panel does not show, click the Photo Bin button at the bottom left of the Editor's main window. Then, under the Photo Bin, click on the thumbnail for the picture you wish to use as the background for your composite image. That picture will then be shown in the Editor's huge preview area. The other picture (or photos) that you have opened in the Editor will still be visible in the Photo Bin window. Simply drag the thumbnail for the appropriate picture into the image preview box to overlay it into the existing image. In other words, you're dragging the relevant thumbnail from the Photo Bin into the image you're now working with. When you let go of the mouse, you'll see that the Layers panel now shows two layers. You may repeat this technique as many times as you want to overlay as many photos as you like.

Merging and flattening layers

If you no longer need to update certain layers, try combining them. There are several reasons why you would wish to blend different layers. For example, if you have numerous adjustment layers, you may wish to combine them into a single layer before making further modifications like sharpening or noise reduction. To merge layers, pick the first layer, hold **Shift**, and then click the final layer you wish to merge (all layers between the first and last will be chosen). After that, right-click the layers and choose Merge Layers. Alternatively, you can select the layers and then hit **Ctrl+E** (or Command+E on a Mac).

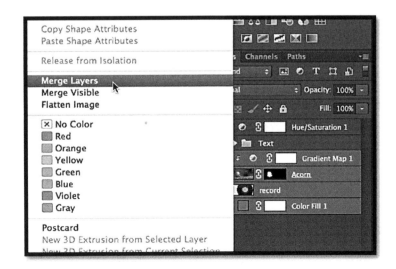

Merging removes the flexibility and control that layers give, so only merge layers if you're certain you don't need to alter them independently. Remember to right-click the layer name rather than the layer icon. The menu will not show otherwise. You can also merge all of your document's layers into a single Background layer. This is referred to as flattening the picture. To do so, right-click any layer and choose Flatten Image. A difficult Photoshop job may be simplified by flattening a picture. It is crucial to remember, however, that you do not need to flatten photos before exporting them. When you save a project as a JPEG or PNG file, all of the layers are automatically flattened since these file formats do not support multiple layers.

Add transparency with Layer Masks

Here are the steps:

1. Load the picture you want to work on into Adobe Photoshop Elements.
2. A background layer can be found in the Layers panel. Right-click on it and choose "**Duplicate Layer**." This step is critical since the original picture should always be kept intact.
3. Select the area you want to make translucent using any selection tool (e.g., Marquee, Lasso, or Magic Wand).
4. Click the "**Add Layer Mask**" button at the bottom of the Layers panel while the chosen region is still active. This symbol resembles a rectangle with a circle within it. Based on your selection, this operation will produce a layer mask.
5. Your layer mask will be shown next to the thumbnail of the copied layer. You can fine-tune the mask even further by using the Brush tool. Select the Brush tool from the toolbar and set the foreground color to black. Painting sections of the layer mask black will make them transparent. If you make a mistake, switch to white in the foreground and paint over the mask to show the sections you wish to preserve.
6. Adjust the overall transparency of the layer by adjusting the layer opacity. Reduce the Opacity slider at the top of the Layers panel to the appropriate level.
7. Once you are pleased with the transparency effect, save your picture. You may want to save it in a format that enables transparency, such as PNG.

Tips:

- **Feathering**: To create a smoother transition between opaque and transparent regions, feather your selection before applying the layer mask.

- **Layer Styles:** Experiment with layer styles to add extra effects to your transparent regions.
- **Undo and History Panel:** If you make a mistake, use the Undo option (Ctrl + Z on Windows, Command + Z on Mac) or check the History panel to go back to a prior state.

Layer masks

You may want just specific elements of a layer to be visible at times. For example, you may wish to remove the background from a layer so that the levels behind it may be seen. While you can use the Eraser tool to delete unwanted sections, this form of destructive editing may be tough to reverse. Layer masks, fortunately, enable you to reveal and hide elements of any layer in a non-destructive manner. Creating a layer mask may be difficult, so let's start with one that's already completed. In the Layers panel, the layer mask is represented by the black-and-white thumbnail to the right of the layer icon. Take note of how the visible portions in the document window correlate to the white areas on the layer mask thumbnail.

Editing a layer mask

Let's try adjusting the Acorn layer mask to better understand how layer masks function.

1. In the Layers panel, click the thumbnail for the layer mask.
2. Then, from the Tools panel, choose the **Brush tool** and set the Foreground Color to white.
3. Drag your picture to expose parts of the layer.

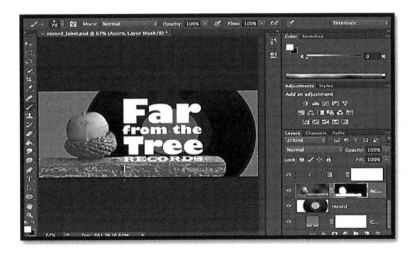

4. Set the Foreground Color to black, then click and drag your picture to hide layers.
5. Continue to use the Brush tool until you're happy with the outcome.

To acquire the greatest potential outcome, you'll need to take your time and work carefully, particularly when refining the margins of the layer mask around an item. It may be useful to change the Brush tool's size, hardness, and opacity.

Creating a new layer mask

You may want to try making your layer masks now that you know more about them.

1. Select a layer, and then click the **Layer Mask button** at the Layers panel's bottom.

2. In the Layers panel, the layer mask will display as a white thumbnail next to the layer icon. The layer mask may then be edited by selecting the thumbnail and using the Brush tool.

3. It's worth noting that you can use numerous layer masks on the same layer. On the other hand, since this might grow difficult, we suggest simply using one layer mask per layer.

Using layer masks with adjustment layers

A layer mask can be used to control which regions of your picture are impacted by an adjustment layer. If you had a Black-and-white adjustment layer, for example, you might use a layer mask to convert select regions to black and white while leaving other parts untouched. Every adjustment layer comes with a layer mask by default, so you won't have to build one. Simply select the layer mask and use the Brush tool to alter it.

Removing a layer mask

1. Drag the layer mask thumbnail to the Trash Can in the Layers panel's lower-right corner.
2. A dialog window will be shown. To remove the layer mask, select **Delete**. Choosing Apply will erase the sections of the layer that are now hidden, so you should avoid it unless you are certain that you no longer want these areas of the picture.

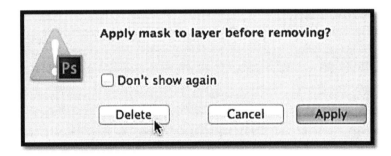

3. You can also temporarily deactivate the layer mask by holding down the Shift key and clicking the thumbnail.

Create non-square graphics

Here are the steps:

1. On your PC, launch Adobe Photoshop Elements.
2. Click on **File > New > Blank File.**

3. Determine the width and height of your graphic. Be careful to add alternative values if you want a non-square form.
4. Customize the resolution and color mode to your liking.
5. Select OK. This will generate a new blank canvas with the dimensions you choose.
6. Adjust the Canvas Size. Go to **Image > Resize > Canvas Size**. The Canvas Size dialog box will be shown.
7. To create a non-square design, change the width or height as required. Check the "**Relative**" box so that you may adjust one dimension without impacting the other.
8. Select an Anchor Point. This defines where your existing picture will appear on the canvas when you resize it. If you're extending the width, for example, you may want to tie it to the left side.
9. Select OK. This resizes the canvas without changing the content.
10. You can now generate or import components for your design now that you have a non-square canvas. Use tools like the Text Tool, Shape Tool, Brush Tool, and so on.
11. Navigate to **File > Save As**. Select a file type (for example, PSD for subsequent editing or PNG/JPEG for web sharing).
12. Give your artwork a file name and store it somewhere.
13. Make any required adjustments and then click OK.

Tips

Use layers

Use layers to arrange and separate various aspects of your design.

Transform Tool

You can resize, rotate, and skew layers with the Transform tool (**Edit > Free Transform**).

Guides

You can use guides (View > New Guide) to precisely align and position components.

Save As Copy

Before making large changes, try using "**Save As**" to make a backup of your work. In this manner, you may always return to the original if necessary.

File formats that support alpha

An alpha channel is a supplementary channel that holds information about an image's transparency. It is often used to create and save masks, selections, and transparency data.

The following file types are commonly supported by Photoshop Elements:

1. **PSD (Adobe Photoshop Document):**

The PSD format is Adobe Photoshop and Photoshop Elements' native file format. Layers, transparency, and alpha channels are all supported. When you save a file in PSD format, all of the layer information, including transparency masks, is preserved.

2. **PNG (Portable Network Graphics):**

PNG is a popular picture format that allows for lossless compression and, more significantly, an alpha channel for transparency. When you save a picture in PNG format from Photoshop Elements, the transparency information is preserved.

3. **TIFF (Tagged Image File Format):**

TIFF is a flexible file format with layers and alpha channels. It is a popular format for high-quality photos that may be utilized in both print and digital settings. When exporting a TIFF file from Photoshop Elements, verify that the right selections for layers and transparency are selected.

4. **PSB (Large Document Format):**

PSB is a PSD format extension that is utilized for bigger files that exceed the PSD file size constraints. PSB, like PSD, has layers and alpha channels.

5. **PDF (Portable Document Format):**

PDF documents may include both raster and vector graphics. When you export a Photoshop Elements file as a PDF, it may contain transparency information, making it appropriate for publications that need transparency.

6. **Gif (Graphics Interchange Format):**

While the restricted color palette of GIF makes it unsuitable for high-quality photos, it does offer transparency. GIF, on the other hand, is more typically used for basic graphics, logos, and animations than for complicated pictures.

Transform and warp a layer

Transforming a Layer

Here are the steps:

1. Open Adobe Photoshop Elements.
2. Open the picture or create a new document containing the layer to be transformed.
3. In the Layers panel, make sure the layer you want to change is selected.
4. Go to the top menu and choose **"Image" > "Transform."**
5. A submenu containing transformation selections such as Scale, Rotate, Skew, Distort, Perspective, and more will be displayed.
6. Select the transformation type that best meets your requirements. For example, choose "**Scale**" to resize the layer.
7. **Carry out the Transformation:**
- The selected layer will be surrounded by a bounding box.
- Hover over any of the bounding box's corners or edges until your cursor changes, then click and drag to modify the size or form.
- To keep the aspect ratio, hold down the "**Shift**" key while dragging.
- To apply the transformation, press "**Enter**" or click the checkbox in the options bar.

Warping a Layer

1. In the Layers panel, choose the layer to warp.
2. To access the Warp Options, go to the top menu and choose **"Edit" > "Transform" > "Warp."**
3. A mesh overlay will be shown over your layer. Hover your pointer over the mesh points to observe how it changes.
4. To warp the layer, click and drag these locations. You can also use the control points between the mesh points for more exact adjustments.
5. To apply the warp, press "**Enter**" or click the checkbox in the options bar.

6. Select "**Custom**" from the warp selections in the settings bar if you need greater control. This enables you to manually position and alter control points for a more personalized warp.
7. When you click on a control point, you'll see handles that you may use to change the warp.
8. To obtain the appropriate warp effect, move, rotate, or scale these handles.
9. To apply the custom warp, press "**Enter**" or click the checkbox.

Frequently Asked Questions

1. How do you select a layer to edit in Photoshop Elements?
2. How do you simplify or flatten a layer?
3. How does the layer work?
4. How do you transform or warp a layer?
5. How do you copy layers from one image file to another?

CHAPTER TEN

CREATE AND EDIT TEXT

Overview

Chapter ten discusses text in Photoshop Elements including the different tools for typing, how to re-edit a text layer, and others.

The Type Tools

Photoshop Elements' type capabilities enable users to add and alter text into their photos.

Here's a comprehensive look at Adobe Photoshop Elements' Type Tools:

1. **Horizontal Type Tool (T)**
   - The main tool for adding horizontal text to your photographs is the Horizontal Type Tool.
   - Select the Horizontal Type Tool from the toolbar or hit the 'T' key to use it.
   - A text box will appear when you click on the picture where you want to begin typing.
   - After that, you can enter your content right into the text field.
2. **Vertical Type Tool (T):**
   - Add vertical text to your photos with the Vertical Type Tool.
   - To use the Vertical Type Tool, go to the toolbar and choose it, or hit 'T' and then pick the vertical type option.
   - Click on the picture where you want to begin your vertical text, and a text box for vertical input will emerge.
3. **Type Mask Tools (Horizontal and Vertical):**
   - With these tools, you can create a text mask, in which the text serves as a mask for an underlying picture or layer.
   - From the toolbar, choose either the Horizontal or Vertical Type Mask Tool.
   - To create a text box, click and drag. The words will fill the box as you enter, and the underlying picture will be shown only inside the text.
4. **Type Mask Reveal Tools (Horizontal and Vertical):**
   - After you've created a type mask, use these tools to expose more or less of the underlying picture inside the text.
   - Choose from the Horizontal and Vertical Type Mask Reveal Tools.

- Adjust the visibility of the underlying picture by clicking and dragging inside the text.
5. **Text on Selection Tool:**
- With this tool, you can add text to a specific region of a picture.
- Make a selection using any selection tool (for example, the Rectangular Marquee Tool).
- Choose the Text on Selection Tool and start typing within the selection.
6. **Text on Custom Path Tool:**
- Use this tool to add text along a specified route or shape.
- Using the Pen Tool or any shape tool, create a custom path.
- To add text, choose the Text on Custom Path Tool and click along the path.
7. **Text Options and Styles:**
- Photoshop Elements has several text formatting and stylistic selections.
- The Type Tool options bar allows you to modify the font family, size, color, alignment, and other text qualities.
- The Character and Paragraph panels provide further text formatting options.
8. **Warped Text**:
- Photoshop Elements lets you add warp effects to text such as arch, bulge, flag, wave, and so on.
- These selections are accessible via the "**Create Warped Text**" button in the Type Tool options bar.
9. **Text Effects:**
- Elements include pre-built text effects that you can use to create innovative and stylish styles for your text.
- To access these effects, click the "fx" button at the bottom of the Layers panel.
10. **Text Layers:**
- In the Layers panel, each text element you add to a picture creates a new text layer.
- Texts layers can be moved, resized, and have numerous layer effects applied to them individually.

Edit type in a type layer

You can change the text and apply layer commands to it once you create a text layer. Text layers allow you to input new text, edit current text, and erase text. When styles are applied to a text layer, the characteristics of those styles are sent down to all text.

A text layer's orientation (horizontal or vertical) may also be changed. The type lines run from top to bottom when a text layer is vertical. The type lines flow from left to right when a text layer is horizontal.

The steps:

1. **Perform one of the following:**

   - Choose the **Horizontal Type tool or the Vertical Type tool** (or choose Move and double-click the text).
   - In Advanced Mode, in the Layers panel, choose the text layer.

   When you click on an existing text layer, the Type tool's insertion point shifts to match the layer's orientation.

2. Insert the insertion point into the text and then perform one of the following:
   - Set the insertion point by clicking.
   - Choose one or more characters to adjust.
   - Enter whatever text you like.
3. Commit the text layer via one of the following methods:
   - In the options bar, click the **Commit button**.
   - Hover your mouse over the picture.
   - Choose a different tool from the toolbox.

Select characters

The steps:

1. Choose a type tool.
2. Choose the text layer in the Layers panel, or click in the text flow to pick a text layer automatically.
3. **Insert the insertion point into the text and then perform one of the following:**
   - Use your mouse to choose one or more characters.
   - Click twice to choose a single word.
   - Use three clicks to select an entire line of text.
   - To select a range of characters, click a place in the text and then Shift-click.
   - To select all of the characters in the layer, go to **Select > All**.

- To choose characters using the arrow keys, hold Shift and hit the **Right or Left Arrow key**.

Choose a font family and style

A font is a collection of characters (letters, numerals, or symbols) that all have the same weight, width, and style. When you choose a font, you may choose the font family (for example, Arial) and the type style separately. A type style is a modified form of a single typeface in a font family (for example, normal, bold, or italic). Each typeface has a different set of accessible typestyles. If a font doesn't have the desired style, you may use faux (false) versions of bold and italic. A fake font is a computer-generated variant of a font that closely resembles another typeface design.

Here are the steps:

1. If you want to adjust the font of the current text, pick one or more characters. To alter the font of all characters in a layer, select the text layer in the Layers panel and then modify the font type, style, size, alignment, and color using the buttons and selections in the options bar.
2. Select a font family from the Font Family pop-up menu in the options bar.
3. **Perform one of the following:**
- In the selections bar, choose a **font style** from the Font Style pop-up menu.
- If the font family you selected does not have a bold or italic style, click the Faux Bold, Faux Italic, or both buttons.

Note: The color of the type you enter is determined by the current foreground color; however, you can change the color of the type before or after you input text. You can adjust the color of individual letters or all types in a layer while changing existing text layers.

Choose a font size

The size of the font controls how big it appears in the picture. The actual size of the typeface is determined by the image's resolution. In a 72 ppi picture, a capital letter in 72-point lettering is around 1 inch high. Since pixels in higher-resolution photos are packed more densely, they lower the size of a particular letter point.

The steps:

1. If you're adjusting the size of existing text, select one or more characters. Select the text layer in the Layers panel to modify the size of all the letters in that layer.
2. Choose between the Horizontal Type tool or the Vertical Type tool.
3. Enter or pick a new Size value in the options bar. You can enter a size that is more than 72 points. The value you input is translated to the unit of measurement of your choice. Enter the unit (in, cm, pt, px, or pica) after the value in the Size text box to use another unit of measurement.

Note: The type's default unit of measurement is points. However, you can change the unit of measurement in the Preferences dialog box's Units & Rulers section. Select a unit of measurement for Type by going to **Edit > Preferences > Units & Rulers**.

Change text color

Adjust the color of the font before or after you input text. You can change the color of individual letters or all types in a layer while changing existing text layers. A gradient can also be applied to text in a text layer.

1. **Perform one of the following:**

- Use a type tool to modify the color of text before typing it.
- To change the color of existing text, choose a type tool and then drag to pick it.

2. Choose the **Color menu** in the options bar to choose a color from a selection of color swatches. Click ⬤ to choose a color and add it to the palette.

Apply style to text

Text effects are available. Any Effects panel effect can be applied to text in a layer.

Here are the steps:

1. Write and commit the text to which you want to apply a style for new content. Under the Tool Options bar, choose one of the available presets.
2. Select a text-containing layer for existing text.
3. Double-click the thumbnail of a style you want to apply to the text in the Effects panel.

Warp type

Warping enables you to distort text to conform to a variety of forms, such as an arc or a wave. Warping affects all characters in a text layer; individual characters cannot be warped. Furthermore, you cannot bend fake bold lettering.

The steps:

1. Select a text layer in the Edit workspace.
2. **Perform one of the following:**
- In the tool selections menu, choose a type tool and click the **Warp button**.
- Select **Layer > Type > Warp Text**.
3. Select a warp style from the Style drop-down menu. The fundamental form of the twisted text is determined by the style.
4. Choose a warp effect orientation: horizontal or vertical.
5. (Optional) Enter values for additional warping options to modify the warp effect's orientation and perspective:
- Bend to determine the amount of warp.
- Horizontal and vertical distortions provide perspective to the warp.
6. Select **OK**.

Unwarp type

Here are the steps:

1. Select a warped text layer.
2. Choose a **type tool** and then click the Warp button in the options bar, or go to **Layer > Type > Warp Text**.
3. Select **None** from the Style drop-down option, then select **OK**.

Change the orientation of a type layer

Follow the steps below:

1. **Perform one of the following:**
   - Choose the text, and then in the options bar, select the **Toggle Text Orientation button**.
   - Select **Layer > Type > Horizontal or Layer > Type > Vertical** after selecting a text layer.

Placing text on a layer

Follow the steps below:

1. Click the **Organizer button** in the Edit workspace's Menu bar. The Organizer is revealed as a result of this.
2. Locate and select your file.
3. In the menu bar, press the arrow to the right of the Fix tab and select **Full Photo Edit** from the drop-down menu, or use the keyboard shortcut Ctrl+I (Windows) Command+I (Mac OS). After you've opened a picture, you'll learn how to create a font layer. To insert a type, you do not need to create a new layer. When you use the Type tool on a picture, Photoshop Elements automatically produces a new type layer.
4. From the Toolbox, choose the **Horizontal Type tool.** To ensure that you have the right tool, click and hold on the Type tool to see the hidden tools.
5. Select anywhere in the image's bottom center. You should notice a new layer titled Layer 1 in your Layers panel, as well as a flashing cursor in the bottom center of your screen.

6. Then enter your desired text.

Formatting a text layer

Learn how to adjust the size and font of text once you've learned how to insert it into a picture.

The steps:

1. Select the full text using the **Horizontal Type tool** by double-clicking on the text layer thumbnail.
2. Now that the text has been chosen, go to the top of the screen and look at the Options bar. The first option on the left allows you to change the font. By clicking on the downward-facing arrow to the right of the font name, you may access the drop-down menu. You can choose whatever font you like, or if you want to follow along, use Hobo Std.

3. Ensure your text is still chosen, and then choose a size from the drop-down option. You can select whatever size you like, or 72 if you want to follow along.

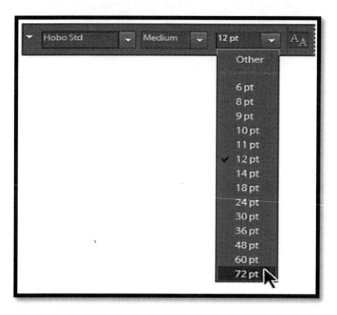

4. Even though the drop-down menu only goes up to 72, you are not restricted to that size. To commit your change, highlight 72 in the Options bar and write 80, then click the green checkmark in the Options bar. The modification should be visible on your screen immediately. If you need to relocate your type, use the Move tool to move it to the center of the picture.

Use your arrow keys

Another method for changing any number value in any field inside Photoshop Elements is to simply click within the field, either to the right or left, or even in the center of a number, and then use your keyboard's up and down arrow keys to alter the value. This way, you can see what size you desire. Try it with your font name as well; you can see how your text will appear in all of the fonts you have installed on your computer!

Editing a text layer

Since text is on its layer, it is editable, even after you have deselected it and closed the document, as long as it is saved in .psd format. You will save the document, shut it, and make some additional modifications to the text in this exercise.

Here are the steps:

1. Proceed to save the .psd file to your PC by going to **File > Save As**. In the Save As dialog box, enter a name in the Name text field, choose **Photoshop** as the format, and save it to the folder. You will now reselect the text, alter its color, and move it.
2. From the Toolbox, choose the **Horizontal Type tool**. Click on the type; a flashing cursor should now appear in the type. To pick the sentence, click three times in a row. You may modify the color of the type now that it has been picked.
3. In the Options bar at the top of the workspace, choose the color block from the drop-down menu. You can select whatever color you like, or if you want to keep things simple, choose black, then click on the color block to exit the color option. To commit the edit, click the **green checkmark** in the Options box. You will move the text now that it is a different color.

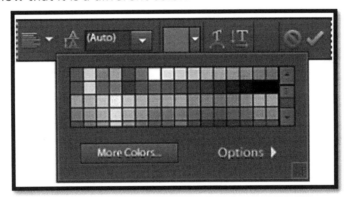

4. Choose the **Move tool** and move the text to the top of the screen while keeping it centered.
5. Select **File > Save**. If prompted, specify a file name and location, then choose **File > Close** to close the file.

The Type Tool Options Bin

Here's an overview of Adobe Photoshop Elements' Type Tool and its options

Set the following Type tool options in the options bar:

Font Family

A font family is applied to new or existing text.

Font Style

Apply font styles like bold to new or existing text.

Font Size

Changes the font size of new or existing text.

Color Menu

Adds a color to new or chosen text.

Leading Menu

Sets the spacing between new or selected text lines.

Tracking

Sets the amount of space between letters in fresh or chosen text.

Faux Bold

To create existing text, use a bold style. If your font does not have a genuine bold style that you can pick from the Font Style menu, use this option.

Faux Italic

The italic style is applied to new or existing text. If your font does not include a genuine italic or oblique style that you can pick from the Font Style menu, use this option.

Underline

Adds an underlining to new text or a portion of existing text.

Strikethrough

A line is drawn through new or chosen existing text.

Align Text

Text alignment is specified. If the text orientation is horizontal, you may align it to the left, center, or right. For vertical text, choose the top, middle, or bottom.

Toggle Text Orientation

Vertical text becomes horizontal, while horizontal text becomes vertical.

Warp Text

Text on the specified layer is warped.

Anti-aliased

Anti-aliasing is used to make text look smoother.

Shape and resize your text

The steps:

1. To begin, launch **Adobe Photoshop Elements**.
2. Begin a new project or open an existing picture to which you'd want to add text.
3. Select the "**Text Tool**" from the toolbar. It generally appears as a capital 'T'.
4. After selecting the Text Tool, click on the picture where you want to add text. You will see a flashing cursor, suggesting that you can begin typing.
5. Start entering the text you want. Before or after typing, you can change the font, size, and color.
6. Once you've chosen the text, you can change its attributes by utilizing the selections in the Text Selections Bar at the top of the screen:
- **Font**: From the drop-down menu, choose a font.
- **Font Style:** Change the font style to normal, bold, italic, and so on.
- **Font size:** Change the font size by using the size drop-down menu or by inputting a particular size.
- **Color**: To change the color of the text, click on the color swatch.
7. To enlarge the text, click and drag one of the text bounding box's corner handles while holding down the "**Shift**" key to maintain the aspect ratio. You can also change the font size in the Text Options Bar.
8. You can further change the text by using the Transform tool. Select the text layer, then go to the "**Enhance**" menu and select "**Transform**" or use the keyboard shortcut (Ctrl+T for Windows, Command+T for Mac). Then, to alter the text, click and drag the corner handles. When you're finished, hit the "**Enter**" key.
9. Use the Text Options Bar's alignment options to position your text horizontally and vertically. You can also place the text manually by clicking and dragging.

10. To apply effects to your text such as drop shadows, bevels, or gradients, go to the "**Layer**" menu, select "**Layer Style**," and then select the required effect.
11. Save your work whenever you're pleased with the text positioning, size, and style. The project file may be saved in Photoshop Elements format (PSE) or exported to a standard picture format such as JPEG or PNG.
12. If you make a mistake, you can undo (Ctrl+Z for Windows, Command+Z for Mac) or redo (Ctrl+Shift+Z for Windows, Command+Shift+Z for Mac) your actions using the "**Edit**" option.

Other transform options

Type on a Selection, Shape, or Path

Use the Text on the Shape tool

Text can be added to any of the shapes accessible in the Text on Shape tool.

Here are the steps:

1. Choose the **Text** on Shape tool. To change the current text tool quickly, select **Option** and then click the current tool.

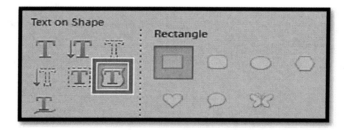

2. Choose the shape to which you want to add text from the available shapes. To make the form, move the pointer over the picture.
3. Hover the mouse over the path until the cursor icon switches to text mode to add text to the picture. To add text, click the point.
4. After you've finished typing, click **Commit** ✓. Text must be typed within some of the forms. By holding Cmd and clicking and dragging the mouse (the text shows as a little arrow), you can move the text about the path or inside/outside. You can drag that cursor into a certain location, and the text path can be within or outside of an area.

Use the Text on the Selection tool

Add text to the contour of a path formed from a selection. When you commit a selection, it is turned into a route where you can write text.

The steps:

1. Choose the **Text on Selection tool**. To change the current text tool quickly, select **Option** and then click the current tool.

2. Place the mouse on the item in the picture and drag it until you have the selection you want. The Offset slider allows you to change the size of your selection.
3. Hover the mouse over the path until the cursor icon switches to text mode to add text to the picture. To add text, click the point. After you've added text, you can edit it just like ordinary text.
4. After you've finished inserting text, click the **Commit button**. Cancel to restart your process.

Make use of the Text on Custom Path tool.

Follow the steps below:

1. Choose the Text on **Custom Path tool**. To change the current text tool rapidly, choose **Option** and then select the current tool.

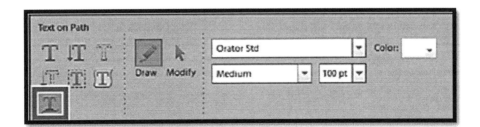

2. Create a custom path around the picture. From the tool options bar, you can commit/cancel the drawn path to redraw it.
3. Click Modify in the tool options bar to adjust or redraw the path. To change the path, use the nodes that appear on it.
4. After you've finished drawing a path, click the mouse at any place along it to add text. Alter the text in the same manner that you would normally change text.
5. After you've finished typing, select the **Commit button**.

Frequently Asked Questions

1. How do you use the type tools in Photoshop Elements?
2. How do you shape and resize your text?
3. How do you type on a selection or path?
4. How do you re-edit a text layer?
5. How do you use the type tool options bin?

CHAPTER ELEVEN
ADD PHOTO EFFECTS AND FILTERS

Overview

Chapter eleven talks about adding photo effects and filters in Photoshop Elements 2024. Here, you can learn how to use the filter gallery, the effects panel, the filters panel and so much more.

The Filter/Adjustments menu

Filters can be used to clean up or modify photographs. Filters can also be used to add distinctive art effects or to generate unique transformations via distortion effects. In addition to the filters offered by Adobe, certain third-party developers' filters are accessible as plug-ins. These plug-in filters display at the bottom of the Filter lists once installed.

Filters can be applied in three ways:

Filter menu

Contains all available filters and allows you to apply them separately.

Filter Gallery

Shows thumbnail samples of what each filter works, similar to how the panel does. The Filter Gallery allows you to apply filters cumulatively as well as individually. You can also rearrange filters and alter the settings of each one to create the desired look. Since it is so versatile, the Filter Gallery is often the best option for applying filters. The Filter Gallery, however, does not include all of the filters provided in the Filter menu.

Filters Panel

Shows thumbnail illustrations of what each filter in the Filter menu performs. In the Expert view, the Filters panel lets you apply filters to individual photos.

Tips for Using Filters

The following information will assist you in comprehending the process of adding filters to your photos

- View the filter's output. Applying filters to a huge picture might take some time. The Filter Gallery makes it easier to see what the filter does. The Filter Options dialog box and the document window both allow you to examine the results of most filters. You may then apply the filter or abort the process without wasting time.
- Filters only affect the active part of a picture. Filters only influence the active, visible layer or a specific part of the layer.
- Filters do not apply to all photos. Some filters cannot be applied to grayscale photos, nor can any filters be applied to bitmap or indexed-color images. Many filters are incompatible with 16-bit pictures.
- You can use the previous filter again. The most recently used filter displays at the top of the Filter menu. Reapply it with the same settings as before to improve the picture even more.

Tips for Creating Filtered Visual Effects

To generate unique visual effects using filters, use the following techniques:

- Highlight the filter boundaries. When applying a filter to a specified area, feathering the selection before applying the filter softens the edges of the filter effect.
- Apply filters sequentially to create effects. To create an effect, apply filters to individual layers or numerous levels in sequence. The effect is blended by selecting various blending modes in the Layers window. A layer must be visible and contain pixels for a filter to impact it.
- Design textures and backgrounds. Create a variety of backgrounds and textures by adding filters to solid-color or grayscale photographs. These textures may then be blurred. When applied to solid colors, certain filters (for example, the Glass filter) have little or no apparent impact, while others yield fascinating effects. Add Noise, Chalk and charcoal, Clouds, Conté Crayon, Difference Clouds, Glass, Graphic Pen, Halftone Pattern, Mezzotint, Note Paper, Pointillize, Reticulation, Rough Pastels,

Sponge, or Underpainting may be used to create these hues. You may also use any of the Texture submenu filters.
- Enhance the image quality and uniformity. When you apply the same filter to each picture, you can hide flaws, edit or improve photos, or make a sequence of images seem identical.

Apply a filter

The steps:

1. **Select the area to which you want to apply the filter:**
- To apply a filter to a complete layer, remove any previously selected areas before selecting the layer in the Layers panel.
- To apply a filter to a section of a layer, choose an area using any selection tool.
2. **Select how to use the filter:**
- To use the Filter Gallery, go to **Filter > Filter Gallery**, pick a category, and then click the filter you want to use.
- To access the Filters panel, go to **Window > Filters**, pick a category, and then double-click the filter you want to use.
- To use the Filter menu, choose **Filter**, then a submenu, and finally, the filter you want to apply. A Filter Options dialog box displays if a filter name is preceded by ellipses (...).
3. Enter values or pick selections if a dialog box opens.
4. **Choose the Preview option if it is present to preview the filter in the document window. Use one of the following techniques to preview the filter, depending on the filter and how you're using it:**
- To zoom in or out, use the + or - buttons in the preview box.
- To choose a zoom percentage, click the zoom bar (where the zoom percentage shows).
- Click and drag inside the preview window to center a particular area of the picture.
- To hide the filter thumbnails, click the **Show/Hide button** at the top of the dialog box. Hitting the hide button widens the preview area.
- Hover your mouse over a filter to hide the effect in the preview picture.
5. Hold down Alt (Option on Mac OS) while moving a slider in the dialog box to get a real-time preview (real-time rendering).
6. To center a particular section of the picture in the preview window, click on the image window. (Not all preview windows will support this.)

Note: The preview is being displayed as shown by a flashing line under the preview size.

7. **If you're using the Filter Gallery or the filter opens in the Filter Gallery, perform one of the following and then select OK:**
   - At the bottom of the dialog box, select the **New Effect Layer button** and choose an extra filter to apply. You may apply several filters by adding multiple effect layers.
   - Drag a filter name to a different place in the list of applied filters at the bottom of the dialog box to rearrange it. Rearranging the order of your filters may drastically alter the appearance of your picture.
   - To remove an applied filter, select it and select the **Delete Effect Layer button**.
8. **If you're using the Filters panel, do the following steps and then select OK:**
   - Select the filter you want to use on your picture.

If time permits, you may undertake one of the following:

- Use the sliders to change the strength of the filter.
- Select the Apply Extra option to apply extra effects, which are available for a select one-click filter (such as Blur).
- Some filters allow for more customization. Select the **Advanced Options option**. Adjust the sliders and pick options in the dialog box to make changes to the filter applied to the picture.

Filter Categories

Use the following filter categories:

Correct Camera Distortion

Corrects typical lens faults including barrel and pincushion distortion, as well as vignetting. In addition, the filter spins a picture and corrects the visual perspective caused by vertical or horizontal camera tilt.

Adjustment Filters

Change the brightness, color, grayscale range, and tonal levels of individual pixels in a picture. Color pixels are converted to black and white.

Artistic Filters

Create a one-of-a-kind effect by simulating a painting's appearance on conventional media.

Blur Filters

Make a selection or a picture softer. This is useful for retouching.

Brush Stroke Filters

Using several brush and ink stroke effects, create a painterly or fine-art style.

Distort Filters

Create three-dimensional and other reshaping effects by geometrically distorting a picture.

Noise Filters

Remove troublesome areas such as dust and scratches by blending a selection into the surrounding pixels.

Pixelate Filters

Clumps of pixels with identical color values can be used to define an image or selection.

Render Filters

In a picture, add cloud patterns, lens flare, fibers, and lightning effects.

Sketch Filters

Texture can be used to provide depth or to create a hand-drawn effect.

Stylize Filters

By shifting pixels and increasing contrast, you can create a painted or impressionistic image.

Texture Filters

Add depth or solidity to the appearance, or go for an organic effect.

Other Filters

Allows you to build your filter effects, edit masks, offset a selection inside an image, and make rapid color changes.

Digimarc Filter

Allows you to see a Digimarc watermark.

The Gallery of Filters

The Filter Gallery (**Filter > Filter Gallery**) allows you to apply filters cumulatively as well as individually. You can also rearrange filters and alter the settings of each one to create the desired look. Since you can apply several filters to a picture using the Filter Gallery dialog box, you have a lot of control over how each filter affects your image. It is versatile and simple to use and the Filter Gallery is often the best option for applying filters.

Texture and glass surface options

Texturizing options are available in the Conté Crayon, Glass, Rough Pastels, Texturizer, and Underpainting filters. These settings make photographs seem as if they were painted on surfaces like canvas or brick, or as if they were seen through glass blocks.

Texture

Specifies the texture to be used. You can also choose a Photoshop file by clicking **Load Texture**.

Scaling

The influence on the picture surface is increased or decreased.

Relief (If available)

Adjusts the surface depth of the texture.

Light (if available)

Set the light source's direction in the picture.

Invert

Reverses the bright and dark hues on the surface.

Enhance performance by using filters and effects

A few filters and effects use a lot of memory, particularly when used on high-resolution photos.

You can boost your performance by using the following techniques:

- Experiment with filters and settings on a tiny portion of the photo.
- Experiment with filters and settings on a smaller, scaled version of your photo. When you're happy with the results, apply the same adjustments to your original picture.
- Clear the clipboard, undo history, or both before running the filter or effect to free up memory. Select **Edit > Clear > [command]** from the menu.
- Close from other apps to free up memory.
- Modify filter settings to reduce the complexity of memory-intensive filters. Cutout, Stained Glass, Chrome, Ripple, Spatter, Sprayed Strokes, and Glass are memory-intensive filters. (For example, increasing cell size reduces the complexity of the Stained Glass filter; increasing Edge Simplicity, decreasing Edge Fidelity or both reduces the complexity of the Cutout filter.)

The Effects, Filters, and Styles panels

The Effects panel

The Effects panel is a centralized spot where you can apply picture effects. In Quick and Advanced mode, the Effects panel is positioned on the taskbar by default. It shows thumbnails of the artwork or effects that can be added or applied to a picture. Most sections include a menu of category selections and subcategories. There are three types of effects available: artistic, classic, and color match.

Using the Graphics panel

The Graphics panel allows you to apply artwork, theme embellishments, and text styles to your photos in a single area. Select **Window > Graphics** to open the Graphics panel.

The following sections of the Graphics panel provide numerous objects that may be used to improve your photographs. You can, for example, choose from a variety of frames, backgrounds, pictures, shapes, and text. A drop-down menu under each tab assists in selecting the appropriate frames, backgrounds, pictures, shapes, or text to replicate. Each section contains thumbnail samples of artwork or effects that may be added or applied to a picture. Most sections include a menu of category selections and subcategories.

Add stylized shapes or graphics to an image

When you add a shape or graphic to a picture, it becomes a new layer and does not affect the original image.

The steps:

1. Select a category (for example, By Event or By Activity) and a subcategory (for example, Baby or Cooking) in the Graphics panel.
2. Select a color for the shape from the toolbox.
3. **Perform one of the following:**
- Select a thumbnail by double-clicking it.
- Click and drag the thumbnail to the picture.
4. To move or resize the form or graphic, implement using the **Move tool**.

Add an artistic background to an image

When you add an artistic background to a picture, the current background layer is replaced. You might, for example, use the selection tools to create a layer that separates your family members from a kitchen background, and then replace the kitchen with a natural background.

The steps:

1. If your picture just has one layer, pick it and go to **Layer > Duplicate Layer**. Give the layer a name and click OK.
2. In the Layers panel, choose the **Background layer**.
3. Click **Backgrounds** from the drop-down menu in the Graphics panel.
4. **Then perform one of the following:**
- Select a thumbnail by double-clicking it.
- Click and drag the thumbnail to the picture.

Add a frame or theme to an image

Frames show a blank (gray) space for the picture when you add a frame or theme to a photo project. Drag a picture from the Photo Bin to the empty spot.

The steps:

1. Select **Frames** from the drop-down menu in the Graphics panel.
2. **Perform one of the following:**
- **Choose a thumbnail > Click Apply**.
- Select a thumbnail by double-clicking it.
- Move the thumbnail to the empty background.
3. Drag or move a picture from the Photo Bin into the frame.
4. Use the slider to resize the picture in the frame or theme border, then select the **Commit or Cancel button** to save your changes.
5. Use the Move tool to center the picture, then click the Commit or Cancel buttons to save your changes.

About photo effects

Photo effects allow you to easily change the appearance of your photographs.

Frame

Apply different effects to the borders of a layer or a section of a layer. A frame also generates a drop zone where you can simply add or alter content.

Image Effects

Effects are applied to a copy of a chosen layer. When you apply the Blizzard effect to a picture, it seems to be snowing. The Neon Glow effect transforms the image into a striking neon image. Image effects such as Oil Pastel and Soft Focus may be used to soften or blur an image. Image effects may also be combined; however, you may be required to flatten layers first.

Textures

Texture layers can be added to a picture. You can apply texture as a background to a new, blank picture or an existing image. You can also build fascinating and appealing photos by organizing layers and experimenting with opacity and other layer tools.

Note: Several photo effects use filters with altered values.

Artistic effects

Transform your photos with effects inspired by legendary works of art or popular art styles with a single click. Choose from a variety of wonderful Artistic effects that you can apply to all or part of your picture, and quickly tweak the results to get the precise appearance you like. In both Quick and Advanced modes, you may apply creative effects.

To add an artistic impact to your picture, do the following:

1. In either Quick or Advanced mode, choose **Open** to upload a picture of your choice.
2. In the right panel, choose **Effects and Artistic** to access a variety of artistic effects.
3. Apply any Artistic effect of your choosing to your picture.

4. **Carry out the following actions:**
- Specify Intensity.
- Keep the original picture colors by choosing Keep original photo colors.
- Select to remove the artistic impact from the photo's subject and/or background.
- Select **Advanced** to recompose the shot or sections of the photo. Mask sections of the shot you want to recompose using the Brush in Tool Options. Size and Threshold may also be specified.

5. To save the picture, go to **File > Save As**, or go to Post to share it on social media.

Classic Effects

Classic effects can be used to improve your images in Photoshop Elements. In the Quick and Advanced modes, choose your preferred effect from 11 Classic effects.

To add the Classic effect to your picture, do the following:

1. Launch Photoshop Elements and open a picture.
2. Select **Effects > Classic** in Quick mode to get 11 vintage effects. Select **Effects > Classic** in Advanced mode to get more than 30 vintage effects.
3. Choose a Classic effect from the drop-down menu and apply it to your picture.
4. Click **Advanced** to recompose the shot or sections of the photo. To recompose a picture, use the Brush tool under Tool Options to mask off the areas you wish to recompose. Size and Opacity may also be specified.
5. To save the picture, go to **File > Save As**, or go to Post to share it on social media.
6. To clear the effects, click the **Reset button** in the top right corner of the panel.

Color Match effects

Use one of the built-in presets or a picture of your own. You can adjust the color, saturation, and brightness further. Investigate the Color Match effect in both Quick and Advanced modes.

Apply Color Match effect in Quick mode

1. To open a picture to which you want to apply the effect, go to **File > Open** or click the **Open button**.
2. Choose from the built-in presets provided in the Color Match section of the Effects panel.

3. Color Match effects are mutually exclusive, and since layers are not generated, any presets applied to the primary input picture will be replaced by the effect of another preset.

If you want to apply one preset over another, you may do it in two ways:

- Save the result of your first preset and use it as an input picture for the next preset.
- Apply the initial preset in **Quick mode > Switch to Advanced mode > In Advanced mode**, use the Quick mode result as your input picture, and then pick the preferred preset to apply.

4. Depending on your needs, you can fine-tune the Saturation, Hue, and Brightness of the picture.

Note: Click the **Undo button** to undo the changes and the redo button to reapply the changes.

5. To save the picture, go to **File > Save As**, or go to Post to post it on social media.

Apply Color Match effect in advanced mode

The steps:

1. To open a picture to which you want to apply the effect, go to **File > Open** or click the **Open button**.
2. Change to **Advanced mode.**
3. Within the Effects panel, you can use either built-in presets or a picture of your own as a Custom preset by choosing the Import photo button in Advanced mode.

Note:

- A custom preset is kept for the duration of the launch session, allowing it to be utilized until the program is closed. It is eliminated when the program is relaunched to save up hard drive space.
- While you can import the Custom preset many times during the same launch session, only the most recently applied Custom preset will be kept and used for the duration of the session. When you import a new Custom preset, the existing one is replaced with the newly imported preset.

4. Depending on your needs, you can fine-tune the Saturation, Hue, and Brightness of the picture.
5. To save the picture, go to **File > Save As**, or go to Post to post it on social media.

Add stylized text to an image

When you add text to a picture, it creates a text layer that allows you to edit the text without impacting the original image. **Here are the steps:**

1. **Click Text from the drop-down menu in the Graphics panel, and then perform one of the following:**
   - Choose a **thumbnail > Click Apply**.
   - Select a thumbnail by double-clicking it.
   - Click and drag a thumbnail to the picture.
2. The Text tool is activated when a text frame appears over the picture. Enter the new text.
3. When you've completed editing the text, either click the **Commit or Cancel buttons** to save your changes.
4. To move or resize the text frame, use the Move tool.
5. (Optional) Colorize the text using the Color panel in the settings bar.
6. When you're finished editing the text, click the **Commit or Cancel buttons** to save your changes.
7. (Optional) Drag a different thumbnail over the text frame to experiment with various text effects.

Add graphics or effects to Favorites

Add a graphic or effect to the Favorites area of the Effects panel if you want to access it fast in the future. Right-click the thumbnail in the Effects or Graphics window and further select **Add To Favorites**.

Frequently Asked Questions

1. How do you use the filter gallery in Photoshop Elements?
2. How do you use the filter/adjustment menu?
3. How do you apply classic effects?
4. How do you apply artistic effects?
5. How do you use the filters and styles panel?

CHAPTER TWELVE

PHOTOSHOP ELEMENTS TRICKS

Overview

Chapter 12 simply discusses the different Adobe Photoshop Elements tricks including swapping out a face, removing blemishes from images, and others.

Swap out a face

A few elements influence whether a face swap will appear well. The most crucial ones are head placement and illumination. The location of the head you want to replace must be comparable to the position of the head you want to replicate. This will give you the most natural-looking results. In Adobe Photoshop, you can bend and distort a flat surface, but not a human face. When you have to bend and twist a face to make it fit, it no longer looks natural. No amount of retouching can change that. Furthermore, the light on both faces must be comparable. Putting a person's head or face in direct sunlight on a person's body in the shade is extremely difficult. If you have photos of similar size and composition, you can easily layer them in Photoshop for a basic face swap.

Simply follow these steps:

1. Begin by importing two images: the main one and the one with the new face you want to use. Make the new face the bottom layer and the main image the top layer.
2. Match the faces in the two photos. Make use of the Auto-Align feature to ensure that the two figures are roughly aligned.
3. Add a layer mask to the top layer that contains your main image. Increase the opacity to 100%.

4. Choose the **Brush tool**. Increase the opacity to 100%. A softer brush style works well for this type of work.
5. Paint over the face you want to swap out on the layer mask with the black brush. The face beneath the layer mask will be visible in real-time as you paint over it.

Swap out a background

Here are the steps:

1. On your PC, launch **Adobe Photoshop Elements**.
2. Select "**Open**" from the "**File**" menu to open the picture you want to work on.
3. Select the "**Quick Selection Tool**" from the left-hand toolbar. It has the appearance of a paintbrush with a dotted circle.
4. Click and drag the tool over the subject you want to save. As required, change the brush size.
5. After you've made your first pick, go to the "**Refine Edge**" option in the top toolbar.
6. Use the refining options such as **"Refine Radius," "Smooth," "Feather,"** and "**Contrast**" to fine-tune your pick.
7. To guarantee accuracy, preview the pick against several backgrounds.
8. After you've made your choice, click the "**Add Layer Mask**" option at the bottom of the Layers panel. The background will be removed, leaving just the subject visible.
9. Click the "**New Layer**" icon at the bottom of the Layers panel to add a new layer.
10. Drag the new layer underneath the layer containing your subject.
11. Choose the new layer, then the background color or picture you want to use. Use the Paint Bucket tool or copy and paste an image into the new layer.
12. Choose the layer containing your subject (the one with the layer mask).
13. Use the "**Move Tool**" to reposition and resize your subject on the new background.

14. On the new background, fine-tune the boundaries of your subject. To manually refine the edges, you may need to use a delicate brush on the layer mask.
15. Check for any visible halos or artifacts surrounding your subject.
16. Make any final color, brightness, or contrast changes to ensure that your subject blends in with the new background.
17. You can also use more components or effects to improve the overall composition.
18. Save your picture after you're pleased with the outcome. Select "**File**" and then "**Save As**" to save the file in the format of your choosing.

Remove warts and blemishes

Various tools and strategies can be used to remove warts and imperfections in Adobe Photoshop Elements.

Follow the steps below:

1. Open **Adobe Photoshop Elements** and choose the picture with the warts or flaws you want to erase.
2. To see the defects more clearly, zoom in on the area with the problem.
3. In the toolbar, look for the Spot Healing Brush Tool. It resembles a band-aid.
4. To pick the tool, click on it or hit 'J' on your keyboard.
5. Match the brush size to the size of the blemish. This can be accomplished by adjusting the Brush Size slider in the settings bar at the top of the screen.
6. With the Spot Healing Brush, choose the imperfection/blemish. Photoshop Elements will evaluate the surrounding pixels and try to blend the imperfections with them.

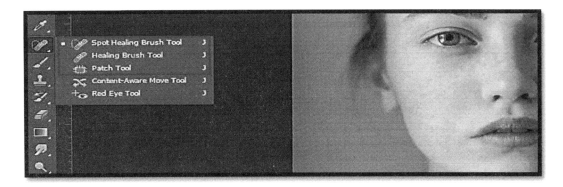

7. Smaller brush sizes and quick, precise strokes may be required for more intricate imperfections or those in detailed locations.

If the Spot Healing Brush fails to provide the required results, use the Healing Brush Tool:

- Select the Healing Brush Tool (it resembles a band-aid with a brush) from the toolbar.
- While holding down the **'Alt'** key, click on an area of the picture that has a texture and color close to the area you want to cover.
- Click on the flaw after releasing the 'Alt' key. This will apply the texture from the clicked region to the imperfection.

You can use the Clone Stamp Tool to have more exact control over the source area:

- Choose the **Clone Stamp Tool** from the toolbar (it resembles a rubber stamp).
- Alt-click on a blemish to clone the sampled area, then Alt-click on the imperfection to clone the sampled area onto it.
8. Zoom out at regular intervals to assess the overall look of the picture. If necessary, use the Spot Healing Brush, Healing Brush, or Clone Stamp tools to make further changes.
9. When you're happy with the effects, save your picture by going to **File > Save or File > Save As**.

Tips:

- **Undo/Redo**: To undo a mistake, use Ctrl+Z (Windows) or Command+Z (Mac). Press Ctrl+Shift+Z (Windows) or Command+Shift+Z (Mac) to undo.
- **Adjustment Layers**: Use adjustment layers to blend the repaired area's color and tone with the remainder of the picture.

Remove big things from your photos

The steps:

1. Open the picture from which you want to delete the huge item in Adobe Photoshop Elements.

2. Right-click on the Background layer in the Layers panel and choose "**Duplicate Layer.**" This generates a duplicate that you can work on without changing the original picture.
3. Outline the item you wish to eliminate using one of the selecting tools. The best tool for the job is determined by the form and intricacy of the item. **The following are examples of common selection tools:**
- **Marquee Selection Tool (M):** Used to choose basic geometric shapes.
- **Lasso (L) Tool**: For freehand selections.
- **Polygonal Lasso Tool (L):** For selections with straight edges.
- **Magic Wand Tool (W):** This tool is used to pick regions of similar hue.
4. After you've made your first decision, use the "**Refine Edge**" option (**Select > Refine Edge**) to fine-tune it. This allows you to fine-tune the edges for a more precise selection.
5. When you're finished with your selection, go to **Edit > Fill Selection**. Select "**Content-Aware**" from the Contents dropdown option in the Fill dialog box. To use the content-aware fill, click **OK**.
6. Use the Clone Stamp Tool (S) if Content-Aware Fill did not deliver the required results or if there are regions that need human correction. Set a source point in a nearby region, then brush over the undesirable item to replace it with the sampled area.
7. Another tool for blending and repairing areas is the Healing Brush Tool (J). Set a source point using Alt-click, then brush over the item to enable the tool to blend the pixels perfectly
8. For quick corrections, use the Spot Healing Brush Tool (J). Simply brush over the item and Photoshop Elements will replace the chosen area with pixels from the surrounding area.
9. Zoom in and thoroughly examine the altered area. To get a natural and seamless effect, make any required modifications using a combination of the tools listed above.
10. Save your adjusted image after you're pleased with the removal. To retain the original picture, consider storing it in a different file type or version.

Add things to your photos

Follow the steps below:

1. On your PC, launch **Adobe Photoshop Elements.**

2. When you choose "**File**" > "**Open**" and browse the picture file, you can open the photo to which you wish to add components.
3. Click the "**New Layer**" button in the Layers panel (typically on the right side of the screen). This assures that your new parts have no direct impact on the original picture.
4. Open a picture of what you want to add in Photoshop Elements if you already have one.
5. Drag the piece onto your main picture using the "**Move Tool**" (shortcut: V). You can also use the "**Selection Tools**" (such as the Rectangular Marquee Tool or the Lasso Tool) to pick and copy the element, then paste it into your main picture.
6. To resize the additional element, use the "**Transform**" tool (Ctrl+T or Command+T).
7. Drag the element to the appropriate location on the image.
8. To apply the change, press **Enter**.
9. If required, use the "**Eraser Tool**" (shortcut: E) to refine the borders of the inserted piece.
10. If you want the piece to merge more perfectly with the background, adjust the opacity of the additional layer.
11. Click on the layer to which the element was added.
12. Click the "**fx**" icon at the bottom of the Layers panel to explore layer styles and effects. This enables you to apply shadows, glows, and other effects to the additional element to improve its authenticity.
13. Once you're happy with the adjustments, save the picture by going to **"File" > "Save" or "Save As."**

Tips:

- **Text and Shapes**: Add text or shapes to your photos using Photoshop Elements' respective tools.
- **Layer Order**: In the Layers panel, pay attention to the layer order. Components on higher levels will display on top of lower-layer components.
- **Blending Modes**: Play around with blending modes to add more aspects. This may aid in achieving various effects and improving blending with the surroundings.
- **Undo and History**: If you make a mistake, you can return to a prior state by using the "**Undo**" command (Ctrl+Z or Command+Z) or by checking the "**History**" panel.

Frequently Asked Questions

1. How do you swap out a face in Photoshop Elements?
2. How do you remove blemishes and warts from images?
3. How do you swap out a background?
4. How do you add objects to your photos?
5. How do you remove big objects from your images in Photoshop Elements?

CHAPTER THIRTEEN
ADVANCED PHOTO EDITING TOOLS

Overview

In this chapter, you will learn all about the multiple advanced photo editing tools in Photoshop Elements and get to see how they are used.

Scan your photos

How to Import Scanner Photos into Photoshop Elements:

1. To import photos from a scanner straight into the Organizer in Photoshop Elements, make sure your scanner is properly connected and set for your computer. This often entails upgrading your scanner driver.
2. Launch the Photoshop Elements Organizer.
3. From the Menu Bar, choose "**File > Get Photos and Videos > From Scanner...**"
4. Alternatively, near the left end of the Shortcuts Bar, click the "**Import**" drop-down.
5. From the drop-down option, choose "**From Scanner...**".
6. Use the "**Scanner**" drop-down menu in the "**Get Photos from Scanner**" dialog box to pick the scanner from which to import the picture.
7. If you see "**None Detected**" in this drop-down list, make sure your scanner is connected to your computer and switched on.
8. The default folder for saving scanned photographs displays under the "**Save Files In**" label.
9. To change this location, launch a "**Browse for Folder**" dialog box by clicking the adjacent "**Browse...**" button.
10. Navigate to and choose the folder where you want to store the scanned picture in this dialog box.
11. To set the new folder destination, click the "OK" button in the "**Browse for Folder**" dialog box.
12. To save the scanned picture, use the "**Save As**" drop-down menu to pick a file format.
13. If you select "**jpeg**," use the adjacent slider to adjust the picture quality.
14. Drag the slider to the left to reduce the quality and the slider to the right to enhance the quality.

15. Click the "OK" button at the bottom of the "**Get Photos from Scanner**" dialog box to scan and import the picture.
16. Depending on the scanner driver loaded, another scanner-specific dialog box may appear, allowing you to configure additional scanner settings.
17. To complete, follow the directions in any dialog boxes that occur.

Screen captures

Follow the steps below:

You must first capture the stuff you want to work with before you can utilize screen grabs in Photoshop Elements. This is possible using your operating system's built-in screenshot utilities. As an example:

Windows

- To capture the complete screen, use the "**PrtScn**" (Print Screen) key.
- Use "**Alt + PrtScn**" to capture just the currently active window.

Mac

- To capture a section of the screen, press "**Command + Shift + 4**"
- To capture the full screen, use "**Command + Shift + 3**".
2. On your PC, launch Adobe Photoshop Elements. If you don't already have it, you may get it from the Adobe website and install it.
3. To start a new project, go to the top menu and select "**File**." Set your project's size and resolution, or use a preset like "**Default Photoshop Size**."
4. Return to the "**File**" menu and choose "**Open**." Navigate to the spot where you saved your screen grab and open it in Photoshop Elements.
5. Crop the picture to the appropriate size using the Crop tool (click 'C' on your keyboard). Other tools and capabilities in Photoshop Elements can also be used to alter the recorded screen, such as changing brightness, contrast, or adding effects.
6. When you're finished making changes, go to "**File**" and choose "**Save**" to save your project. Select "**Save As**" instead if you wish to save the picture in a different format or location.
7. You may need to export the picture if you want to use the recorded screen in another program or share it online. Click "**File**" and then "**Export**" or "**Save for Web**" to pick the settings that are best for you.

8. After you've adjusted the export options, click "**Save**" to save the final altered picture.

Divide Scanned Photos

Here are the steps:

1. On your PC, launch Adobe Photoshop Elements. If you don't already have it, you may get it from the Adobe website and install it by following the installation instructions.
2. Scan and save your images to your PC. Make sure you know where you stored the scanned photos. Go to "**File**" > "**Open**" in Photoshop Elements and go to the folder containing your scanned photos. Choose the file and press "**Open**."
3. If your scanned images are all in one image file, you'll need to start a separate project for each one. To do so, go to "**File**" > "**New**" > "**Blank File.**" Enter the measurements for your new project (width and height) depending on the size of each picture you wish to generate. Ascertain if the resolution is acceptable for print or online usage.
4. Select the "**Crop Tool**" (shortcut key C) from the toolbar on the left. You may use this tool to designate the region you want to save in your new project.
5. The Crop Tool settings can be changed in the options bar at the top. Make sure the "**Delete Cropped Pixels**" option is off. The cropped regions will be conserved rather than wasted.
6. Create a cropping box around the first picture in the scanned image by clicking and dragging. Adjust the box's size and location until it covers the area you want to save. When you're finished, hit **Enter** to apply the crop.
7. To prevent overwriting the original picture, go to "**File**" > "**Save As**" and save the cropped photo with a new name. Select a file format (such as JPEG or PNG) and quality level.
8. Steps 3–7 should be repeated for each picture in the scanned image. Make a new project for each picture, choose the area using the Crop Tool, and then save each cropped photo individually.
9. Close the original scanned picture without saving modifications after you've separated all of the scanned photos.

Download photos from your digital camera

The steps:

1. Connect your digital camera to your computer using the included USB connection. Make sure your camera is switched on and in the proper setting for transferring photos.
2. On your PC, launch Adobe Photoshop Elements 2024. If you don't already have the program, you may get it from the Adobe website and install it.
3. There are two key components of Adobe Photoshop Elements: the Organizer and the Photo Editor. The Organizer will be used to download photos. In the top-left corner of the screen, click the "**Organizer**" button.
4. Locate the "**Get Photos & Videos**" button in the Organizer, which is usually in the upper left or the File menu.
5. Select "**From Camera or Card Reader**" from the dropdown menu under "**Get Photos & Videos**."
6. A dialog window with a list of linked devices, including your digital camera, will appear. Choose your camera from the drop-down menu.
7. Adobe Photoshop Elements will show thumbnails of your camera's photos. You can import all photographs or just a subset of them.
8. Select the "**Get Media**" option to import all photos.
9. To import certain photos, mark the checkbox next to each thumbnail with a check mark. Then, choose "**Get Media**" from the drop-down menu.
10. A new dialog box will display once you pick the photos. You may pick where to save the images on your computer, whether to sort them into folders, and other options here. Tailor the settings to your tastes.
11. When you've finished configuring the import options, click the "**Import**" button to begin the download. Adobe Photoshop Elements will copy the photos you've chosen from your digital camera to your computer.
12. Following the completion of the import procedure, you can analyze and arrange your photographs in the Organizer. For easy administration, Adobe Photoshop Elements includes capabilities for tagging, labeling, and arranging your photographs.
13. You can open your photos in the Photo Editor to edit or improve them by choosing the photo and clicking the "**Edit**" option.

Camera RAW Installation

Raw files from many cameras are supported by Adobe Photoshop Elements. When you open a raw file in Photoshop Elements, it is initially opened in Adobe Camera Raw.

Download and install the Adobe Camera Raw plug-in

To install the Adobe Camera Raw plug-in, follow these steps:

- In Photoshop Elements or Elements Organizer, go to **Help > Install Camera Raw**.
- In Photoshop Elements, go to **File > Open in Camera Raw**.

An Overview of Photoshop Elements' Camera Raw Dialog Box

When you open a camera raw file in the Photo Editor for processing, it opens the Camera Raw dialog box in Photoshop Elements. The Camera Raw dialog box includes the tools and options for importing and processing raw camera data.

Buttons at the top of Photoshop Elements' Camera Raw Dialog Box

The Title Bar located at the upper part of the Camera Raw dialog box in Photoshop Elements shows which Camera Raw you have. Below that is a bar that displays the camera raw file name as well as the camera model used to shoot the shot. The "**Convert and save the image,**" "**Open preferences dialog,**" **and** "**Toggle full-screen mode**" **buttons** are located at the right end of this bar. You can access the "**Save Options**" dialog box by clicking the "**Convert and save image**" button, which allows you to save a copy of the camera raw image as a DNG file with the settings you select. However, you can save and convert a duplicate of the picture while bypassing the "**Save Options**" dialog box by holding down the "**Alt**" key on your keyboard and then clicking the "**Convert and save image**" button.

When you click the "**Open Preferences Dialog**" button, the "**Camera Raw Preferences**" dialog box appears. If necessary, dismiss this dialog box by clicking the "**Cancel**" button. Finally, pressing the "**Toggle full-screen mode**" button in Photoshop Elements toggles the Camera Raw dialog box between the full screen and a smaller version of the dialog box.

Tools at the Right Side of the Camera Raw Dialog Box in Photoshop Elements

The Camera Raw dialog box toolbar is located on the far right side of the Camera Raw dialog box in Photoshop Elements. The toolbar has buttons that allow you to modify and adjust the picture while it is being processed. From top to bottom, the buttons are: "**Edit**," "**Crop & Rotate**," "**Red Eye Removal**," "**More image settings**," and, at the bottom, the "**Zoom Tool**" and "**Hand Tool**." Depending on whatever tool is chosen in the toolbar, tabbed panels on the right side of the dialog box display the **"Edit," "Crop & Rotate," or "Red Eye Removal" tool**. The current picture's histogram may be found in the upper-right corner of Photoshop Elements' Camera Raw dialog box, displaying the tonal range of the image at its current settings. When you use the "**Edit**" settings and make changes to the tabs in the Edit Panel, the data in the histogram instantly updates.

In the sample picture to the left, there are two buttons in the upper-left and upper-right corners of the histogram that you may click to turn clipping warnings on and off. Clipping warnings display in the preview picture as shaded red or blue regions when enabled. These areas show where the image's highlights or shadows will be clipped based on the current settings. The left button is for "**Shadow clipping warning**" while the right button is for "**Highlight clipping warning**." The RGB and picture information are located above and below the histogram. Slide your cursor over the preview picture to see the matching RGB information for that place in the image preview at the top of the histogram. When the "**Edit**" tool is chosen in the Camera Raw dialog box's toolbar in Photoshop Elements, three collapsible and expandable tabs display in an Edit Panel on the right side of the dialog box. Use these tabs to display or hide the corresponding options and sliders. The tabs are labeled **"Basic," "Detail," and "Calibration"** from top to bottom.

Buttons in the lower-left corner of Photoshop Elements' Camera Raw Dialog Box

In Photoshop Elements, the "**Fit in view**" button, the "**Zoom to specified level**" button, and the "**Select zoom level**" drop-down are located below the preview picture on the left side of the Camera Raw dialog box. Click the "**Fit in view**" button to fit the picture in the preview window. To fit the preview picture in the window, in Photoshop Elements, double-click the "**Zoom tool**" button in the toolbar on the right side of the Camera Raw dialog box. Choose a magnification level from the "**Select zoom level**" drop-down to use when you click the preview picture with the Zoom Tool. Hold down the "**Ctrl**" key on your keyboard and then click and drag over the area in the preview picture to magnify to adjust the magnification when the Zoom Tool is selected. When the "**Edit**" button in the toolbar is chosen, the Zoom Tool is the default tool in the Camera Raw dialog box in Photoshop Elements. Hold your cursor over the preview picture and click to zoom in to the region where you click when it is chosen. Click again to zoom out to fit the picture in the preview area. When the Zoom Tool is not chosen, just click the **"Fit in view" or "Zoom to specified level" button** to zoom in or out.

Buttons underneath/below the Preview Image in Photoshop Elements' Camera Raw Dialog Box

A 5-star scale appears just below the preview picture in Photoshop Elements' Camera Raw dialog box. You can set a star rating for the current picture by clicking or dragging on this scale. To designate a picture for deletion, select the "**Toggle mark for deletion**" button, which looks like a trash can, to the right of the stars. The "**Cycles between Before/After views**" button is located to the right of this same bar. You may use this button to cycle the camera raw picture preview between the five "**Before/After**" views to customize how changes to the camera raw file display in the preview area. Alternatively, click and hold the button to bring up a pop-up menu with these view options. Then, in the menu that opens, choose the "**Before/After**" view to use. If you modify the picture in one of the "**Before/After**" views, you can switch the settings between the two photo versions by clicking the adjacent "**Swap Before/After settings**" button, or you can copy the changes to the "**Before**" image by clicking the "**Copy current settings to Before**" button. To apply the current or default settings to the "**After**" version of the picture, click the "**Toggle to default/current settings**" button.

Buttons at the bottom of Photoshop Elements' Camera Raw Dialog Box

Select the "**Help**" button at the left end of the bar at the bottom of the dialog box to view a web page using the Camera Raw dialog box in Photoshop Elements. To the right of that, use the "**Bit Depth Settings**" drop-down to choose the bit depth for the camera raw picture file. Select the "**Done**" button in the lower-right corner to make any process settings changes to the chosen camera raw picture and dismiss this dialog box without opening the image in the Photo Editor. Alternatively, click the "**Cancel**" button to cancel your changes and dismiss this dialog box. If necessary, hold down the "**Alt**" key on your computer and then click the "**Reset**" button that replaces the "**Cancel**" option to reset this dialog box. Choose the "Done" button in the lower-right corner to make any process settings changes to the selected camera raw picture and dismiss this dialog box without opening the image in the Photo Editor. Alternatively, click the "**Cancel**" button to cancel your changes and dismiss this dialog box. If necessary, hold down the "**Alt**" key on your computer and then click the "**Reset**" button that replaces the "**Cancel**" option to reset this dialog box. Click the "**Open**" button to implement your changes by changing the picture's metadata and opening the image in the Photo Editor. Hold down the "**Alt**" key on your keyboard and then click the "**Open Copy**" button that substitutes the "**Open**" button to open the chosen picture in the Photo Editor without altering the image's metadata.

Edit in Camera RAW

Open and process camera raw files

The steps:

1. Select **File > Open** in the Edit workspace.
2. Proceed to find and open one or more camera raw files. The histogram in the Camera Raw dialog box displays the image's tonal range at the current settings. The histogram is automatically updated as you change the values.
3. (Optional) Modify the picture view by using controls like the Zoom tool and selections like Shadows and Highlights, which display clipping in the preview area.
4. When you choose Preview, you'll get a preview of the picture with the settings modifications you've made. Deselecting **Preview** shows the camera's raw picture with the current tab's original settings merged with the settings in the concealed tabs.
5. Select the **Rotate Image buttons** to rotate the image 90° counterclockwise or 90° clockwise.
6. Select your preferred option from the Settings menu in order to use the settings applied in the previous camera raw picture. Using the same settings is beneficial if you want to quickly process photos with identical lighting circumstances.
7. Configure the white balance selections. The RGB values of pixels in your picture may be monitored as you alter them in the Camera Raw dialog box. Place the Zoom, Hand, White Balance, or Crop tools on top of the preview picture to show the RGB values immediately under the pointer.
8. Tonal changes can be made using the Exposure, Brightness, Contrast, and Saturation sliders. Click **Auto** to undo your manual modifications and make the

adjustments automatically. To reset all selections to their default values, press Alt (Option on Mac OS) and choose **Reset**.

9. **Perform one of the following:**
   - Choose **Open Image** to open a copy of the camera raw image file (with the camera raw settings applied) in Photoshop Elements. You can change the picture and save it in a format supported by Photoshop Elements. The original camera raw file is not changed.
   - Select **Cancel** to cancel the changes and dismiss the dialog box.
   - Click **Save Image** to save the edits to a DNG file.

Note: Adobe's suggested standard format for camera raw data is the Digital Negative (DNG) format. DNG files are excellent for preserving camera raw photos since they include the raw camera sensor data as well as information on how the image should appear. DNG files can be used to store camera raw picture settings instead of sidecar XMP files or the camera raw database.

Adjust sharpness in camera raw files

The Sharpness slider increases the picture sharpness to get the desired edge definition. Sharpening is a variant of the Adobe Photoshop Unsharp Mask effect. This adjustment finds pixels that vary from surrounding pixels by the threshold you define and raises the contrast of the pixels by the amount you provide. The Camera Raw plug-in determines the threshold to apply when opening a camera raw file depending on the camera model, ISO, and exposure compensation. You can choose whether sharpening should be applied to all photos or only previews.

Here are the steps:

1. Zoom in to at least 100% on the preview picture.
2. Select the **Detail option**.
3. Sharpening can be increased or decreased by moving the Sharpness slider to the right or left. Sharpening is disabled when the value is set to zero. In general, reduce the Sharpness slider setting for clearer pictures.
4. If you don't intend to perform any editing in Photoshop Elements, use the camera raw Sharpness slider. Turn off the camera raw sharpening if you want to modify the picture in Photoshop Elements. After all other editing and resizing are finished, utilize the sharpening filters in Photoshop Elements as the last step.

Reducing noise in camera raw images

Controls for decreasing picture noise—the superfluous visual artifacts that diminish image quality—can be found on the Detail tab of the Camera Raw dialog box. Picture noise comprises luminance (grayscale) noise, which causes a grainy appearance in a picture, and chroma (color) noise, which appears as colored artifacts in the image. Photos produced at high ISO rates or with less capable digital cameras may have visible noise. Grayscale noise is reduced by sliding the Luminance Smoothing slider to the right, while chroma noise is reduced by moving the Color Noise Reduction slider to the right. For a better look, preview photographs at 100% while applying Luminance Smoothing or Color Noise Reduction modifications.

Save changes to camera raw images

Changes made to a camera raw file can be saved. The Camera Raw dialog box saves your adjustments to the camera raw picture as a.dng file. Saving the file does not open it in Photoshop Elements automatically. Use the Open command to open a camera raw file, then edit and save it as you would any other picture.

The steps:

1. Apply modifications to one or more Camera Raw photos in the Camera Raw dialog box.
2. Save the image by clicking the **Save Image button**.
3. If you're storing more than one camera raw file, choose where to store the file and how to label it in the store Options dialog box.

Tips:

- **Embed Fast Load Data**: Inserts a significantly smaller copy of the raw picture into the DNG file to speed up previewing the raw image.
- **Use Lossy Compression**: This reduces the file size of your DNG file while causing quality degradation. Recommended exclusively for raw photos that will be archived and will never be used for printing or production (other usage).
- **Embed Original Raw File**: Stores all of the raw picture data from the original camera in the DNG file.

4. Save the file.

Open a camera raw image in the Edit workspace

After processing a camera raw picture in the Camera Raw dialog box, you can open it in the modified workspace and modify it.

Follow the steps below:

1. Proceed to apply changes to one or more Camera Raw photos in the Camera Raw dialog box.
2. Select the **Open Image option**. The Camera Raw dialog box is closed, and the image is shown in the Edit workspace.

Camera raw settings

Zoom tool

When you click inside the preview picture, the preview zoom is set to the next preset zoom setting. To zoom out, use **Alt-click** (Option-click on Mac OS). Zoom in on a certain region by dragging the Zoom tool in the preview picture. Double-click the Zoom tool to return to 100%.

Hand tool

If the preview picture is set to a zoom level greater than 100%, it will be moved. While using another tool, hold down the spacebar to access the Hand tool. To fit the preview picture in the window, double-click the Hand tool.

White Balance tool

To eliminate color casts and change the overall color of the picture, set the region you click to a neutral gray tone. To reflect the color alteration, the Temperature and Tint values change.

Crop tool

Removes a section of a picture. Drag the tool around the preview picture to pick the area you wish to preserve, and then hit **Enter**.

Straighten tool

The Straighten tool is used to realign a picture vertically or horizontally. This tool also resizes or crops the canvas to allow for picture straightening.

Red Eye Removal

Removes red eyes from flash images of humans and green or white eyes from photos of pets.

Open the Preferences dialog box

This command displays the Camera Raw Preferences dialog.

Rotate Buttons

Rotates the image either clockwise or counterclockwise.

Set custom camera settings

When you open a camera raw file, Photoshop Elements examines the file's metadata to determine which camera model made it and then applies the proper camera settings to the picture. If you often make the same modifications, you may modify your camera's default settings. You can also customize the settings for each camera model you possess, but not for numerous cameras of the same type.

- Select the ≡ icon and choose **Save New Camera Raw Default** to store the current settings as the default for the camera that generated the picture.
- To use the Photoshop Elements default camera settings, click the ≡ icon and choose **Reset Camera Raw Default**.
- To remove prior settings, select the ≡ icon and click **Clear Imported Settings**.

Process Multiple Files

Here are the steps:

1. To begin, launch Adobe Photoshop Elements.
2. Make sure that all of the files you want to process are in a specified folder. This makes them simpler to find and pick throughout the batch process.
3. Navigate to the "**File**" menu and choose "**Process Multiple Files**."

4. In the "**Process Multiple Files**" dialog box, specify the source of your files first. Navigate to and choose the folder holding your photographs by clicking the "**Choose**" button.
5. When a folder is selected, all of the files contained within that folder are displayed. Select the files to be processed by checking the boxes next to their names.
6. Designate a location for the processed files. You have the option of saving them in the same folder or creating a new one. To select the destination folder, click the "**Browse**" button.
7. You have the option of renaming the files during the batch process. Photoshop Elements offers several renaming options, including adding a prefix, suffix, or a combination of the two. Configure the naming options to suit your needs.
8. Pick a file format for the processed files. JPEG, PNG, and other file formats are supported by Photoshop Elements. Choose the appropriate format from the drop-down menu.
9. Depending on what you want, you may also have the option of resizing images, applying filters, or adjusting the quality settings. Investigate these options and tailor them to your specific requirements.
10. When you've finished configuring everything, select the "**Run**" button to start the batch process. Photoshop Elements will save the specified changes to the destination folder after applying the specified changes to each selected file.
11. Once the batch process is finished, go over the processed files to ensure that the changes were applied correctly. You can go back and change the settings for future batches if necessary.
12. Close the application and save any changes made during the batch process.

Photoshop Elements Preferences and Presets

New File Presets

Pop-up panels appear in the Tool Options bar in Advanced Mode, allowing access to predefined libraries of brushes, color swatches, gradients, patterns, layer styles, and custom shapes. Presets are the items in each library. When pop-up panels are closed, they show a thumbnail image of the currently selected preset. You can configure a pop-up panel to display presets by their names, as thumbnail icons, or both names and icons. You can also load different preset libraries using the Presets Manager.

Use preset tool options

The steps:

1. Choose the tool that you want to use.
2. Open the pop-up panel from the Tool Options bar. (Pop-up panels are only available for certain tools.)
3. **Perform any of the following:**
- To choose a preset, click an item in the preset library.
- To save a brush, open the pop-up panel menu, select the **Save Brush command**, enter a name in the provided dialog box, and click OK.
- Proceed to save the gradient or pattern by opening the panel menu, selecting **New Gradient or New Pattern**, then entering a name in the provided dialog box and click OK.
- To rename a brush, gradient, or pattern in a panel, open the pop-up panel menu, select Rename, enter a new name, and click OK.
- To remove a brush, gradient, or pattern from a panel, select it, open the pop-up panel menu, and then select the **Delete command**. You can also click a brush or gradient while holding down **Alt** (Option in Mac OS).
- Open the pop-up panel menu to save a library of brushes, gradients, or patterns. Choose Save Brushes, Save Gradients, or Save Patterns from the menu, then enter a name for the library file and click Save.
- To add a library of brushes, gradients, or patterns, open the pop-up panel menu, select the Load command, then select the library file and click Load.
- The Load command adds the brush library to the available brushes. When you select a preset library of brushes, it replaces your current set of brushes.
- Select **Append** to add assets from a library to an existing library. Select the library file to be added and press the Append button.
- To replace a panel's current gradients, open the pop-up panel menu, select a library file from the bottom section of the menu, and click OK. You can also use the Replace command; navigate to a library file, then select **Load**.
- Select **Preset Manager** from the pop-up panel menu to load a different library of brushes, gradients, or patterns to replace the current set of brushes, gradients, or patterns.
- To restore the default set of brushes, gradients, or patterns, open the pop-up panel menu and select **Reset**.

Change the display of items in a pop-up panel menu

The steps:

1. **Perform one of the following:**
   - To change the display of one panel, open the pop-up panel menu by clicking the menu icon in the pop-up panel's upper-right corner.
   - To change the display for all panels, open the Preset Manager by selecting **Edit > Preset Manager** and then clicking the **More button**.
2. Choose a view option:

Text Only

Each item's name is displayed.

Large Thumbnail or Small Thumbnail

Each item is represented by a thumbnail.

Small or Large List

Each item's name and thumbnail are displayed.

Stroke Thumbnail

A sample brush stroke and brush thumbnail are shown. (This option is only accessible for brushes.)

Note: Not all of the selections listed above are available for all pop-up panels.

Use the Preset Manager

The Preset Manager (**Edit > Preset Manager**) in Advanced Mode allows you to manage the libraries of preset brushes, color swatches, gradients, styles, effects, and patterns available with Photoshop Elements. You can, for example, save a collection of preferred brushes or restore the default defaults. Each library type is a file with its own file extension and default location. Preset files are installed on your computer in the Photoshop Elements software folder's Presets folder.

Note: In the Preset Manager, you can remove a preset by choosing it and clicking remove. You may always use the **Reset command** to restore a library's default elements.

Load a library

The steps:

1. Select Brushes, Swatches, Gradients, Styles, Patterns, or Effects from the Preset Type option in the Preset Manager.
2. **Then perform one of the following:**
- Select **Add**, then choose a library from the list, and finally click **Load**. To load a library from another location, browse to that folder and then pick the library. Preset files are placed on your computer by default in the Presets folder inside the Photoshop Elements software folder.
- Select a library from the bottom area of the menu by clicking the **More button**.
3. When you're done, click the **Done button**.

Restore the default library or replace the currently displayed library

1. Select the **More button** in the Preset Manager and choose a command from the menu:

Reset

Restores the type's default library.

Save a library subset

1. Shift-click to choose multiple contiguous presets or Ctrl-click (Command-click on Mac OS) to select multiple noncontiguous presets in the Preset Manager. Only the presets that have been chosen are stored in the new library.
2. Select **Save Set**, and then give the library a name. If you want to store the library somewhere other than the default location, browse to the new location before saving.

Change the name of a preset

1. **Do one of the following in the Preset Manager:**
- Choose a preset from the list and select **Rename**.
- Select a preset from the list by double-clicking it.
2. Give the preset a new name. You are requested to provide several names if you select numerous settings.

Frequently Asked Questions

1. How do you scan your photos?
2. How do you install Camera RAW in Photoshop Elements?
3. How do you process multiple files?
4. How do you download your photos from your digital camera?
5. How do you use file presets in Photoshop Elements 2024?

CHAPTER FOURTEEN
LEARN ABOUT YOUR PHOTOSHOP ELEMENTS FILE

Overview

Chapter fourteen discusses learning about the multiple Photoshop Elements files and how they are used. Simply check out important information and details about your Photoshop Elements file window.

The Info Bar

In Adobe Photoshop Elements, the Info Bar is a panel that displays real-time information about your picture, such as the cursor's current location, color values, and image size.

Here's how to take advantage of the Info Bar:

1. On your computer, launch Adobe Photoshop Elements. If you don't already have it, you can get it from the Adobe website and install it.
2. Open the picture you want to work on by choosing **"File" > "Open"** and then the image file.
3. The Info Bar is often found around the bottom of the workspace. If it isn't visible, you can make it visible by going to the "**Window**" menu and choosing "**Info**" from the dropdown menu.
4. **Understand the Info Bar**:

The Info Bar provides numerous details regarding your picture, such as:

- **Mouse Coordinates**: Displays the X and Y coordinates of the image's pointer.
- **Color Readouts**: Shows the color values of the pixel beneath the cursor in different color modes (RGB, CMYK, and so on).
- **Image Dimensions:** Displays the image's width and height in pixels.

5. **Use Color Readouts**. Color readouts are especially helpful for selecting and altering colors. The Info Bar displays the color values in the selected color mode when you move your mouse over the picture. By right-clicking on the Info Bar and choosing the appropriate mode, you may change the color mode.
6. Change the units used to show the dimensions. Right-click the Info Bar, chooses "**Units**," and then selects your desired unit (pixels, inches, centimeters, and so on).

7. Use color samplers to monitor particular sections of your picture. In the toolbar, choose the eyedropper tool, and then select the picture where you want to create a color sampler. The color values for that location will be shown in the Info Bar.
8. To reset or alter the display selections of the Info Panel, click on the little menu symbol in the top-right corner of the Info Bar. You can choose which information is shown here.
9. Temporarily shut the Info Bar by clicking the "**x**" symbol in the top-right corner of the Info Bar. To bring it back up, go to the "**Window**" menu and select "**Info**."

Why does a "100% zoom" video fill only part of my computer screen?

Adobe Photoshop Elements is mainly intended for picture editing, and although it does have some basic video editing features, it may not handle video footage as well as specialist video editing software. When you encounter a circumstance in which a "100% zoom" video does not cover your full computer screen, various variables may be at play.

Here are some probable explanations:

Mismatch in Resolution

The video resolution may differ from the resolution of your computer screen. Even at 100% magnification, a movie with a lower quality than your screen may seem smaller and not cover the full screen. Check the resolution of your video and make any necessary adjustments.

Pixel Aspect Ratio

Different pixel aspect ratios (PAR) in videos might alter how they are shown. If the video's pixel aspect ratio does not match that of your screen, black bars will appear around the movie, making it looks smaller.

Project Settings

Adobe Photoshop Elements may have project options that affect how your video is shown. Check the project options, including resolution and aspect ratio, to confirm they correspond to your intended output.

Display Settings

The display settings on your computer may affect how the video is shown. Check your computer's display settings to ensure they match the video resolution.

Zoom Controls

When playing a video, the zoom level in the editing interface may not appropriately represent the real size of the video. Check that the zoom controls are set correctly and that the preview window appropriately depicts the final result.

Software Restrictions

When it comes to managing video content, Adobe Photoshop Elements may have limits. It may not have the same video editing capabilities as specialist video editing software, which may cause some complications.

Hardware Acceleration

Hardware acceleration settings may also be important. If the graphics hardware on your computer isn't optimized for video playback, it may alter how the video is shown.

Update Software

Make sure you're using the most recent version of Adobe Photoshop Elements. Software upgrades often contain bug fixes and enhancements that may solve video playback difficulties.

File Format Compatibility

The video file format may also affect how it is shown. Ascertain that Adobe Photoshop Elements supports the video file type you want to use.

Examine the Output Settings

Check that your project's output settings are appropriately adjusted. This covers settings like frame rate, aspect ratio, and resolution.

The Status Bar

In Adobe Photoshop Elements, the status bar is situated at the bottom of the program window. It offers vital project information such as the current tool, zoom level, and other characteristics.

Here's a step-by-step instruction for using the status bar in Adobe Photoshop Elements:

1. To begin, launch Photoshop Elements.
2. When you click "**File**" in the menu bar and select "**Open**" to open an existing project or "**New**" to create a new one, you can open an existing project or create a new one.
3. Find the Status Bar. The status bar is usually at the bottom of the Photoshop Elements window. It shows numerous details regarding your project.
4. Understand the Status Bar Components:

Several components in the status bar give information about your project. The following are examples of common components:

Document Information

- Displays the name of the currently active document.
- Displays the currently selected layer as well as the overall number of layers in the document.

Zoom Level

- Displays your project's current zoom level.
- To alter the zoom level, click the zoom percentage and choose a new value from the drop-down menu.

Tool Information

- Displays the tool's name that is presently chosen.
- Some tools may show extra selections or settings in this section.

Scratch Sizes

- Displays information about how much RAM Photoshop Elements is using. When the scratch disk is active, it also shows user information.

Color Resolution and Mode

- Displays the current document's color mode (e.g., RGB, CMYK) and resolution.

Notification and Status Area

- Shows messages and alerts, such as cautions or information about current processes.
5. To activate a tool in the toolbar, click on it. The name of the chosen tool will be shown in the status bar.
6. Adjust the zoom level by choosing a new number by clicking on the zoom percentage in the status bar
7. Change what information appears in the status bar. For any modification selections, go under the preferences or settings menu.
8. Keep an eye on the notification box for any vital project messages or cautions.
9. After you've made modifications to your project, save it by going to "**File**" and then "**Save**" or "**Save As.**"

The Info Panel

Activating the Info Panel

1. On your computer, launch Adobe Photoshop Elements.
2. Go to **File > Open or File > New** to start a new project or open an existing picture.
3. Go to the menu bar and choose **Window > Info** to open the Info Panel. This will open the Info Panel, which is usually located on the right side of the workspace.

Understanding the Info Panel

The Info Panel shows different details about the currently active picture. The following are frequent items that you may encounter in the Info Panel:

Coordinates

When you move your mouse over a picture, the Info Panel normally shows the X and Y coordinates. This is useful for pinpointing certain places in your picture.

Color Information

When you hover over a color, the Info Panel provides information about that particular color. RGB (Red, Green, and Blue) values are included, as are HSB (Hue, Saturation, Brightness) or CMYK (Cyan, Magenta, Yellow, Key/Black) values.

Document Information

The Info Panel shows document-specific information such as width, height, and resolution. This might help you determine the overall size and quality of your picture.

Using the Info Panel

Cursor Position

Move your mouse over the picture and the Info Panel will change in real-time, displaying your cursor's current coordinates.

Color Sampling

Use the **Eyedropper tool** to click on a particular place in your picture to sample a color. The color information for that point will then be shown in the Info Panel.

Measuring Distance

The Info Panel is used to estimate the distance between two spots by clicking on one and then holding down the Shift key while clicking on the second. The distance between the two locations will be shown in the Info Panel.

Setting Preferences

You can change the information shown in the Info Panel. Customization options may be found in the Preferences or Settings menus.

Closing the Information Panel

To close the Info Panel, go to **Window > Close Panel** or click the 'x' icon on the Info Panel.

File Info

File information is often referred to as "**File Info**" in Adobe Photoshop Elements, and it enables you to examine and update metadata linked with an image file. Metadata comprises information such as the author's identity, copyright information, the date the file was generated, and other pertinent information about the file.

In Adobe Photoshop Elements, you can obtain file information as follows:

1. Open Adobe Photoshop Elements 2024.
2. Open the picture file you want to examine or update the file information for.
3. In the top-right corner of the screen, choose "**File**."
4. Click the drop-down menu and choose **"File Info" or "File > File Info."** A new dialog box will appear, with many tabs or sections containing metadata information. The most common tabs are **"Description," "Keywords," "Origin," "IPTC," "Camera Data,"** and others.
5. You can examine and change detailed information about your picture by clicking on each tab. You can see fields where you can enter or change data. You may, for example, add a title or description under the "**Description**" tab. The "IPTC" option allows you to input information such as the author's name, copyright status, and keywords.
6. Once the appropriate changes have been made, click the "OK" or "**Save**" button to save the revised file information.

Frequently Asked Questions

1. What is the info bar and how do you use it in Photoshop Elements?
2. How do you use the status bar?
3. How do you use the info panel?
4. How do you use the file info section in Photoshop Elements?

CHAPTER FIFTEEN

MANAGE YOUR FILES WITH THE ORGANIZER

Overview

In this chapter, you will learn how to manage your files with the organizer in Photoshop Elements and also get acquainted with the media browser to perform tasks such as adding your metadata, searching catalog using filters, and others.

Adaptive Grid vs. Details View

Adaptive Grid

Grid Functionality

- Adaptive Grid most likely refers to a function that adapts the grid overlay on your picture dynamically depending on zoom level and image size.
- Grids are often used in design and picture editing to aid with alignment and composition.

Zoom Level Sensitivity

- As you zoom in and out of a picture, the Adaptive Grid can change its spacing and look to stay helpful and unobtrusive.
- This is especially useful when working on intricate modifications that need both close-up and overview views.

Friendly User Interface

- The word "**Adaptive**" implies a user-friendly method in which the grid adjusts to the user's activities to improve the editing experience.

Customization

- Users may be able to modify grid settings such as grid color, opacity, or grid style (for example, rule-of-thirds, golden ratio).

Details View

Zooming in for Precision

- Details View most likely refers to a mode or function that enables users to zoom in on a particular area of a picture for detailed editing.
- Use this mode when you need to work on tiny details, such as repairing minor flaws or making exact selections.

Pixel-Level Editing

- In the Details View, users can edit at the pixel level, making it simpler to remove imperfections, change minor features, and refine complicated areas of a picture.

Previewing Changes

- While working in Details View, users can preview changes in real time, ensuring that changes are correct and acceptable.

Navigating within the Detail

Tools and shortcuts may be available for simple navigation inside the detailed view, making it easier to move about when working on complex areas of a picture.

Contextual Controls

Details View provides a more concentrated and specialized workspace by giving particular controls and selections essential to fine-tuned editing.

Auto Curate

Manually selecting your finest images from a collection or album may be a challenging and time-consuming endeavor. Elements Organizer uses Auto Curate to intelligently evaluate your photographs and choose the finest ones in a single click.

After Elements Organizer has auto-curated your photographs, you can use them to create amazing photo projects like slideshows, photo books, and calendars. You can also add photos to albums, post them on social media, or just browse through them to relive your favorite experiences.

Using Auto Curate

The steps:

1. First of all, choose **Auto Curate** in the upper-right corner of the window in the Media view.

2. Set the Auto Curate slider to the desired number of photos. You can also input the number of images you want in the text box.

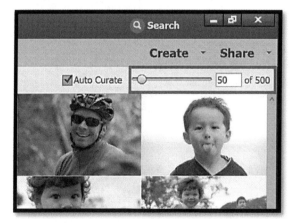

Note:

- Auto Curate only works with images.
- Auto Curate can be used with a minimum of 10 photographs and a maximum of twenty thousand photos.

3. Elements Organizer shows your finest images in the grid based on the number of photos you've selected.

The Media Browser area

1. Typically, the Media Browser is found inside the Photoshop Elements workspace. It might be a distinct panel or window accessible via the menu or toolbar.
2. Once launched, the Media Browser enables you to browse your computer's file system or linked devices for media assets such as photos.
3. Preview photos and other media files immediately in the Media Browser. This might assist you in rapidly locating the files you need to work with. When you've located the necessary file, you may choose it for further editing.
4. The Media Browser is often used to immediately import media files into your Photoshop Elements project. This makes importing external material into your editing environment easier.
5. The Media Browser usually supports a wide range of file types, including popular picture formats like JPEG, PNG, and TIFF. Depending on the version of Photoshop Elements, it may also support various media formats.
6. The Media Browser is intended to simplify your workflow by allowing you to view and import material without leaving the Photoshop Elements environment.

The Back or All Media buttons

Back Button

The "**Back**" button is often used to go through the history of actions in Photoshop Elements. This might be beneficial if you wish to undo or return to a prior editing state.

All Media Button

On the other hand, the "**All Media**" option is often used to examine all of the media assets (pictures and videos) in your current project or catalog. It displays a list of all the media you've imported or are working with.

Manually add to and update your Organizer Catalog

Manually add photos

1. To begin, launch Adobe Photoshop Elements.
2. In the Photoshop Elements workspace, choose the "**Organizer**" tab or icon.
3. To import photos into the Organizer, choose "**File**" > "**Get Photos and Videos**" or click the "**Import**" button.

4. Select the place where you want to save your images and the photos you want to add.
5. Once the photos are imported, you can organize and classify them by adding tags, captions, and other information.

Update the Organizer Catalog

Use the following procedures to update the Organizer Catalog with new photos or changes:

- To add new photos to the Organizer, use the import feature. Follow the instructions outlined before.
- Organize the new photos by using tags, ratings, descriptions, and other information.
- You can change the information of existing images in the Organizer by choosing them and clicking on the "**Info**" panel. This enables you to change captions, tags, and other information.
- If you've made major modifications or the catalog seems to be out of sync, you may wish to rebuild it. Keep in mind that recreating the catalog may take some time.
- Always back up your Organizer Catalog before making substantial changes or revisions. Within the program, look for the option to generate a backup.
- Check to see whether your Adobe Photoshop Elements program is up to date. Updates may contain improvements and bug fixes that impact the functioning of the Organizer.

Switch between Album and Folder Views

The names "**Album**" and "**Folder**" in Adobe Photoshop Elements may refer to distinct organizing layouts for your photos.

Changing the Album and Folder Views

1. Go to the Organizer workspace in Adobe Photoshop Elements. This is the location where you manage and arrange your images. There are tabs, panels, or selections on the left or top of the workspace in the Organizer.
2. Look for a panel or section that has picture organization selections. There might be tabs such as "**Albums**" and "**Folders**."

3. Switch to the Album view by clicking on the "**Albums**" tab, or the Folders view by clicking on the "**Folders**" tab.
4. Photoshop Elements has a navigation window that allows you to navigate between various viewpoints. In the navigation bar, look for selections such as "**Album View**" and "**Folder View**."
5. Look for dropdown menus or menu bar selections that enable you to convert between Album and Folder displays.
6. There are keyboard shortcuts for toggling between perspectives on occasion. Check the program documentation or support pages for any accessible keyboard shortcuts.
7. Change the workspace in certain versions of Photoshop Elements. Check the settings or preferences to see whether you can alter how albums and folders are displayed.

Sync your media to the Cloud

Using Cloud Storage Services

1. Select a cloud storage provider such as Google Drive, Dropbox, OneDrive, or Adobe's Creative Cloud storage.
2. On your computer, install the desktop program for the cloud storage provider of your choice.
3. Within your cloud storage, create a folder just for your Photoshop Elements media.
4. Open Adobe Photoshop Elements, find your media files and transfer or copy them to the appropriate folder inside your online storage.
5. Some cloud storage providers provide automatic synchronization. If available, enable this functionality so that any changes made in the cloud folder are mirrored on all devices.

Using Adobe Creative Cloud (if Elements is available)

1. Make sure your Adobe Photoshop Elements version is up to date.
2. Use your Adobe ID to sign in to Adobe Photoshop Elements.
3. Look through the program settings or settings to see if there are any cloud syncing or Creative Cloud integration possibilities.
4. If your device supports cloud syncing, follow the on-screen prompts to configure and sync your media.

Add your metadata

Information about data is referred to as metadata. Metadata in the context of digital photographs comprises information about the photo such as the date it was shot, the camera settings used, and even information about the camera itself. This data is saved in the picture file and may be accessed and examined using a variety of software tools. Adobe Photoshop Elements enables users to examine and update picture information.

Add Metadata

1. Firstly, open Adobe Photoshop Elements.
2. Select the picture to which you want to add metadata and click **Open**.
3. Select "**File**" from the top menu.
4. Click the "**File Info**" dropdown menu. The File Info dialog box will appear.
5. The File Info dialog box has tabs for numerous sorts of information, such as Description, Camera Data, IPTC, and others. Proceed to fill in the fields with the necessary information. This might contain the title, author, copyright, keywords, and other information.
6. Once the required information has been entered, click "OK" to save the modifications.
7. To display the metadata, return to the "**File Info**" option and double-check the information you submitted.

Common Metadata Types

They include the following:

IPTC Metadata

IPTC metadata (International Press Telecommunications Council) contains information such as title, description, keywords, and copyright.

EXIF Metadata

EXIF (Exchangeable image file format) metadata provides camera-captured data such as date and time, camera settings, and, if available, GPS information.

XMP Metadata

Adobe's XMP (Extensible Metadata Platform) standard for creating, processing, and reading standardized and custom metadata for digital documents and data sets.

Search your catalog using Filters

Here are the steps:

1. To begin, launch Adobe Photoshop Elements.
2. The Organizer module in Photoshop Elements is used to manage and organize your media assets. By clicking on the "**Organizer**" button or choosing it from the menu, you can access the Organizer.
3. Make sure you're in the "**Catalog**" view, which organizes and displays your media files.
4. Search for a section or toolbar that offers filtering selections for your media files. This is often seen at the top or side of the Organizer.
5. You will see filtering options such as date, keyword, tags, ratings, and more. Choose the filter criteria you want to use.
6. You may narrow down your search even more by combining different criteria. For example, you can filter by date and keywords at the same time.
7. Once the filters have been applied, the Organizer should present the results that fit your criteria.
8. If necessary, the option to reset or clear filters to display all items should be available.

Manage your files with Keyword Tags

Adding Keyword Tags

1. Launch Adobe Photoshop Elements.
2. Open the **Photoshop Elements library** and import the photos you want to arrange. Select **"File" > "Get Photos and Videos" > "From Files and Folders"** and then go to the location of your photos.
3. In the Organizer workspace, choose the photos to tag with keywords. To pick several photos, hold down the **Ctrl or Shift key**.
4. Open the Keyword Tags Panel. The Keyword Tags panel is located on the right side of the screen. If it isn't visible, open it by going to **"Window" > "Keyword Tags"** from the menu.

5. To add keywords, go to the Keyword Tags panel and click the "+ Add Keyword Tag" button. Enter the keyword(s) of interest and hit Enter. You can enter several keywords separated by commas.
6. Select the photos to tag, then drag & drop the required keyword(s) from the Keyword Tags panel onto the chosen photos. Alternatively, you may right-click on the photos in question, choose **"Add Keyword Tags**," and enter the required keywords.

Searching and Managing Keywords

1. **Keyword Search**: Use the search box in the Keyword Tags panel to identify photos that contain specified phrases. When you enter a term, Photoshop Elements will provide related results.
2. To edit or remove keywords, choose the image(s) containing the term you want to change. Right-click a term in the term Tags window and choose "**Edit**" or "**Delete**."
3. **Organize Keywords:** To better organize your tags, create keyword categories or groups. To add a new category, right-click on the Keyword Tags panel and choose "**New Category**."
4. **View Keyword Tags in Gridview**: In the Organizer, go to the Grid mode to see your photos with their related keyword tags. To access this view, click the "**Grid**" button on the toolbar.

Manage your photos by Place

The steps:

1. Launch Photoshop Elements.
2. Import your photos into the Organizer by choosing "**Get Photos and Videos**" from the "**File**" menu or by dragging and dropping them onto the Organizer workspace.
3. Make sure you're in the "**Media**" view in the Organizer workspace.
4. Select "**Map**" from the "**View**" menu to activate the Map view.
5. Choose the photos you want to link with a certain place.
6. Drag and drag the photos you want to use into the map.
7. You can also designate a location by right-clicking on the chosen photos, selecting "**Place on Map,**" and then clicking on the map.
8. To locate particular places, use the search box in the Map view. Enter an address or a place name, and Photoshop Elements will find it on a map.

9. After linking images with places, you may see them in the Map view by location. When you click on a map marker, the images linked with that place will be shown.
10. Use tags in the Organizer to better arrange your photos. Add location-based tags to help you discover photographs later.
11. Use the "**Filter**" options in the Organizer to filter images depending on location. You can filter photos by location by using the "**Filter**" drop-down menu.
12. If you need to update the location of a picture, right-click on it, choose "**Location Info**," and make the appropriate adjustments.
13. If your images have geo-tagging information, you may export them with it intact. This is helpful for online picture sharing since some platforms show photographs on a map based on geo-tags.

Manage your media files by Date or Event

Organizing by Date

1. Launch Photoshop Elements.
2. Select "**Organizer**" as your workspace.
3. In the menu, click "**File**" and then "**Get Photos and Videos**" to import your media files into the Organizer.
4. In the Organizer, choose the "**Date View**" option. This will sort your photos by the date they were taken.
5. Within the Date View, you can further sort your media by clicking on the column headings, such as "**Date**" or "**Time**."
6. Add tags or captions to your media files to help you discover them later. This is accomplished by choosing a file and clicking on the "**Info**" tab.

Organizing by Event

- You can tag images from the same event in the Organizer. Choose the images you want to include in an event, then click the "**Add a Tag**" button to add a new tag to the event.
- Select "**Tags View**" to view all of your tagged things. You can simply search and access media files related to various events here.
- Albums can be used to organize images connected to a certain occasion. To make a collection, go to the "**Albums**" menu, select "**New Album,**" and then add photos from other folders.
- Arrange your albums in the order you choose by dragging and dropping them.

- Use the Organizer's search bar and filters to easily find photographs connected to a given event.

Instant Fix a photo

The steps:

1. First of all, launch Adobe Photoshop Elements.
2. Select the picture to be repaired by navigating to "**File**" > "**Open**" and choose it.
3. Select "**Enhance**" from the top menu bar.
4. Select "**Auto Smart Fix.**" This tool automatically changes your phone's brightness, contrast, and color balance to improve its overall look.
5. You can also use the **"Quick Fix**" feature. This gives a streamlined interface with sliders for lighting, color, and sharpness adjustment.
6. If necessary, go to the "**Enhance**" menu, select "**Adjust Lighting**," and then "**Levels**" or "**Brightness/Contrast.**" Adjust the sliders to enhance the photo's overall lighting and contrast.
7. To fine-tune the colors in your picture, go to the "**Enhance**" menu, select "**Adjust Color**," and then select "**Adjust Hue/Saturation**" or "**Adjust Color Curves**."
8. To improve picture sharpness, go to the "**Enhance**" menu, choose "**Adjust Sharpness,**" and use the sliders to sharpen the image.
9. Once you're happy with the changes, save them by navigating to "**File**" > "**Save**" or "Save As."

Back up your Organizer Catalog

The Organizer Catalog in Adobe Photoshop Elements is where your media assets (such as images and movies) are grouped and maintained. It's a good idea to back up your Organizer Catalog regularly to avoid data loss in the event of an unforeseen problem.

Here's how to make a backup of your Organizer Catalog:

1. Go to your computer's desktop and launch **Adobe Photoshop Elements 2024**.
2. Click the "**Organizer**" tab in the Photoshop Elements workspace to open it. This is where your media files are organized and managed.
3. In the Organizer, find the catalog you want to back up and click it. If you have several catalogs, choose the one you want to backup.
4. In the top-left corner of the Organizer window, click the "**File**" menu.

5. From the File menu, select "**Backup Catalog**." This option is usually at the bottom of the menu.
6. Choose Backup settings. A dialog box will pop up, enabling you to choose your backup settings. Select a spot on your computer or an external disk to store the backup file. Depending on your options, you may also be able to include media files in the backup.
7. Once you've chosen a backup location and any extra selections, click the "OK" or "**Save**" button to begin the backup process.
8. Depending on the size of your catalog, the backup procedure may take some time. Allow the procedure to finish without interfering.
9. Once the backup is finished, browse to the place you provided to confirm that the backup file is there and that it was correctly made.

Frequently Asked Questions

1. How do you use the media browser area in Photoshop Elements?
2. How do you add your metadata?
3. How do you search your catalog using filters?
4. How do you use the back or all media buttons?
5. How do you sync your media to the Cloud?
6. How do you auto analyze your media?
7. How do you instantly fix a photo?
8. How do you manage your files with keyword tags?
9. How do you manage your media files by date or event?

CHAPTER SIXTEEN

CREATE FUN PIECES

Overview

Want to create fun pieces in Photoshop Elements 2024? This chapter talks about how to create different fun pieces in Photoshop Elements including creating a slideshow, creating a photo reel, how to create a greeting card and so much more.

Create an Organizer Slideshow

Create slideshows

The steps:

1. **Launch an album or catalog in the Media view and choose Slideshow in the following ways:**
   - Select **Slideshow** from the taskbar.
   - Move to the top right of the screen, click **Create** and then **Slideshow**.

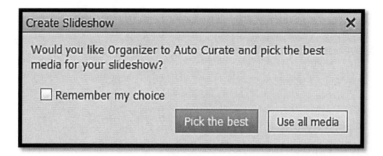

2. You can also build a slideshow by right-clicking anywhere on the screen in the Media view and selecting Create a Slideshow.
3. Choose **Pick the best** to have Elements Organizer automatically compile your finest photos.

Note: Alternatively, in the upper-right corner of the screen, choose **Auto Curate**. Adjust the slider to the desired number of photos, and then click **Slideshow** on the taskbar.

4. The auto-curated media files are used to generate a slideshow preview in the Slideshow window.

Note:

- The first picture in the slideshow is the text slide, which shows the presentation's title and subtitle.
- The slideshow preview is of poor quality. When you export the slideshow, a better-quality video is available.

Manually select photos and videos

The step:

1. In the media grid, choose the photos and videos you want.
2. **Choose Slideshow using one of the following ways:**
- Click **Slideshow** in the taskbar.
- In the upper-right corner of the screen, click **Create** and then Slideshow.
- Choose **Create a Slideshow** from the context menu when you right-click anywhere on the screen in Media view
3. A slideshow preview is created in the Slideshow window using the specified media files. The slideshow preview is of a lesser resolution. When you export the slideshow, a better-quality video is available.

Create a Photo Collage

Create photo collages

Perform the following steps to make a photo collage:

1. Open two or more pictures in Photoshop Elements. You can also select photos in the Elements Organizer. A maximum of 8 photos can be picked to make a photo collage.

2. Select **Create > Photo Collage**. Based on the number of open photos, an appealing collage is automatically constructed. Using sophisticated auto-crop, the most noticeable element of the picture (face) is targeted and put in the collage frames.
3. (Optional) Select a layout for your photo collage. The arrangement ideas are provided depending on the number of photos in your collage. You can choose a layout across four categories: Landscape, Portrait, Facebook Cover, and Instagram.
4. Add, subtract, replace, and swap photos from your collage.
   - **Add a photo:** Select **Computer** to upload photos saved on your computer. Or, click Organizer to choose photos from your collection or albums.

   - **Replace a photo:** Right-click on the photo you want to change. From the context menu, select **Replace Photo** to open the Photo dialog and choose the appropriate photo from your computer to replace.
   - **Remove a picture:** Right-click on the photo you wish to delete. From the context menu, select **Remove Photo**.
5. When you add or delete a picture from your collage, a new layout is instantly put into the composite.
6. (Optional) Double-click on a picture to reveal the heads-up display (HUD). Use the HUD to rotate your picture left or right, zoom in or out, swap the photo, or you can even remove the photo. Once you've made the necessary adjustments, click the green check mark to save your work.
7. (Optional) Select **Graphics** in the lower-right corner to select a background or a frame. Double-click on the appropriate background or frame to put it in your collage.
8. (Optional) Select **Advanced Mode or Basic Mode** to pick how you want to see and change the photos you want to work with. In the Basic mode, you can add text and move text or pictures.

In the Advanced mode, you have the whole toolbox and layer option. You can use the options to modify the photographs and alter layers.

9. **Do one of the following to save the photo collage:**
   - In the Taskbar, click **Save**. You can save your picture collage in several formats such as Photoshop, BMP, JPEG, PNG, and more.
   - Select **File > Save**. By default, the collage/project is stored in your Pictures folder, however, you can save the collage/project to another place.
   - Select Ctrl+S (Windows) or Command+S (Mac OS).
10. **Carry out any of the following to print the photo collage:**
    - In the Taskbar, select **Print**.
    - Select **File > Print**.
    - Click Ctrl+P (Windows) or Command+P (Mac OS).

Create a Photo Reel

Follow these steps to create a Photo Reel:

1. Select **File > Open** to open preferred photos for creating Photo Reel. To make a Photo Reel, a minimum of two photographs is necessary.
2. Click **Create > Photo Reel**.
3. All the chosen photographs will be organized in frames displayed in Timeline. Drag and drop to rearrange the photos.

Note: Add extra photos to the Timeline by choosing the **Add media** from Computer or Organizer options offered in the Layout section.

4. Within the arrangement tab, select a photo arrangement that matches the unique criteria of your favorite social network. Standard settings for Instagram, Facebook, YouTube, TikTok, Snapchat, Twitter, and Threads are supplied in the Layout panel.

5. Customize the display time unique to each picture frame appearing in the photo Reel by tapping over the time indicated on the photo thumbnail. Select **Apply to all checkboxes** to apply at the same time across all your photos.
6. Choose the three-dot symbol accessible above the thumbnails to alter various settings linked with each picture frame.
7. Add the relevant text to your photos with the Type tool. You can further alter the features of the text like font, font size, font style, color, leading, tracking, alignment, and more based on your needs.

8. **Apply the required effect to your photos by using any of the suggested workflows:**
   - Select the preferred Effects thumbnail and apply the effect exclusively to the chosen picture.
   - Apply the selected effect to all your photographs by choosing Apply to all photos for a consistent appearance.
9. If you want to reverse the imposed effect, click **No Effect**. Change the level of the applied effects by utilizing the intensity slider accessible inside the Effects panel.
10. Choose the required graphics from the Graphics panel with a single click on the thumbnails.
11. Click **Export > Save** to save the Photo Reel in MP4 or GIF format to share with other people easily.

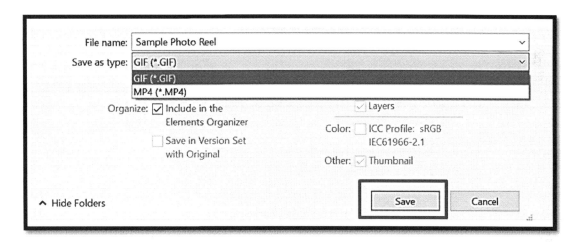

Create a Quote Graphic

Follow the steps:

1. Open Adobe Photoshop Elements 2024.
2. Go to **"File" > "New" > "Blank File."**
3. Set the dimensions for your graphic. Choose a size suited for social networking sites or any other platform where you want to post the image.
4. You can either build a solid color background or import a picture. For a solid color background, use the **"Paint Bucket"** tool to fill the background layer. For an image background, go to **"File" > "Place"** to import an image.
5. Choose the Text tool from the toolbar (T).

6. Click on the canvas where you want to insert your text.
7. Then proceed to enter your quote.
8. Adjust the font, size, color, and other text settings using the selections on the toolbar or the Text panel.
9. Highlight the text to apply formatting selections.
10. Adjust the font, size, color, and style as required.
11. Try various typefaces to discover one that compliments your quote.
12. Experiment with effects or styles to make your text more visually attractive.
13. Right-click on the text layer in the Layers panel.
14. Select "**Blending Options**" to obtain effects like drop shadow, stroke, etc.
15. To improve your quote graphic, try adding ornamental elements or icons.
16. You can find free icons or shapes online, or you may build your own using Photoshop Elements features.
17. Once you're pleased with your quotation graphic, save your work.
18. Go to **"File" > "Save As"** and select a format (e.g., JPEG or PNG) according to your requirements.
19. You can now publish your quote graphic on social media, your website, or any other platform.

Create Photo Prints

Follow the steps below to create photo prints:

1. Open Adobe Photoshop Elements 2024.
2. Open the picture you want to print by going to "**File**" > "**Open**" and choosing your image.
3. Go to **"Image" > "Resize" > "Image Size."**
4. Set the proportions of your picture depending on your desired print size. Make sure the resolution is set to at least 300 pixels per inch (ppi) for high-quality printouts.
5. If required, use the Crop tool (shortcut: C) to modify the composition of your picture for printing.
6. Use the "**Enhance**" option to make color and contrast changes if required.
7. Also use options like "**Auto Levels**," "**Auto Contrast**," or manually adjust brightness and contrast.
8. Go to **"Filter" > "Sharpen" > "Unsharp Mask"** to boost the sharpness of your picture.

9. Adjust the settings until you obtain the required sharpness. Be cautious not to over-sharpen.

Select the Print Layout

1. Go to "**File**" > "**Print**" to open the Print dialog box.
2. In the Print dialog box, pick your printer and paper size.
3. Select the layout selections such as single pictures or numerous photos per page.

Set Print Options

1. Configure print settings including orientation, color management, and paper type.
2. Make sure you check out the "**Print Resolution**" option. Ensure it matches the resolution you specified previously in the Image Size dialog.

Preview and Adjust

1. Use the print preview option to see how your picture will appear on paper.
2. Make any required modifications, such as scaling or positioning, to meet your print arrangement.

Print

1. Once happy with the preview, click the "**Print**" option.
2. Follow the on-screen directions to finish the printing process.
3. After printing, check the actual print for color accuracy, sharpness, and general quality.
4. If required, go back to Photoshop Elements to make corrections and reprint.

Create a Photo Book

Photo albums are fantastic souvenirs for your memories. With numerous size and theme selections, Photoshop Elements makes it simple to create picture books.

The steps:

1. Choose **Create > Photo Book**.

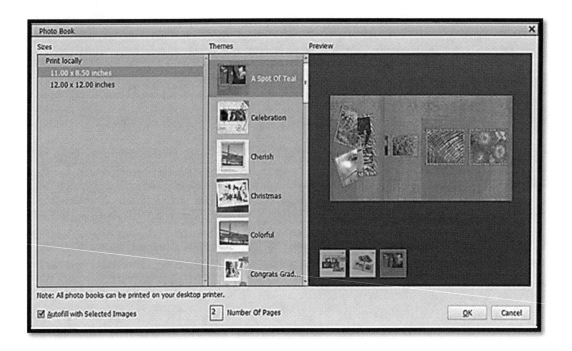

2. **Perform any of the following in the Photo Book dialog box and click OK:**
- Select a size for the photo book.
- Choose a theme.
- Choose **Autofill with selected images** if you want to use images selected in the Photo Bin.
- Set the number of pages (2 to 78) for the photo book.
3. The project opens the following selections in the lower-right corner:
- **Pages**: Displays you the pages of the photo book
- **Layout**: Displays the arrangement of the photo book
- **Graphics**: Allows you to modify the background, frames, and graphics in the photo book.

Carry out the following actions:

- Add photos to your photo book.
- Add the background.
- Include frames if you wish to include multiple photographs on one page.
- Add visuals as required.

4. (Optional) Select **Advanced Mode or Basic Mode** to choose the mode in which you want to see and change the images you want to work with. In the Advanced mode, you have the entire toolbox and layer option. Use the options to modify the photographs and alter layers.
5. **Do one of the following to save the picture book:**
- In the Taskbar, click **Save**.
- Select **File > Save**. By default, projects are stored in your My Pictures folder, however, you can save them in another place.
- Press Ctrl+S (Windows) or Command+S (Mac OS).
6. **Carry out one of the following to print the picture book:**
- Choose **File > Print**.
- Press Ctrl+P (Windows) or Command+P (Mac OS).

Note: If a picture included in the photo book is relocated from its original position on your computer, you cannot print the book. However, you can still save the project.

Create a Greeting Card

Here are the steps:

1. Choose **Create > Greeting Card**.

2. **Perform any of the following in the Greeting Card dialog box and click OK:**
- Select a size for the greeting card.
- Choose a theme.

- Select **Autofill with selected images** if you want to use images selected in the Photo Bin.
3. **The project opens the following selections in the lower-right corner:**
- **Pages**: Displays the pages of the greeting card.
- **Layout**: Displays the arrangement of the greeting card.
- **Graphics**: Allows you to modify the background, frames, and graphics in the photo book

Carry out the following actions:
- Add photos to your greeting card.
- Add the background.
- Include frames if you want to add multiple photos on one page.
- Add visuals as required.
7. (Optional) Select **Advanced Mode or Basic Mode** to choose the mode in which you want to see and change the images you want to work with. In the Advanced mode, you have the entire toolbox and layer option. Use the options to modify the photographs and alter layers.
8. **Do one of the following to save the greeting card:**
- In the Taskbar, click **Save**.
- Select **File > Save**. By default, projects are stored in your My Pictures folder; however, you can save them in another place.
- Press Ctrl+S (Windows) or Command+S (Mac OS).
9. **Carry out one of the following to print the greeting card:**
- Choose **File > Print**.
- Press Ctrl+P (Windows) or Command+P (Mac OS).

Note: You cannot print the greeting card if a picture featured in it is relocated from its original place on your computer. You may, however, still save the project.

Create a Photo Calendar

Create photo calendars using Photoshop Elements to display your images.

Here are the steps:

1. Choose **Create > Photo Calendar**.

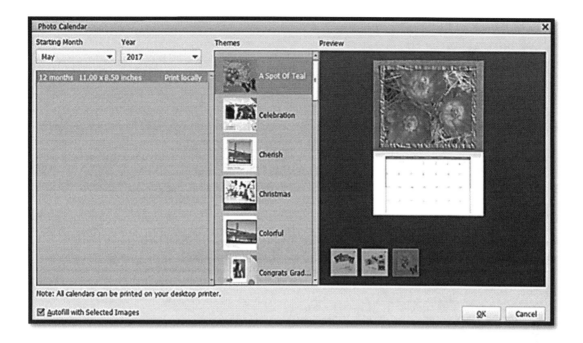

2. **In the Photo Calendar dialog box, enter the following information and click OK:**
- Choose a beginning month and year.
- Decide on a calendar size.
- Decide on a theme.
- Choose **Autofill with selected images** if you want to use images from your Photo Bin.

3. **In the lower-right corner, the project opens with the following options:**
- **Pages**: Displays the photo book's pages.
- **Layout**: Displays the picture book's layout.
- **Graphics**: Allows you to change the photo book's background, frames, and graphics.

Carry out the following actions:

- Include photos on your calendar.
- Create the background.
- Use frames to add additional photos to a single page.
- If required, provide visuals.
4. (Optional) Select either **Advanced Mode or Basic Mode** to examine and change the photos you wish to work with. The whole toolbox and layer options are

available in Advanced mode. The selections allow you to modify photographs and adjust layers.

5. **To save the calendar, do one of the following:**
   - Click **Save** in the Taskbar.
   - Select **File > Save**. Projects are stored in your My Pictures folder by default, but you can save them elsewhere.
   - On Windows, use Ctrl+S, on Mac, Command+S.
6. **To print the calendar, choose one of the following options:**
   - Go to **File > Print**.
   - On Windows, use Ctrl+P, on Mac, Command+P.

Note: You cannot print the calendar if a picture featured in it is moved from its original position on your computer. Meanwhile, you can still save the project.

Create Prints and Gifts

The steps:

1. Open Adobe Photoshop Elements.
2. To start a new project, go to the top menu and select "**File**."
3. Select the appropriate size and resolution for your project. Consider the dimensions that are appropriate for the type of print or gift you're making (for example, a canvas print, greeting card, or photo book).
4. Click "**File**" and then "**Open**" to import the images for your project.
5. Use tools like the Crop Tool, Adjustment Layers, and Filters to arrange and edit your images as needed.
6. To add text to your project, use the Text Tool. Change the font, size, and color to match your design.
7. To add creative elements, experiment with different brushes, shapes, and drawing tools.
8. To improve the overall appearance of your project, use filters or adjustments.
9. Save your project by clicking "**File**" and then "**Save As**." Select a suitable file format (for example, PSD) to preserve layers and editing capabilities.
10. Once you're happy with your design, save it for printing.
11. Select "**File**" and then choose "**Export**" or "**Save As**."
12. Select a suitable file format for printing (e.g., JPEG or TIFF).
13. Set the resolution to the specifications of your preferred printing service.
14. Upload your exported file to an online printing service or a nearby print shop.

15. Select the print size, paper type, and any other customization options that the printing service provides.
16. To complete your order, simply follow the instructions.

Frequently Asked Questions

1. How do you create an organizer slideshow in Photoshop Elements?
2. How do you create a photo collage?
3. How do you create a photo reel?
4. How do you create a quote graphic?
5. How do you create a photo calendar?
6. How do you create prints and gifts?
7. How do you create a photo book?

CHAPTER SEVENTEEN

SHARE YOUR PHOTOS AND VIDEOS

Overview

Here comes the last and final chapter. Chapter seventeen discusses sharing your photos and videos on Photoshop Elements 2024.

Save Changes

Take one of the following actions:

- Select "**Save**" from the File menu.
- Select Ctrl+S (Windows) or Command+S (Mac OS).

Save changes with a different file format, name, or location

The Save as option, which is located in the File menu, allows you to choose several settings for saving picture files. These settings include the format, whether the saved file should be included in the Elements Organizer catalog, and whether or not layers in an image should be preserved. You may have access to additional settings depending on the format that you choose.

1. Choose from the following options:
- Select "**Save As**" from the File menu.
- Select Ctrl+Shift+S (Windows) or Command+Shift+S (Mac OS).
2. Select the following settings for saving the file, and then click the **Save button**:

Note: Some file types bring up an additional dialog box that has additional selections.

File Name

Provide the file name for the picture that has been saved.

File Format

Choose the file format that the picture will be stored in.

Add the Elements Organizer

It is necessary to include the saved file in your catalog for it to be seen in the Photo Browser. It is important to note that the Elements Organizer does not handle all of the file types that are supported in the Edit workspace. EPS is one of the formats that prevents you from selecting this option when you save a file in one of these formats.

Save In Version Set with Original

The file is saved, and then it is added to a version set in the Photo Browser. This helps to maintain order among the many versions of the picture. Unless Include In The Organizer is chosen, this option is not accessible to be selected.

Layers

Every layer in the picture is preserved. It is possible that the picture does not have any layers if this option is either deactivated or unavailable. If you see a caution symbol next to the Layers checkbox, it means that the layers in your picture will be automatically merged or flattened depending on the format that you choose. Sometimes, all of the layers are combined into one. Change the format you're using to keep the layers intact.

As a Copy

It will save a copy of the file while maintaining the open state of the present file. Specifically, the copy is saved to the folder that contains the file that is presently open.

ICC Profile

Create a color profile that is embedded in the picture for certain file types.

Thumbnail

The data for the file's thumbnail files is saved. This choice is accessible in the Preferences dialog box when the **Ask when saving option for Image Previews** is selected as the option to be performed.

Use Lower Case Extension

This function allows you to change the case of the file extension.

Share your photos via email

There are different methods including:

Using Photoshop Elements Organizer

1. Launch Adobe Photoshop Elements on your computer.
2. Use the Organizer to search for and select the images that you want to share with others.
3. To choose photos to add to the email, click on the photos you want to include. While clicking on numerous photos, you can choose multiple photos by holding down the Control key (on Windows) or the Command key (on Mac) simultaneously.
4. Select the symbol that represents the email. The "Email" icon or option should be found. This is often found in the menu or the toolbar of the program.
5. Select Your Email Client Photoshop Elements may prompt you to select your default email client, which may be anything like Outlook, Mail, or another similar program. Decide which one you will use.
6. When you click the "**Compose Email**" button, a new email message together with the photos you chose will open up. After that, you will be able to construct your email, including the recipients, the topic, and any other messages.
7. When you are ready to send your email, you can send it by clicking on the "**Send**" or "**Send/Receive**" button. This will send the email along with the photographs that you have attached.

Using Adobe Photoshop Elements Editor

1. Launch Adobe Photoshop Elements by opening Photoshop Elements.
2. Launch the Editor and launch the picture that you wish to share with others.
3. From the Editor menu, select "**File**," then "**Share**," and **lastly "Attach to Email**." This will attach the documents to your emails.
4. Like the Organizer technique, you can be requested to select the email client service that you use by default.
5. You will see a new email message open with the picture that you have attached. Create the email you want to send, including the recipients, the subject, and any extra messages.

6. After you have finished composing your email, you can send it by clicking on the "**Send**" or "**Send/Receive**" button. This will send the email along with the picture that you have attached.

Share your photos on Flickr

Using Flickr

1. In the Editor, choose the **Share dropdown menu** and select **Flickr** from the list. If the photos that are presently open have not been saved, you will be requested to save the pictures automatically. Please choose OK to continue.
2. For Photoshop Elements to be able to operate with Flickr, you will need to provide permission when you have not previously shared with Flickr. Ensure you follow the steps that appear on the screen to permit Photoshop Elements to upload photographs to your Flickr account.
3. **Through the Flickr dialog, choose the selections that you want to apply to the picture or series of photos that you are uploading:**
- Add or delete photos to be posted to Flickr by selecting the plus (+) or minus (-) sign that is located above the Items preview area. This will allow you to add or remove photos.
- With Set, you can post a collection of photos. For slideshows on Flickr, this is the approach to take. Make changes to the Set settings after you have selected the checkbox labeled "**Upload as a Set**." You have the option of building a new Set or selecting an existing one. The Set has to have a name and a description provided.
- **Audience**: To regulate or limit the visibility of the Set to users from outside the Set, use the **Who can see these photos? option**.
- **Tags**: To tag the album, you will need to provide a list of keywords.
4. Once the photos have been uploaded, the Flickr dialog box will provide two buttons:
- Check out Flickr. Clicking on this button will cause your web browser to open and display the photographs that you have uploaded. From the online browser, you may copy the URL of your Flickr photographs and paste them into Dropbox.
- To end the dialog, use the Done button.

Share your video on Vimeo

The steps:

1. To begin, launch your project in Photoshop Elements. Your video project should be opened once you have launched Adobe Photoshop Elements.
2. To make any required edits to your video, you can make use of the editing tools that are included in Adobe Photoshop Elements.
3. When you are pleased with the changes you have made, go to the "**File**" menu and choose either "**Export**" or "**Save As.**"
4. The first step is to choose an appropriate format and settings for your video. MP4 files that have been compressed using H.264 are a common format for sharing on the web.
5. To save the output video file, you will need to choose a place on your computer and then click either "**Save**" or "**Export**."

Setting up a Vimeo upload

1. You should open your web browser and go to Vimeo.
2. If you do not already have an account, you will be required to create one. You should log in if you have an account.
3. On Vimeo's website, you should look for a button labeled "**Upload**" and then click on it.
4. Using Adobe Photoshop Elements, choose the video file that you exported from the program.
5. Ensure that you provide the necessary information, including the title, description, and privacy settings for your video where applicable.
6. You can begin the process of uploading your film to Vimeo by clicking on the button.
7. Upon completion of the upload, Vimeo will begin processing the video automatically. According to the size and duration of your video, this might take a considerable amount of time.
8. After the processing is complete, you will be able to examine your movie and make any necessary edits. Click the "**Publish**" or "**Save**" button whenever you are ready to publish or save your work.
9. Vimeo will provide you with a link to your film after it has been published on its platform. You are free to distribute this link to other people.

Share as a PDF Slideshow

The steps:

1. Launch Photoshop Elements and arrange the pictures that you want to include in your slideshow in the appropriate order.
2. Go to the File menu, then choose **New**, and then select **Blank File**.
3. Make sure that the dimensions of your slideshow are set. For instance, if the dimensions of your photos are typical, you can choose these dimensions: 1920 by 1080 pixels.
4. Place your photos on the blank file by dragging and dropping them.
5. Ensure that they are arranged in the sequence that you choose for your presentation.
6. You can create transitions between photos by heading to **Window > Effects** and choosing Transitions. This will allow you to set up transitions between images.
7. Specify the length of each picture's display in the Transitions panel if you want each image to be shown for a certain amount of time.
8. You should save the file for your project in the format of Photoshop Elements (PSE).

Exporting as Images

- To create a slideshow, choose **File > Export > Slideshow**.
- Determine a place to store the photos that have been exported.
- Set the file format to JPEG or another picture format, whatever you like.
- Select the **Export option**.

Creating a PDF from Images

Use External Software

- When you have finished exporting your slideshow as photos, you can use third-party software to convert them into a PDF format.
- Merge numerous photos into a PDF using a variety of tools, some of which are available online and some of which are available offline. For instance, Adobe Acrobat is a product that is often used for this particular function.

Online Converters

- The first step is to upload your photos to an online converter that is capable of converting images to PDF format. This particular service is provided by several different websites.

Storing Media in the Cloud

A general set of actions to do this is as follows:

1. The first step is to select a cloud storage service that would be suitable for your needs. Cloud storage services such as Google Drive, Dropbox, Microsoft OneDrive, and Adobe Creative Cloud Storage are very popular selections.
2. **Transfer the Media to the Cloud:**
- If you do not already have an account with the cloud storage provider that you have selected, you should create one.
- You should upload your media files (such as pictures, movies, and so on) to the cloud storage service. The service will typically give either a web interface or a desktop program for users to use to do this task.
3. Launch Adobe Photoshop Elements after all of your media assets have been uploaded to the cloud.
4. You can establish a connection to your cloud storage by heading to the **'File'** menu in the Organizer workspace, selecting **'Connect to Elements Account,'** and then selecting the provider that you are using.
5. To import files from your linked cloud storage, you need to make use of the Organizer. Within the Elements Organizer, you will be able to access and organize your media files thanks to this feature.
6. To edit photos, open them from your cloud storage inside Photoshop Elements.
7. Select the option to save your altered files back to the cloud storage location while you are saving your files.

Frequently Asked Questions

1. How do you share your photos via email?
2. How do you share your video on Vimeo?
3. How do you share your photos on Flickr?
4. How do you store your media in the Cloud?
5. How do you share your file as a PDF slideshow?

CONCLUSION

Photoshop Elements 2024 now enables users to make short reels (vertical films) using only a few photographs, as well as add graphics, scripts, and other effects to the video. Additionally, the upgrade makes it simple to add numerous creative decorations to images. Furthermore, the Photoshop Elements 2024 license includes free access to Adobe Stock images. Object removal is another popular function. Power lines, pedestrians, and other objects that distract from the focus of a picture may be removed with a single brush stroke. Another popular tool is background replacement, which allows you to effortlessly swap one background with another. Photoshop Elements 2024 has a new variety of backgrounds to pick from. The option to modify face characteristics is very popular in Photoshop Elements. Open closed eyelids automatically, correct red-eye, whiten teeth, flip frowns upside down, fine-tune facial tilt, smooth skin, and more. There are also artistic elements like watercolor and drawing effects. Aside from that, there are tools for making calendars, greeting cards, picture collages, and slideshows to share.

While the automated process is at the heart of Photoshop Elements, this does not diminish the fact that Photoshop Elements is a powerful picture editing tool. It has everything from simple touch-up tools to complicated features like the motion function, which allows you to move a specific area of a picture. Simply choose the motion's direction and speed, then save the shot as an MP4 or GIF file to post on social media.

INDEX

1

101*101 average, 130
11*11 average, 129

2

2024 version of Photoshop Elements, 1

3

3*3 average, 129
31*31 average, 130

5

5*5 average, 129
51*51 average, 130

6

6GB of hard-disk space, 33

A

A layer in Photoshop Elements, 21
A raster file, 10
A vector file, 11
About photo effects, 299
Absolute vs. Relative, 221
Access free Adobe Stock pictures to broaden your creative options, 4
Accessing the Hub, 39
Actions, 3, 4, 63, 123, 124, 213
Adaptive Grid, 336
add layers, 32
ADD PHOTO EFFECTS AND FILTERS, 291
Add Text guided edit, 81
Adding a Border, 221
adding blank space, 20

Adding Guides, 45
Adding Keyword Tags, 343
Adding layers, 250
Adding Text and Graphics, 30
Adding Texture, 167
addition to Photoshop, 27
addition to resizing photos, 20
additional capabilities, 1
additional editing possibilities, 23
Additional Foreground, 134
Additional options, 189
Additional Suggestions, 219
Adjust Anti-Aliasing Settings, 158
Adjust color curves, 91
Adjust Edge, 215
Adjust Sharpness, 242, 346
Adjust sharpness in camera raw files, 320
Adjust the color of the font, 280
Adjust the image size, 220
Adjust the opacity, 21, 23
adjusting the resolution of an image, 8
Adjustment Filters, 294
adjustment layer, 91, 130, 161, 230, 250, 260, 262, 263, 271
adjustment layers, 21, 25, 27, 28, 130, 208, 230, 262, 263, 267, 271, 308
Adjustment layers, 28, 30, 250
Adjustments, 62, 72, 77, 215, 226, 227, 291
Adobe After Effects, 27
Adobe Creative Cloud Storage, 368
Adobe Illustrator, 15, 27, 32
Adobe InDesign, 27
Adobe Lightroom, 31
Adobe Photoshop is a raster-based software application, 15
Adobe Premiere Pro, 27
Adobe Sensei AI, 1, 211
ADVANCED PHOTO EDITING TOOLS, 312
Align menu, 139, 141
Align Text, 286
Alignment tool, 116
Alignment Tool, 114, 115, 121
All layers, 130
All Media Button, 339

Alpha, 22, 23, 24
alpha channel, 22, 23, 24, 273
alpha channels, 22, 23, 273
Amount, 145, 154, 244
an artistic background, 298
Anchor Points, 221
Anti-aliased, 158, 209, 287
appearance of squares on graph paper, 14
Apply a filter, 293
Apply a Light Touch, 170
Apply an Effect, Texture, or Frame, 77
Apply style to text, 280
appropriate applications and contexts, 10
Arrange menu, 138
Arrange menus, 141
arrange multiple windows, 136
Artboard, 16
Artboard and canvas sizes, 16
artboards active, 16
Artistic effects, 300
artistic elements, 369
Artistic Filters, 295
As a Copy, 65, 363
Assign a color to a layer or a group, 253
Auto Selection tool, 50, 86
automated process, 369
Automatic cropping, 198
Automatic cropping recommendations, 198
automation, 1

B

B&W Color Pop, 78
B&W Detail, 96
Back Button, 339
background color, 20, 53, 76, 102, 126, 131, 132, 134, 175, 205, 206, 232, 253, 306
Background Eraser, 177
Background Gradient button, 106
Background Layer, 21, 192, 242
basic image editing application, 1
Basic Workspace, 58
Basics, 78, 81, 82, 85, 86, 88
Begin with the Home screen, 41
Bicubic, 19
Bicubic Sharper, 19
Bicubic Smoother, 19
Bilinear, 19

Bin Actions, 27
Black & White, 78, 92
Black and White, 28, 92, 95, 98, 99, 145, 237
Blend Images, 122
Blend it in, 243
Blending, 22, 26, 119, 120, 162, 165, 167, 195, 243, 310, 354
Blending Modes, 22, 26, 165, 195, 310
Blue, 5, 91, 93, 226, 231, 236, 334
blue pixels, 232
Blur Filters, 295
Blur tool, 51
Blur Tool Tips, 165
Blur, Smudge, and Sharpen, 164
BMP, 67, 351
Border Preset button, 100
Brighten Eyes, 112
Brightness and Contrast" and "Sharpen, 78
Brightness/Contrast, 28, 226, 232, 233, 237, 346
brush tool settings, 178
Burn tool, 52

C

Camera, 89, 294, 315, 316, 317, 318, 319, 320, 321, 322, 323, 328, 335, 342
Cancel, 83, 84, 91, 106, 108, 289, 299, 304, 316, 318, 320
Canvas Resizing, 223
Canvas size, 16, 17, 221
Canvas size and picture size, 16
Cascade, 136
CCITT, 69
Change colors in specific areas of a photo, 239
Change or exchange photographs, 102
Change text color, 280
change the canvas size, 20, 221
change the color and thickness of the stroke, 187
Change the guides and grid settings, 47
Change the name of a preset, 327
Change the orientation of a type layer, 282
Change the rulers' zero origin and settings, 46
Change the tool preferences, 55
Change your general preferences, 55
Changing Image Size, 18
Changing the Album and Folder Views, 340
Changing the Canvas Size, 20
Changing the picture size, 17

Channel Mixer, 28
Choose a font family and style, 279
Choose a font size, 279
Choose a language, 34
Choose a tool, 54, 56
Choose an image sky or background with one click for easier editing, 3
Classic, 74, 301
Clone Stamp, 7, 51, 86, 161, 162, 163, 203, 308, 309
Clone Stamp Tool, 86, 161, 162, 163, 308, 309
Clone Stamp tool (S, 51
Close the windows, 137
cloud storage inside Photoshop Elements., 368
Cloud storage services, 368
Cloud Storage Services, 341
CMYK, 25, 31, 329, 333, 334
Collage, 122, 349, 350
Color Balance, 28, 226, 230
Color Channels, 25
Color Correction, 26
Color Depth, 5
Color Grading, 30
Color Information, 5, 334
Color Modes, 25
Color Picker, 25, 53, 102, 111, 126, 127, 134, 136, 175, 181
Color Replacement tool, 52
color spectrum, 25, 126, 228
Color Swatches, 63, 131, 132, 133
Colorize Photo, 238, 239
colors of the shapes., 184
Combine photos, 121
Combine Shapes, 186
Commit button., 106, 278, 289, 290
Commit current operation button, 83, 84
Common Metadata Types, 342
Community and Updates, 40
companion app, 1
Compatibility, 13, 31, 331
Compatibility and conversion, 13
Complex Image Manipulation, 207
Compositing, 29
compressed JPEGs, 4
comprise fixed dots, 14
concealing, 214, 250
CONCLUSION, 369
Confirm that you have a valid Adobe ID., 34
connecting, 186, 250

Cons, 31
Constraining Proportions, 221
Content-Aware, 54, 123, 157, 158, 159, 160, 202, 309
Content-Aware Move tool, 54
Contextual Controls, 337
Contiguous, 175, 177, 180, 181, 229
Continue editing - In Quick, 83
Continuous, 175, 177
Contract, 210
Contrast, 78, 91, 93, 145, 214, 215, 226, 233, 234, 306, 319, 354
Convert the Background layer into a regular layer, 252
Cookie Cutter tool, 54, 55, 199
Coordinates, 329, 333
Copy a selection using commands, 140, 142
Copy and paste selections into the picture., 250
Copy layers from one image file to another, 266
Copy Merged, 140, 142, 143
Copy selections with the Move tool, 139, 142
Copying selections or layers, 139, 142
Correction of Geometric Distortion, 122
Create a Greeting Card, 357
Create a high-pass layer, 242
Create a new layer from part of another layer, 251
Create a new layer group, 253
Create a Photo Book, 355
Create a Photo Calendar, 358
Create a Photo Reel, 351
Create a Picture Stack, 107
Create a Quote Graphic, 353
CREATE AND EDIT TEXT, 276
Create and name a new blank layer, 251
Create and share fast-moving Photo Reels, 2
CREATE FUN PIECES, 348
Create non-square graphics, 271
Create photo collages, 349
Create Photo Prints, 354
Create Prints and Gifts, 360
Create stylish photo text for shareable posts, 4
Create Texture, 156, 160
Creating a new layer mask, 270
Creating a PDF from Images, 367
creative possibilities in Photoshop, 29
Crop to a selection boundary, 197
Crop to Remove Background, 204
Crop tool, 55, 72, 196, 197, 198, 199, 200, 227, 313, 322, 354
Crop tool,, 72, 227

Current and Below no adjustment, 130
Current layer, 130
Custom, 45, 53, 54, 58, 59, 60, 94, 104, 110, 197, 250, 275, 277, 289, 303
Custom guidelines, 45
Custom Method, 110
Custom Shape tool, 53
custom workspace, 59
Custom Workspace, 58, 59, 60, 250
Customizable Buttons, 179
Customization, 334, 336
Customize workspace, 43
Cut and paste a selection into another photo, 217
Cylindrical, 122

D

Darken Eyebrows, 112
Decontaminate Colors, 145, 214
Define a feathered edge for a selection tool, 209
Define a feathered edge for an existing selection, 210
Defringe Layer, 232
Defringe Layer swaps, 232
dehaze or colorize a shot, 3
Depth of Field, 109, 110
Depth of Field Guided Editing, 109
Desaturate, 170
Deselect, 197, 210, 217, 233, 237, 240, 262
desktop program, 341, 368
Detail Smart, 51
Detailed Corrections, 208
detailed instructions, 39
determined, 5, 8, 9, 14, 44, 45, 182, 189, 220, 279, 281, 309
Diffuse Glow option., 92
Digimarc Filter, 296
Digital Art, 22
digital photographs, 13, 15, 220, 342
digital work, 25, 179
Discontiguous, 175, 177
discount on the current license purchase, 1
Discover eye-catching contemporary fonts, 3
Discover one-click photo Quick Actions in one place, 3
Display & Cursors., 56
Display / Hide, 104
Display an image at 100%, 135
Display Bounding Box, 141
Display driver for Microsoft DirectX 12, 33

Display Highlights on Rollover, 138, 141
Display resolution, 33
distinct purposes in design, 10
Distort Filters, 295
Distribute menu, 139, 142
Distribute the menu, 141
Divide Scanned Photos, 314
Document Information, 332, 334
Document Size area, 19
Dodge tool, 52
Done, 88, 107, 109, 121, 318, 327, 365
dotted line, 189, 213
download and install the new software, 2
Download photos, 315
Download photos from your digital camera, 315
downloading, 2, 33
downloading and installing, 2
Downsizing, 6
Drag to resize, 56
Draw a line, 186
Draw an arrow, 190
Dropbox, 341, 365, 368
Duplicate your layer, 242
DxO PhotoLab, 31

E

easy-to-use features, 1
Edges, 167, 173, 175, 205, 206
edit photos, 42, 43, 368
Edit type in a type layer, 277
Editing a layer mask, 269
Editing a text layer, 284
Editing and Manipulation, 6
editing applications, 8, 22
Editing Shapes, 184
editing talents, 23
Editing using the Lomo Camera Effect, 89
Effect, 5, 77, 78, 88, 89, 97, 99, 104, 106, 108, 121, 169, 294, 353
Elements edition, 1
Elements Hub, 39, 40
Elements Organizer, 57, 60, 61, 65, 102, 113, 115, 116, 118, 119, 155, 267, 312, 316, 337, 338, 348, 349, 362, 363, 364, 368
Ellipse, 53, 183
Elliptical Marquee, 20, 50, 148, 192, 207, 209
enhanced UI, 1

Enter the line width in pixels., 189
Erase Refinements tool, 146
Eraser Tool, 108, 120, 177, 179, 180, 194, 310
Eraser Tools, 175
Erasing with a Pencil, 195
establish a connection, 368
exchange experiences, 40
exhibit exceptional clarity, 8
EXIF Metadata, 342
Expand, 15, 210, 211
expand the picture, 20
Experiment on a Duplicate Layer, 172
Experiment with Blend Modes, 172
Experiment with Different Techniques, 167
Expert settings, 40
Explore and customize Auto Creations, 41
Exporting as Images, 367
Exposure, 28, 62, 103, 117, 118, 119, 120, 161, 171, 172, 173, 319
eyedropper, 127, 128, 129, 130, 330

F

Faces, 116
facilitating faster, 13
fantastic place, 43
Faux Bold, 279, 286
Faux Italic, 279, 286
favorite social channels, 2
Favorites, 58, 64, 304
Feather, 89, 145, 209, 210, 214, 215, 216, 306
Feathering, 209, 210, 214, 216, 268
Features, 112, 246, 247
features and online content, 33
File Alternatives, 30
File Benefits and Drawbacks, 31
File Compression, 68
File Conversion to Other Formats, 30
File FAQs, 32
File formats that support alpha, 273
File Info, 61, 335, 342
File Size, 6, 11, 31, 87
File sizes, 13
Filename, 65
Files in the Photographic Process, 29
Fill layers, 29, 249
Filter Categories, 294
Filter Gallery, 238, 291, 292, 293, 294, 296

Filter menu, 291, 292, 293
final picture transmission, 28
final size of the file, 16
fine-tune brightness, 2
fine-tune facial tilt, 369
Fit, 87, 100, 101, 135, 204, 317
Fit an image to the screen, 135
Fit Photo to Canvas, 100
FIX AND ENHANCE YOUR PHOTOS, 224
Flexibility, 31
flip frowns upside down, 369
Font Family, 279, 285
Font Style, 279, 286, 287
Format, 31, 65, 67, 68, 273, 331, 362
Formatting a text layer, 283
formerly Adobe Systems Incorporated, 27
Frame, 77, 106, 299
Frames, 62, 72, 76, 77, 101, 299
free access to Adobe Stock images, 369
free hard disk space, 33
Freehand Drawing, 195
Frequently Asked Questions, 38, 69, 77, 124, 206, 219, 223, 248, 275, 290, 304, 311, 328, 335, 347, 361, 368
Friendly User Interface, 336
Full-Size Brush Tip, 56
Fun Edits, 78, 99, 101, 103, 104, 107, 124
Function, 6, 171, 207, 208
Function in Image Editing, 6
Functions, 183, 184, 208

G

Gaussian, 164
generate a visual representation, 11
GET TO KNOW PHOTOSHOP ELEMENTS 2024, 39
GET TO KNOW THE PHOTOSHOP ELEMENTS TOOLBOX, 126
GETTING STARTED, 2
Google Drive, 341, 368
Gradient Map, 28
Gradient tool, 53
graphic design, 11, 177
Graphic Design, 22
graphic design and illustration, 11
Green, 5, 91, 93, 226, 231, 334
greeting cards, 39, 369
Grid Functionality, 336

Grid Overlay, 199
Grow your skills along the way with Guided Edits, 4
guided edit, 4, 78, 79, 81, 85, 86, 89, 90, 93, 95, 97, 98, 99, 101, 103, 110, 124
Guided Edit Mode, 79
Guided Edits, 4, 39, 78, 80, 89, 98, 99, 106, 113
GUIDED EDITS, 78
Guided mode, 42, 43, 58, 78, 82, 85, 92, 94, 96, 109, 110, 112
Guided Mode, 42, 88
Guides, 45, 47, 272
Guides and Rulers, 45
Guides or Grids section, 47

H

Hand tool, 55, 71, 135, 137, 140, 143, 146, 154, 322
Hand Tool (H), 49
Hardware Acceleration, 331
Haze Removal, 240
Healing Brush, 72, 159, 160, 308
Healing Brush tool, 51, 159, 160
hexadecimal value, 25, 126
High Key, 97, 98
High Key guided, 97
highest possible resolution, 8
Highlight, 119, 233, 292, 317, 354
High-Quality, 31
Histogram, 63, 235
History, 63, 228, 269, 310
Hold the Shift Key, 186
Home Screen, 40, 60
Horizontal and Vertical, 276
Horizontal Guides, 45
Horizontal Type Mask, 53
Horizontal Type Tool, 82, 276
How do you add objects to your photos?, 311
How do you add your metadata?, 347
How do you adjust lighting?, 248
How do you auto analyze your media?, 347
How do you convert photos from black to white?, 248
How do you copy layers from one image file to another?, 275
How do you create a photo book?, 361
How do you create a photo calendar?, 361
How do you create a photo collage?, 361
How do you create a photo reel?, 361
How do you create a quote graphic?, 361
How do you create prints and gifts?, 361
How do you cut and paste a selection into another photo?, 219
How do you instantly fix a photo?, 347
How do you know if an image is a vector?, 15
How do you manage your files with keyword tags?, 347
How do you manage your media files by date or event?, 347
How do you re-edit a text layer?, 290
How do you remove and replace color?, 248
How do you remove blemishes and warts from images?, 311
How do you search your catalog using filters?, 347
How do you shape and resize your text?, 290
How do you share your file as a PDF slideshow?, 368
How do you share your photos on Flickr?, 368
How do you share your photos via email?, 368
How do you share your video on Vimeo?, 368
How do you simplify or flatten a layer?, 275
How do you store your media in the Cloud?, 368
How do you sync your media to the Cloud?, 347
How do you transform or warp a layer?, 275
How do you type on a selection or path?, 290
How do you use haze removal?, 248
How do you use selection to protect an area?, 219
How do you use the background eraser tool?, 206
How do you use the color picker option?, 206
How do you use the cropping tools?, 206
How do you use the marquee selection tools?, 206
How do you use the red eye removal tool?, 206
How do you use the shape tools?, 206
How do you use the smart brush tools?, 206
How do you use the sponge, dodge and burn tools?, 206
How do you use the type tool options bin?, 290
How do you use the zoom and hand tool?, 206
How does the layer work?, 275
How layers work, 249
How to Create and Edit, 32
How to create and edit an alpha, 23
How to Find the Pencil Tool, 194
How to save files for the web, 66
How to Simplify a Photoshop Layer, 265
How to use it, 183
How to Use It, 153, 183, 184
How to Use the Dodge Tool, 171
How to use the eyedropper tool, 127

Hue/Saturation, 28, 226, 227, 228, 229, 230, 238, 260, 262, 346

I

icons, 3, 41, 43, 56, 250, 262, 263, 324, 354
Image downsizing, 6
Image Enlargement, 6
Image File Formats, 7
Image Preparation for Print, 30
image quality, 9, 11, 12, 67, 293, 321
Image Resizing, 222
Image Size, 16, 17, 18, 19, 38, 139, 142, 205, 220, 222, 263, 354, 355
image size expands, 17
Image Size vs. Canvas Size, 16, 220
images and videos, 41
images encountered, 13
image's or selection's transparency settings, 22
impact on pixel fidelity., 7
Impressionist Brush tool, 52
including RGB, 25, 31
Increase Contrast, 93, 112
Increase Contrast option, 93
Indicate the installation site, 34
Install Photoshop, 34
Instant Fix a photo, 346
Intel 6th Generation, 33
Intel processor 6th Generation, 33
Internet access, 33
intricate details, 8, 11
INTRODUCTION, 1
Invert, 28, 97, 210, 297
IPTC Metadata, 342
Is a Portable Document Format (PDF) classified as a raster or vector format?, 15
Is Adobe Photoshop vector-based software?, 15
Is the size of an artboard and a canvas the same?, 16

J

K

Key attributes, 10, 11
Key Concepts, 21
Keywords, 80, 335, 344

L

Large Files, 6
Lasso (L) tool, 50
Launch Adobe Photoshop Elements, 44, 194, 223, 343, 364, 368
Layer groups, 29
Layer Mask, 22, 214, 217, 229, 244, 268, 270, 306
Layer masks, 22, 269
Layer Opacity, 21
Layer Preservation, 31
Layer styles, 21
Layer Styles, 21, 269
Layer Visibility, 21, 258
Layering Images, 266
Leading Menu, 286
LEARN ABOUT YOUR PHOTOSHOP ELEMENTS FILE, 329
Learn and Support, 40
Levels, 26, 28, 91, 226, 234, 235, 266, 346, 354
Light (if available), 296
Light or Dark Interface?, 44
Limitations, 11, 12
Limits, 175, 177
Line, 53, 186, 187, 188, 189, 190, 191, 192, 194
Live Shapes Controls, 189
Load a library, 327
Load Swatches, 133, 134
Location, 171, 345
Long Edge, 87
Loss of Detail, 6
Low Key, 98, 99
lower pixel count yields, 10
LZW (Lemple-Zif-Welch), 68

M

Magic, 7, 20, 50, 52, 143, 145, 147, 150, 151, 158, 179, 180, 207, 208, 209, 214, 215, 216, 218, 219, 229, 239, 268, 309
Magic Wand tool, 20, 50, 207, 209
Magnetic Lasso, 50, 147, 148, 149, 150, 209
Make a copy of an existing layer., 250
Make a layer the Background layer, 253
make picture editing a breeze, 1
making calendars, 369
making picture editing faster, 3

Manage action files, 124
Manage your files with Keyword Tags, 343
MANAGE YOUR FILES WITH THE ORGANIZER, 336
Manage your media files by Date or Event, 345
Manage your photos by Place, 344
Manually select photos and videos, 349
Mask it off, 244
Masking and Layering, 208
Match effect, 301, 303
Match Location, 136
Match tone and color to create new feeling, 2
Match Zoom, 136
mathematical equations, 11
mathematical equations and geometric shapes, 11
Measurement Units, 220
Measuring Distance, 334
Measuring Units, 46
Medium Gray, 44
Menu alignment, 141
Merge numerous photos into a PDF, 367
Merging and flattening layers, 267
meticulous control, 11
Microsoft OneDrive, 368
Midtones, 226, 231
Modify, 49, 54, 200, 210, 214, 290, 297, 319
modify face characteristics, 369
modify the sharpness of painting cursors, 56
More icon, 60
motion function, 369
motion's direction and speed, 369
Move tool, 49, 55, 137, 138, 139, 140, 141, 142, 143, 254, 284, 285, 298, 299, 304
Move Tool, 48, 55, 103, 108, 137, 182, 184, 185, 186, 202, 254, 306, 310
Move tool options, 138, 141
MP4 or GIF file, 369
multi-layered document, 262
Multi-Photo Text Guided Editing, 101

N

natural appearance., 167
Navigating within the Detail, 337
Nearest Neighbor, 19
necessitating a comprehensive comprehension, 10
New additions, 2
new editing experience, 1, 2, 3
New Guide, 45, 272

New Layer button, 191, 251
new Photo Reels, 2
new variety of backgrounds, 369
newer CPU with SSE4.1 capability, or AMD equivalent., 33
No Restriction, 196, 197, 223
Noise Filters, 295
Non-Professional, 9
Normal, 56, 164, 166, 182, 189, 195, 243, 251, 259, 260
Normal Brush Tip, 56
Notification and Status Area, 333
numerous pages, 16

O

Object removal, 369
Object Removal Guided Edit, 85
on Shape, 53, 82, 83, 84, 288
On the next screen, click **Continue**., 34
On the Welcome screen, click the **Activate Now button**., 37
On White/On Black, 215
One-Click Select Subject, Background, or Sky, 211
Online Converters, 368
Only 64-bit versions of Microsoft, 33
Opacity, 58, 93, 95, 104, 120, 147, 159, 160, 189, 195, 197, 268, 301
Open a camera raw image in the Edit workspace, 322
Open and process camera raw files, 319
Open Closed Eyes, 112, 155
Open multiple windows of the same image, 136
Organizing by Date, 345
Organizing by Event, 345
Other Adobe Services Integration, 40
Other Filters, 296
Other Panels, 63
Other transform options, 288
Out Of Bounds, 105, 106
Out of Bounds" Guided Edit effect, 105
Output, 7, 145, 214, 331
overlapping rectangles or boxes, 202
Overlay, 22, 110, 145, 147, 172, 195, 215, 243

P

Paint Bucket tool, 52, 132, 218, 306

Panel Bin, 43, 57, 58, 59, 60, 63
Panel menus, 58
Panorama, 121, 123
Paste one selection into another, 140, 143
Pattern, 4, 51, 53, 163, 181, 292, 325
Pattern Stamp tool, 51
Pattern tool, 53
PDF, 15, 67, 273, 367, 368
Pencil tool (N), 54
Perfect Portrait, 112
Perspective, 54, 55, 121, 122, 200, 274
Perspective Crop tool, 54, 55, 200
phenomenon, 14
Photo Bin, 26, 27, 60, 61, 62, 71, 78, 82, 85, 101, 102, 103, 110, 113, 115, 116, 118, 120, 121, 136, 137, 155, 266, 267, 299, 356, 358, 359
Photo Bin or Tool Options button, 26
Photo Creations, 39, 67
Photo Editing, 22
Photo editing software, 11
Photo Editor, 36, 41, 43, 44, 65, 315, 316, 318
Photo Filter, 28
Photo layering, 266
Photographic, 29, 31, 67
photography, 13, 27, 30, 43
Photomerge, 78, 113, 114, 115, 116, 117, 118, 119, 120, 121
photo's boundaries, 205, 206
Photoshop Document, 27
Photoshop Elements 2023 license, 1
Photoshop Elements 2024 by Adobe, 1
Photoshop Elements 2024 license, 369
PHOTOSHOP ELEMENTS TRICKS, 305
Photoshop has a plethora of filters, 7
Photoshop Space, 191
Photoshop users, 7, 127
picture Bin, 26, 86, 115, 120
picture collages, 369
Pixar, 68
Pixel Aspect Ratio, 330
Pixel Blending, 114, 115
Pixel Characteristics, 5
Pixel Difficulties, 6
pixel dimensions of the respective projector, 10
Pixel Editing, 7
Pixel Filters, 7
Pixel layers, 28, 262
Pixel Manipulation and Layers, 7

Pixel Output and Export, 7
Pixel Selection, 7
Pixelate Filters, 295
pixelation, 6, 10, 12, 14
Pixel-Level Editing, 337
Pixels, 5, 6, 7, 135, 186, 188, 189, 260, 314
pixels per inch, 6, 8, 9, 10, 12, 221, 222, 354
Pixilation, 6
Placing text on a layer, 282
PNG, 7, 10, 28, 30, 31, 32, 68, 174, 178, 222, 268, 272, 273, 288, 314, 324, 339, 351, 354
Polygon, 53, 185
Polygonal Lasso, 50, 147, 148, 149, 209, 309
Pop effect, 95
popular consumer photo editing, 1
popular consumer photo editing program, 1
popular function, 369
Popular one-click changes, 3
popular tool, 369
Pop-up sliders within panels, 58
Portable Document Format, 15, 67, 273
possibilities, 29, 30, 44, 55, 103, 137, 175, 187, 198, 238, 341
post on social media, 369
Posterize, 28
Power lines, 369
powerful file format, 27
powerful picture editing tool, 369
ppi, 8, 9, 279, 354
Precise, 56
Precision Editing, 179
Preferences, 44, 47, 55, 56, 66, 127, 178, 197, 225, 247, 280, 316, 323, 324, 334, 363
Premium Elements 2024, 1
Presets, 100, 104, 324, 326, 327
Pressure Sensitivity, 178
Preview and Adjust, 355
Preview Changes, 227
Previewing Changes, 337
Principles of photo and graphics editing, 5
Print, 8, 62, 87, 88, 228, 313, 351, 355, 357, 358, 360
Print Bin Files, 62
Print output, 87, 88
Print Resolution, 8, 355
Print Resolution vs. Web Resolution, 8
Proceed to click and drag., 188
Proceed to sign in with your email and password., 37
Process Multiple Files, 323, 324

processing and editing, 29
productivity, 22
Professional Publications, 9
professional-grade printers, 9
Projector / Powerpoint, 10
project's artboard, 16
Pros, 31
Proximity Match, 156, 160
PSD, 27, 28, 29, 30, 31, 32, 38, 67, 272, 273, 360
PSD files, 27, 28, 29, 30, 32

Q

QUICK AND GUIDED PHOTO EDITING, 70
Quick Edits, 39
QUICK FIXES AND EFFECTS, 71
Quick Mode, 42
Quick Selection Tool, 48, 50, 151, 239, 306

R

Radius, 145, 146, 185, 210, 214, 215, 242, 244, 306
Range, 172, 173, 226, 230
Raster graphics, 10, 11
Raster images, 10, 11, 14
Raster vs. vector graphics, 10
RAW editor like Lightroom, 29
RAW Installation, 316
Realism, 11, 179
Recognizing the PSD File Format, 27
Recommendations, 222
recommended resolution, 8, 9
Recompose tool (W, 54
recomposition, 202
recomposition process, 202
Rectangle, 183, 184
Rectangular, 50, 53, 147, 148, 198, 209, 216, 217, 277, 310
Rectangular Marquee, 50, 147, 198, 209, 216, 217, 277, 310
Red, 5, 72, 91, 93, 154, 155, 226, 231, 317, 323, 334
Red Eye Removal tool, 72, 154, 155
redesigned user interface, 1
Redo and Undo, 218, 219
Reducing noise in camera raw images, 321
Refine Edge button, 96
Refine Edge dialog box, 214, 215, 216

Refine Effect, 95
Refine Selection, 50, 143, 151, 152
Refine Shape, 89
Refine the automatic selection, 213
Refine the edge of your selection, 213
Refining the edges of a selection, 144
Relaunch the app, 41
Relief (If available), 296
Remove a Color Cast, 78
Remove actions, 124
Remove any unwanted sections of your line, 193
Remove big things from your photos, 308
Remove Blemishes, 112
Remove Color Cast command, 90
Remove imperfections, 242
Remove JPEG artifacts for a more natural appearance, 4
remove pixels, 6, 20, 207
Remove spots and small imperfections, 156
Remove the color, 242
Remove troublesome areas, 295
Remove unwanted objects with content-aware healing, 157
Remove warts and blemishes, 307
Removing a layer mask, 271
Removing an unwanted object, 157
Render Filters, 295
reposition, 60, 103, 306
Reposition, 122
Resample Image, 19, 220, 222
resampling, 19
Resampling, 220
resampling approach, 19
resampling approaches, 19
Reset a swatch library to its default color swatches, 133
Reset actions, 124
Reset All Tools, 56
Reset Tool, 56
Resize Guided Edit, 86
Resize the window while zooming, 135
RESIZE YOUR IMAGES, 220
Resolution, 6, 8, 9, 12, 18, 196, 201, 221, 330, 333
resolution and quality, 8
Restore the default library or replace the currently displayed library, 327
Restore the tool's default settings, 56
Reveal Layer, 145

revised version, 1
RGB Color, 25
RGB color correcting, 26
RGB stands for the main colors of light, red, green, and blue, 25
RGB Values, 5
right of the Channels screen, 24
Right-click on the document and select, 254
RLE (Run Length Encoding, 68
Rotate Buttons, 323
Rounded Rectangle, 53, 183, 184
Rounded Rectangles Tool, 184

S

Sample, 112, 129, 130, 151, 155, 156, 160
Sampling Ring, 131
Saturate, 170
Saturation, 95, 119, 161, 226, 228, 229, 302, 304, 319, 334
Save Bin as an Album, 62
Save challenging options for later use., 23
Save files to the Cloud, 64
Save in Version Set with Original, 65, 233, 237
Save or File, 64, 308
Save/Save As, 65
Scalability, 11, 12
Scaling, 296
Scan your photos, 312
Scene Cleaner, 114, 115
Scratch Sizes, 332
Screen captures, 313
Search window, 80
Search your catalog using Filters, 343
Select a Border, 110
Select a layer to edit, 253
SELECT AND ISOLATE AREAS, 207
SELECT AND ISOLATE AREAS IN YOUR PHOTOS, 207
Select characters, 278
Select Layer, 91, 138, 141, 251, 253, 281, 282
Select **New Channel**, 24
Select options from the Tool, 55
Select **Photo Editor** from the menu that displays., 36
Select Subject, 143, 211
Selecting Editing, 207
Selection Brush tool, 50, 86, 146, 209
Selections, 20, 151, 158, 165, 172, 192, 207, 210, 219, 287

Selective Color, 29
Separate picture components, 23
Set custom camera settings, 323
Set the appearance of a pointer, 56
Set the resolution of your picture here, 222
Set the width of your line, 187
several advantages, 11, 12
Shadows, 91, 119, 226, 231, 233, 319
Shake Reduction, 247
Shape and resize your text, 287
Shape layers, 29
Share, 83, 88, 89, 90, 106, 107, 108, 364, 365, 366, 367
Share as a PDF Slideshow, 367
SHARE YOUR PHOTOS AND VIDEOS, 362
Sharpen tool, 51
Sharpening the Tool, 168
Shift Edge, 145, 215
SHIFT key, 148, 150
Short Edge, 87
Show Bounding Box, 138
Show Crosshair In Brush Tip, 56
Show Open Files, 26, 27, 118, 120
Show Regions, 113, 115, 116, 120
Show sampling ring, 128
Show Strokes, 113, 115, 116, 120
Shrink to Fit box,, 87
Simple, 109, 119
Simple Method, 109
simple touch-up tools to complicated features, 369
Simplify or Flatten a Layer, 265
single brush stroke., 369
six-digit code, 25
size of 2 gigabytes, 28
size of the artboard or canvas, 16
Sketch Filters, 295
slideshows, 41, 337, 348, 365, 369
Slim Down, 112
small colored squares, 10
Small or Large List, 326
small picture tweaks, 1
Smart Brush tool, 51
Smart object layers, 29
Smart Radius, 145, 214, 215
Smart Tone, 224, 225, 248
smartphones operating on the Android and iOS platforms, 1

Smooth, 112, 145, 152, 153, 209, 210, 214, 215, 245, 306
smooth skin, 3, 369
Smudge tool, 51, 168
Smudge Your Image, 167
Softening, 167
Software Restrictions, 331
sophisticated version, 1
spanning one horizontal inch, 8
Special Edits, 78, 109, 110, 112
specialized software, 13
Specialized Software, 31
specific area of a picture, 369
specific points, 11, 185
Spherical, 122
Sponge tool, 52, 172
Spot Healing Brush tool, 51, 156, 157, 159
Standard, 56, 228, 352
Star, 53
storage devices, 33
Storing Media in the Cloud, 368
Straighten a picture automatically, 206
Straighten tool, 54, 203, 204, 205, 206, 323
straightforward video editing, 1
straightforward video editing application, 1
Strength, 112, 152, 164, 166, 168, 170
Strikethrough, 286
stroke a selection, 218
Stroke Variations, 184
Stroke Width, 188
Style button, 112
Styles, 63, 64, 277, 297, 327
Stylize Filters, 295
stylized shapes or graphics to an image, 298
stylized text to an image, 304
subtract from a selection, 143
Subtract from selection", 152, 153
Supported file formats for saving, 66
Supports several image modalities, 31
Swap out a background, 306
Swap out a face, 305
Switch between Album and Folder Views, 340
Sync your media to the Cloud, 341
system requirements, 2
System requirements, 33
System Requirements, 33

T

Tablet Input, 178
Teeth Whitening Tool, 72
Text and Border Overlay Guided Edit, 110
Text and Shapes, 310
text frames by doing one of the following, 102
Text layers, 29, 277
Text on Path Tool, 82
Text Only, 326
Text Overlay, 111
Text Tool, 158, 272, 287, 360
Text Vertical Type, 53
Texture, 77, 293, 295, 296, 299
Texture and glass surface options, 296
Texture Filters, 295
Textures, 62, 72, 75, 77, 299
Texturizing options, 296
the "**Ungroup**" option., 15
The ability to save PDFs as raster files, 15
The Active Layer, 257
The actual dimensions and resolution, 17
the actual process of downloading and installing Photoshop Elements 2024., 2
THE ADVANCED PHOTO EDITING WORKSPACE, 125
the artboard and canvas sizes, 16
The Blur Tool, 164
The brush tool, 24
The Burn Tool, 172
The characteristics of screen images, 9
The Cookie Cutter Tool, 199
The Crop Tool, 196, 314
The Crop tool and method, 198
the dialogue box., 19
The Dodge Tool, 171
The Editor workspace, 40
The Elements Hub, 39, 40
The Eraser, 175, 176
The Eyedropper tool's options, 129
The Eyedropper/Sampler Tool, 127
The Gallery of Filters, 296
The Gradient Tool, 182
the **green Mark**, 192
The Healing Brushes, 72
The Info Bar, 329
The Layer Name, 256
The Layer Row, 256
The Layer Search Bar, 261

the Layers panel, 249, 250, 255, 256, 259, 262, 264
The majority of PDFs, 15
The Media Browser area, 339
The Meme Maker Guided Edit, 99
The Move & Scale Object Guided Edit, 85
The Name Tab, 255
The new match color tool, 1
The option to modify face, 369
The Painterly Guided Edit effect, 103
The Panel Bin, 57, 58
The Pattern Stamp Tool, 163
the Pencil Tool, 120, 194, 195
The Pencil Tool, 194
The Perfect Portrait Guided Edit, 112
The Photo Bin, 26, 61, 71, 102
The Photo Bin/Tool Options section, 26
the pixel layers symbol, 262, 263
the pop-up window, 24
The primary distinction, 17
the PSD file format, 27
The recommended resolution, 8
The Recompose Tool, 202
The resolution of an image, 8, 10, 14
the RGB color channels, 22
The Save/Save As dialog box and how to use, 64
The Search Bar, 261, 262
The Select menu, 210
The **Settings icon**, 42
The Shape Tools, 183
The Sharpen Tool, 167
The Smudge Tool, 165, 166, 167
The Sponge Tool, 169, 170
The Sponge, Dodge, and Burn Tools, 169
The standard resampling procedure, 19
The Status Bar, 332
The Straighten Tool, 203
The Tool Options, 126
The Toolbox, 47, 147, 148
The Tools Options Bin, 26
The Type Tool, 72, 111, 277, 285
The usage of PPI, 9
The vector graphic, 11
the web or various devices, 9
The Welcome Screen, 41
The Zoom Tool, 134
Things you need to Know, 5
third-party tools, 27
three channels, 23, 25

three-color channels, 25
Threshold, 28, 244, 300
Thumbnail, 66, 257, 263, 264, 326, 363
TIFF, 7, 28, 30, 31, 68, 273, 339, 360
TIFFs or JPGs, 29
Tilt Sensitivity, 178
Toggle Text Orientation, 282, 287
Tolerance, 150, 175, 177, 178, 180, 181, 229, 241
Tonal Range, 171
Tool Information, 332
Toolbox, 47, 48, 71, 147, 148, 149, 150, 151, 152, 192, 194, 282, 285
Toolbox in the Quick mode, 47
Tracking, 286
Transfer the Media to the Cloud, 368
Transform and warp a layer, 274
Transform Selection, 192
Transform Tool, 272
Transforming a Layer, 274
transforming an existing layer, 29
translucent background, 23
Transparency and Brightness, 5
Transparent Areas, 123
Try something new, 218
Turn off pop-up blockers in your browser., 34
two-pixel layers visible, 262
Type layers and shape layers, 250
Type Mask Reveal Tools, 276
Type Mask Tools, 276
Type Tool, 48, 100, 277, 285
Type tool (T), 53
Type Tools, 83, 276
Types of Files and Extensions, 14
Types of Guides, 45
Types of Rulers, 46
Typing Tools, 194

U

unchosen sections, 214
Underline, 286
Understanding the Dodge Tool, 171
Undo and Redo, 195
Units & Rulers., 47, 280
Unsharp Mask, 244, 245, 320, 354
Unwarp type, 282
Update Software, 331
updated image dimensions, 19

upgraded capabilities, 1
Usage, 22
usage of Adobe Photoshop, 15
usage of digital cameras, 14
Use a selection to protect an area, 216
Use a tool, 54
Use Context Menus, 43
Use External Software, 367
Use grids to improve cropping results, 199
Use keyboard commands and modifier keys, 43
Use layers, 165, 218, 272
Use preset tool options, 325
Use the Blur Tool, 164
Use the Burn Tool, 172
Use the Photo Ratio, 196
Use the Preset Manager, 326
Use the Recompose Tool, 202
Use the Tab Key, 254
Use the taskbar, 60
Use the Text on Path tool, 84
Use the Text on the Shape tool, 288
Use the Type tool or a shape tool., 250
Use your arrow keys, 284
User-Friendly Interface, 40
Uses, 13
using a variety of tools, 367
Using Guided Edits, 4
using new backgrounds, 4
Using Rulers for Accuracy, 46
Using the settings in the toolbar, 184
Using the Sponge Tool, 170

V

Variations, 226
variety of picture editing activities, 39
Vector File Types, 14
vector files, 11, 12, 13, 14, 15
Vector files, 11, 12, 13
vector graphics, 10, 12, 13, 14, 15, 28, 273
Vector graphics, 11, 14, 38
Vertical Guides, 45
vertical line, 205, 206
Vertical Type Mask, 53, 276
Vertical Type Tool, 82, 276
very popular selections, 368
Vibrance, 28
Video Editor, 41

Video layers, 29
Vignette button, 89
Vignette Effect Guided Edit, 88
Vignette Removal, 122
visual quality of the image, 8

W

Warp Text, 82, 281, 282, 287
Warp type, 281
Warped Text, 277
Warping a Layer, 274
watercolor, 369
watercolor and drawing effects, 369
Web, 8, 9, 26, 31, 66, 67, 87, 126, 222, 313
web browsers, 13, 68
web images, 9, 10
Weight, 187, 188, 189
What do these panels do, 62
What is a native PSD file?, 27
What is a raster file?, 10
What is a vector file?, 11
What is an Image Size?, 17
What is Anti-Aliasing?, 157
What Is Photoshop Canvas Size?, 16
What Is the Distinction Between Canvas and Image Size?, 17
White Balance tool, 322
Why does a "100% zoom" video fill only part of my computer screen?, 330
Width and Height, 87, 196, 197, 222
With the new Artistic Effect settings, you can turn images into works of art, 5
work in a variety of picture formats, 7
Work with Panels, 58
WORK WITH PHOTOSHOP ELEMENTS LAYERS, 249
Workflow Customization, 179

X

XMP Metadata, 343

Z

ZIP, 69
Zoom Controls, 331
Zoom in for more detail, 171

Zoom Level, 332, 336
Zoom Level Sensitivity, 336

Zoom tool, 71, 134, 135, 146, 154, 228, 317, 319, 322
Zooming in for Precision, 337

Made in the USA
Monee, IL
11 December 2024

73280503R00225